THE ULTIMATE
DOORS COMPANION

Printed by: MPG Books, Bodmin, United Kingdom

Published by: Sanctuary Publishing Limited, Sanctuary House,
45-53 Sinclair Road, London W14 0NS, United Kingdom

Web site: www.sanctuarypublishing.com

Edited by: David Mead

ISBN: 1-86074-288-2

THE ULTIMATE
DOORS COMPANION

Doug Sundling

"Rock 'n' roll should corrupt you to think."

Alice Cooper, late 1980s

ACKNOWLEDGEMENTS
getting it straight...

After graduating from high school, I went to college in the summer of 1973 and found, in the library of Ball State University, a cosmos of information on The Doors written by others – eons removed from the world of small town USA in America's heartland. My mind was expanded. Ever since, I have been revising both many assumptions I have made and a lot of information I have gathered about The Doors. In short, correcting mistakes. But getting it straight isn't all that easy, evident in the following two examples:

Doors keyboardist Ray Manzarek was born in 1939. But somewhere, in some early rock 'n' roll reference book, the year of his birth was cited as 1935. Henceforth, a preponderance of other authors and reference books use 1935.

In *The Lizard King: The Essential Jim Morrison* (published in 1992) Jerry Hopkins, who had been writing about The Doors for 25-plus years, wrote that 'Runnin' Blue' was released as a single from the album *Morrison Hotel* (p129). 'Runnin' Blue' is song number two on side two of *The Soft Parade*, the album that preceded *Morrison Hotel*. The reason I include this minor miscue from Hopkins (and not more grievous miscues by others who have written on The Doors or on Morrison) is I have always had a high regard for Hopkins because of his insistence on presenting information as accurately as possible.

Though we live in an age of information, it is also a world of deadlines and myriad layers of diversions and intents. And survival isn't always to the meticulous. As Hopkins wrote about Oliver Stone's attempt to tell The Doors' story on film, 'a gonzo journalistic attitude doesn't allow facts to get in the way of a good story'. Yet, I welcome comments, suggestions, additions, corrections, etc.

I am deeply indebted to Kerry Humpherys for allowing me access to his extensive archives of Doors material. Kerry is the editor-in-chief of *The Doors Collectors Magazine* (a quarterly) and sells various types of Doors-related items from an extensive catalogue. Kerry can be contacted at: TDM Inc, PO Box 1441, Orem, Utah 84059-1441 USA. Phone: 800-891-1736.

CONTENTS

INTRODUCTION: A DOOR OPENS

What were The Doors saying as artists? The details of personal stories about The Doors (or of Jim Morrison) or speculation on such stories has been but a casual interest to me; what The Doors expressed through their music has always been more important.

My journey with The Doors began when Jim Morrison's ended. On my 16th birthday my parents gave me, as I had requested, my first Doors album, *LA Woman*. I had thought if I liked two cuts on an album (in this case, the two radio tunes, 'Love Her Madly' and 'Riders On The Storm') then that album was worth having. When the opening of 'The Changeling' hit my restless 16-year-old spirit, I was enthralled until the final wave of thunder in 'Riders On The Storm'. Then I played the album again...and again...and...

Three days later, Jim was dead.

I have never viewed Jim Morrison as a demigod, as a 20th-century Dionysus, or The Doors as a greater-than-life entity. From my 16th birthday onward, I have looked to The Doors as fellow artistic spirits who had successfully forged a path to express a creative vision we share. Consequently, I haven't had the problem I see of so many Doors fanatics: when the worshippers leave their adolescent view of life, the god becomes all too human.

Having now outlived Morrison, I understand what Jim's – and The Doors' – artistic vision can't portray: the wisdom that comes with having lived into your thirties, into mid-life, into old age. That perspective of life never came to Morrison, for like a fiery and intense burst of brilliance, like so many artistic spirits who choose not to burn the candle at both ends but with a blowtorch in the middle, Jim, though very gifted, paid a dear price for being a jerk.

But on my 16th birthday, I had peered through an opened door inside me and a journey had begun. I collected all The Doors' recordings and bootlegs I could find and began a decade-long research into all the mainstream and underground literature I could unearth on them. In 1979, life having diverted me onto other paths, I put aside this research at the same time that there began a resurgence in The Doors, spurred by three events:

(1) the release of Francis Ford Coppola's movie, Apocalypse Now, which uses 'The End' to open its imagery of the Vietnam War;

(2) the publication of Jerry Hopkins' and Danny Sugerman's *No One Here Gets Out Alive*;

(3) the release of *An American Prayer*, an album on which the three surviving Doors blended their music to some resurrected tapes of Jim reading poetry.

In the summer of 1985, needing to write a thesis to fulfil my requirements for a master's in English, I resurrected that research and composed a paper entitled, *The Poetic Imagery And Themes In The Works Of James Douglas Morrison*. That title sounded better – at that time – on the proposal sheet submitted to the department head than *The Poetry Of Jim Morrison, Lead Singer Of The Doors*.

While I was teaching at college and corrupting youthful minds with such topics as 'The Poetics Of Rock 'n' Roll', I met in the spring of 1987 Diana Maniak (later to marry and become Diana Bittner). Also enamoured of The Doors, she provided insights and inspiration to help me finish a critique of their six studio albums. By the spring of 1990, we had finished the manuscript and distributed homemade copies of the book.

In 1996, *The Doors Artistic Vision* was published by Castle Communications of London. The editing and formatting of the manuscript didn't create my intended book, and in retrospect my manuscript was overtly wordy. In 1999, Jeff Hudson of Sanctuary Publishing (which had bought Castle) contacted me in regards to reissuing the book. After a flurry of activity, we managed to put together this revised edition.

To read this critique of the lyrical and musical themes of The Doors' songs isn't to read the way the band created. This critical rendering of The Doors' artistic vision is a variation of their musical rendering of the western dream. Just as this critique is a piecing together of many artistic impressions by The Doors, it is also a way of painting a portrait of America and of being human in the 20th century, a portrait similar to the one The Doors render. Instead of destroying the secrecy and mystery with the light of exposure, hopefully this critique develops an understanding of why the artistic vision of The Doors remains a viable portrait of modern life. Critical analysis should heighten understanding and thus the power and impact of any artistic vision of life – of what it means to be human.

May the book offer a concise overview of one of the more potent and enduring artistic visions that emerged from the Sixties. May it stimulate you to think.

And so, ladies and gentlemen, The Doors.

Jim Morrison: vocals (8 December 1943 – 3 July 1971)
Ray Manzarek: keyboards (12 February 1939 –   )
Robby Krieger: guitar (8 January 1946 –)
John Densmore: percussion (1 December 1944 –   )

The Studio Albums (Elektra Records):

The Doors (January 1967)
Strange Days (October 1967)
Waiting For The Sun (July 1968)
The Soft Parade (July 1969)
Morrison Hotel (February 1970)
LA Woman (April 1971)
Absolutely Live [double live album] (July 1970)
13 [compilation of hits] (November 1970)

chapter 1

THE DOORS' ARTISTIC VISION

"A successful rock group has to combine technical virtuosity
with a savage kind of grace."
Richard Goldstein in *Critique*, 1969 NET (National Education Television)
special on The Doors

Why do The Doors continue not only to survive, but also thrive? Jim Morrison's notoriety can't be responsible for the lasting power of The Doors. When the god became all too human, Jim fell from the Dionysian throne on Mt Olympus and back to Earth with a thud.

That doesn't keep selling this music.

The Doors' artistic vision keeps the music alive. On each of the six studio albums, the group composed a well-rendered portrait of their artistic vision that evoked both reaction and transformation. Art is revolutionary; unfortunately, most of what is called 'art' nowadays is merely something being marketed for consumption, not transformation.

The intensity and uniqueness of The Doors' artistic vision emerged from the four members functioning as a cohesive, creative spirit, although their artistic achievements have been overshadowed by the hype begot by Morrison's six-year presence on the American rock 'n' roll scene. But Morrison, as an artist, a shamanic spirit of sorts, understood symbols and their relationships in the context of our culture and how he expressed them became the hallmark of The Doors' legacy.

A shamanic spirit understands how to travel on this esoteric landscape of symbols and values of the shaman's culture. To render pictures from this landscape, Morrison used short snatches of poetic imagery and themes that could grasp the fast-paced, temporal-oriented contemporary mind. He understood the power of obscurity. Tantalise with a short, beautiful or terrifying burst of imagery. Arouse curiosity. Excite with sexual tension.

With drug imagery. With the threat of violence. Of unknown fears. Of death. Then leave the mind in a state that it seeks to complete the aroused experience.

> "Great poets are insurgents.
> They are in revolt against
> the limitations of reason and logic."
> Wallace Fowlie, *Rimbaud (A Critical Study)* (pp230-31)
>
> Hank Zevallos: "Why do you write lyrics
> and what are you trying to do with them?"
> Jim Morrison: "Achieve clarity and alter fate.
> Deepen a strange hue in the clan tartan."
> Jim Morrison (interview), *Poppin* (March 1970 p47)

The other three Doors didn't simply play music to accompany Jim's lyrics. In essence, all four were shamanic, knowing how to tap into the culture's matrix of values and symbols without needing to intellectualise. That is not to say The Doors didn't intellectualise their songs; they had to on some levels, piecing together the artistic impressions each member grasped at: a lyrical image, an organ interlude, a guitar riff, a drum cadence. (While all four had attended college, two of The Doors, Ray Manzarek and Jim Morrison, had *earned* college degrees – a rarity among rock musicians.)

Most of the songs started with an idea from Morrison and occasionally from the group's guitarist, Robby Krieger. And then, as keyboardist Ray Manzarek explained in the radio special, *History Of Rock 'n' Roll*, the four of them worked like a "communal brain" and the songs then evolved from "all four guys putting their input into the song."[1]

The other three Doors – Manzarek, Krieger and drummer John Densmore – meshed their musical expressions to Morrison's poetic imagery and themes. And all four were aware of this. After describing the universal rejection of the group's initial acetate six-song demos (recorded before Krieger joined the group) in his book, *Riders On The Storm*, Densmore wrote: "Incredible, I thought. They just don't understand our vision. They don't get it!"[2] Well, a quick listen to the demos would easily convince most people why their vision wasn't understood.

The creative guidance Morrison provided as the main lyricist became

1 *History of Rock ' n' Roll*, aired 29 April 1978, WOWO Radio, 1190 AM, Fort Wayne, IN.
2 John Densmore *Riders On The Storm: My Life With Jim Morrison And The Doors* (New York: Delacorte Press, 1990) p46.

quite evident upon his death. The group cut two more albums, but the albums lacked the spirit and impact of the previous works; as Manzarek reflected, the three of them could make music, "but somehow the whole lyrical, vocal thing just wasn't right without Jim."[3] In a 1972 interview with *ZigZag* magazine, Krieger stated when Morrison was in the group, "it was like the band with the voice of God up front."[4] Morrison's verbal imagery and themes set the tone of the six original studio albums.

Each of The Doors had a creative role, determined by individual instinct and collectively by the group's dynamics. The Doors' *sound* is unique because of how all four fit their roles together. In the video, *The Doors: A Tribute To Jim Morrison*, Krieger stated that on stage, instead of performing a show or an act, they tried to do *reality*: "the music was what we were really feeling." The relationship between the music and the musicians was direct; hence, The Doors' sound cannot be duplicated and has not given rise to any new styles. Except for the fourth album, their music doesn't sound like anything or anybody else. It is rare to even hear the exact sound within a repeated pattern of a song. The moment guided the creative input by each member and no two moments are ever the same. Yet these images and themes piece together, forming a coherent picture of the band's artistic vision, a reflection that isn't always clear and can be described many different ways.

Their message echoed Timothy Leary's aphorism for the times: turn on, tune in, and drop out. An avid reader, as were all The Doors, Morrison absorbed Friedrich Nietzche's discourse in *The Birth Of Tragedy* on the conflict of Apollonian-Dionysian duality in art as manifested in the tragic struggle of the hero. He took to heart the archetypal hero figure so characterised in Joseph Campbell's works who risks the journey to bring wisdom or insight back to his culture. He wrote Professor Wallace Fowlie of North Carolina a letter of gratitude for his translation of the works of French poet Arthur Rimbaud whose short, intense life was a 19th-century inspiration for Morrison. William Blake's aphorism that if the doors of perception were cleansed, everything would appear to man as it truly is, infinite begot Aldous Huxley's book, *The Doors Of Perception*, describing his mescaline-induced seeking; *The Doors Of Perception* begot Morrison's seeking which begot The Doors' artistic vision.

The Doors insisted their work was art and each album they created was a unified composition, as Ray Manzarek told me, a conceptual album. And

3 *History Of Rock 'n' Roll.*
4 John Tobler *The Doors In A Nutshell; 64 Quick Questions,* (ZigZag, September 1972) p29.

the albums together portray the maturing of artists creating the art to express their vision. Worthwhile to note is Manzarek's comment on the compilation albums released by Elektra: "We never wanted those compilations albums released at all."[5] Their music was originally recorded onto vinyl discs. The vinyl album had two sides and each of The Doors albums recognised a beginning on side one, a closing on side one, either a restating of the theme or a transition to open side two and an ending.

Not all conceptual albums follow a smooth, chronological ordering which takes the listener comfortably through a storyline. Organisational patterns have been traditional modes of moving chronologically through event one to the last sequential event, such as The Who's *Tommy* and Pink Floyd's *The Wall*; thematic statements which take the listener through a kaleidoscope of images, such as The Beatles' *Sgt Pepper's Lonely Hearts Club Band* and many of Frank Zappa's albums (notably the early ones with the Mothers Of Invention (ie *Freak Out*); or extended metaphors, such as the Moody Blues' albums, notably *Days Of Future Past*.

A conceptual album results from artists consciously creating an album within an intended structure (which exemplifies the original notion of a concept album as the term came into use in the 1960s) or from a producer who arranges songs from the artist's repertoire to reflect an intrinsic theme. This latter process typifies The Doors under the guidance of producer Paul Rothchild, who produced the first five albums.

So, what characterises the music of The Doors?

First, the instrumentation. The prominent use of an electric organ was unique, as was the lack of a bass player and use of only one guitarist. Though The Doors used bass players in the studio, the lack of a bass player in the group contributed to The Doors creating songs with a sound that was haunting and ethereal. It was standard practice to use different guitar players for different styles; guitarist Robby Krieger did it all and incredibly well. Having a jazz background, drummer John Densmore brought an essential quality of blending to mold The Doors' *sound*. Never just a time-keeper, he commented on whatever the other three were doing.

Then there was Morrison's voice. His sensual crooning, sarcastic laughter and screams are all givens. Rothchild said of Morrison's voice, "He was a rock 'n' roll Bing Crosby; the first crooner of the new era." In *Wilderness: The Lost Writings Of Jim Morrison, Volume I*, Jim wrote in a poem that his voice was, at best, a "scream" or a "sick croon" with the "squeaks" and

5 Tobler, *The Doors In A Nutshell*, p29.

"furies" of a repressed teenager's "nasal whine"[6]. Despite a lack of training, Morrison demonstrated a good sense of control and appropriateness of phrasings and feelings to get maximum audience impact.

In popular music, vocals usually carry the melody and instrumental parts mold into layers underneath the singer. At the bottom is a bass line. The guitar line can be either rhythm or lead with a piano or organ in supporting capacity. This didn't characterise The Doors.

None of The Doors limited himself to one particular musical role; they *never* played in predictable or well-defined layers, but in swirls. The music swirls because the relationship between the four performing musicians constantly changes. One player would throw out a bass line or rhythm and everybody would build on that before the texture shifted subtly and the ensemble fell together in a different configuration. Because of these dynamics, The Doors were innovative in their sound.

The first three albums – *The Doors*, *Strange Days*, and *Waiting For The Sun* – produced in less than 18 months, are musically equivalent as the group's music matured with an overall sound that is generally psychedelic, but daring and still lurking in the shadows. Despite the use of an orchestra and a sell-out to pop idioms in the fourth album, *The Soft Parade*, The Doors' sound begins to shift to a blues theme. On the fifth and sixth albums, *Morrison Hotel* and *LA Woman*, the sound becomes more gutsy and closer to the blues. The artistic vision matured, and these later albums have to be approached differently, which many critics failed to do as they compared these later albums to the group's initial burst of music.

The swirling tempest of anger and urgency which characterised the initial albums had slowed to a blues style and the music became more relative to life that all humans experience. Closer to the street. The Doors' essence was still there, but the fist-clenching anger was replaced with wisdom gained from experience which allowed for deeper feeling to emerge.

A comparison of the bootleg recordings from the gigs by The Doors at The Matrix in San Francisco in March of 1967 (before they exploded on the national scene) with the live recordings on the 1983 release, *Alive, She Cried*, gives a good indication of what being thrust into the mass market did to The Doors' sound. The Matrix recordings reflect the kind of intimate nightclub scene where people came to sit back, slowly get stoned, *listen* to the band tell you how it is, applaud, and then drift home. The pleasant applause and a cordial Morrison at the microphone seem so distant from

6 Jim Morrison *Wilderness: The Lost Writings Of Jim Morrison, Volume I* (New York: Villard Books, 1988), p205.

the soon-to-be raucous, arena-filled concerts. And the sound which was still contoured to fit the intimacy of the nightclub would blossom into the amplified renderings of the live performances that grace the album *Alive, She Cried*, released in 1983.

> In a May 1967 review of The Doors at the Whisky-A-Go Go for the Los Angeles Times, Pete Johnson wrote that their consistently spirited music was "too raw for comfort" and the symbolism in their lyrics bordered "on tastelessness," but they had nurtured their own "distinctive style, melting jazz improvisation, a hard rock beat and free-wheeling word imagery." (18 May 1967, Part IV, p13.)

The picture of life The Doors painted from their artistic perspective may appear to be puzzling and fragmentary, mostly because of Morrison's rich rendering with universal symbols rather than specific ones. Like all art, a work of art renders a different impression on each beholder. The different impressions evoked by The Doors spread from one end of the emotional and intellectual spectrum to the other, from "it's all the sophomoric psychedelic babble of a bozo laureate" to "he's a god," and for the most part, each are valid renderings of The Doors.

Much of Morrison's lyrics, and perhaps no one has done better, capture vividly the adolescent alienation, desperation and isolation which so characterise our modern times. But beyond this perspective, The Doors rendered an artistic vision of the fragmentary nature of twentieth century society, a fragmenting that creates disquieting despair in even the most basic sanctuaries of a house or of love. Not only did their music consistently portray the fears of life, but also the hopes. And their artistic vision remains a vivid portrait of the landscape we move across.

Art tells stories about being human, being alive, about aspiring beyond the day-to-day mundane. A piece of art invokes both its own story and one that unfolds within whoever ponders that piece. And each one of these albums tells a story. Listeners should use discretion – and their own imaginations.

"It is easily understood
why such a feeble culture hates a strong art:
it is afraid of being destroyed by it."
Friedrich Nietzsche, *The Birth Of Tragedy*

chapter 2

BREAKIN' ON THROUGH:
the debut album

"Jim's great talent was to do something that made you respond as who you really were. He made you drop your guard. He provoked you."
Bill Siddons, Doors manager, in Westwood One Radio Special,
Rock 'n' Roll Never Forgets: Jim Morrison

There was a magical tension in the 1960s, a whirlwind of social, polit-ical and creative forces. Political and social winds kept the vibrant air swirling with tensions and creative energies, especially of the young, tossed and turned in those winds, sensitive to an uneasiness with the traditional Western way of life. Creative expression in turn, focused and honed itself upon this growing sense of uneasiness.

The first wave of the post-WW II generation had matured to young adulthood. Under the shadow of the nuclear bomb and fallout from WW II, American society had spent almost two decades rebuilding a sense of security while maintaining its new position as leader of the Free World. The generation that came of age in the Sixties had grown up in an unreal world of technological wizardry which was a very real everyday world to them.

They questioned traditional paths. As Don J Hibbard and Carol Kaleialoha noted in their book, *The Role Of Rock*, this generation "revi-talised and garbed in mod clothing" the Christian ethic of "love thy neigh-bour" as an alternative to the Cold War rhetoric of "us vs them": a broth-erhood of love where people treated others as equals, "everyone viewed as a brother or sister involved in the experience of living."[1] Moreover, the youth, especially the artists, perceived what Hibbard, Kaleialoha and oth-ers did: "the ludicrousness of an American economic system with no social purpose other than its own self-preservation and expansion."[2] Yet this same dissident generation could live off the fat of society and enjoy

1 Don J Hibbard and Carol Kaleialoha *The Role Of Rock* (Englewood Cliffs, NJ: Prentice-Hall Inc, 1983) p 48.
2 Ibid, p43.

the fruits of both worlds of technology and of freedom that such affluence begot – and do so without becoming part of the system.

Here within laid the fertile soil for strange times.

The early Sixties had been a turbulent mixture of the charm of Camelot and impending darkness of the nuclear shadow, of the energetic post-WWII generation coming of age, and the lingering, entrenched values of moral and political providence shaped by The Great Depression and two world wars. The election of John F Kennedy as President in 1960 signalled the arrival of youthful energy and idealism. It ushered in of an age of Camelot, but the Americanised version of royalty quickly became a trial of political will with the Bay of Pigs Invasion fiasco and the building of the Berlin Wall in 1961. The Cuban Missile Crisis of October 1962 cast the imminent shadow of Soviet nuclear bombs parked just beyond the tip of Florida and aimed at the US mainland. Rachel Carson's book, *Silent Spring*, a well-documented indictment of the indiscriminate use of pesticides and other chemicals (particularly DDT) signalled that the threat to this age of American Camelot wasn't just coloured red by Soviet communism. In 1963, Americans had to deal with events that shook the post-WWII compliancy: the assassination of civil rights leader Medgar Evers in June, the emergence of Martin Luther King Jr (which was consummated by his "I have a dream" speech during the Washington DC Freedom March for job opportunity and employment equality in August), and the vacant senselessness of John F Kennedy's assassination in November, followed two days later by Jack Ruby's killing of Lee Harvey Oswald on live television. The age of JFK's Camelot with all its flaws became the backroom reality of political arm-twisting of LBJ.

On 7 February 1964, The Beatles arrived at Kennedy Airport in New York City. They appeared on the *Ed Sullivan Show* and began a phenomenally successful tour – and conquest – of America. The court of Camelot shifted to the upbeat and sanguine music of the mop tops. In movie theatres, the American public was entertained by Julie Andrews and Dick Van Dyke in Walt Disney's *Mary Poppins* and by Peter Sellers and George C Scott in Stanley Kubrick's *Dr Strangelove* (whose Cold War and nuclear sabre-rattling rhetoric would echo with a frightening clarity during the Reagan presidency of the 1980s). With the success of the second and third James Bond films, *From Russia With Love* (1963) and

Goldfinger (1964), the superhero – both Agent 007 and the actor Sean Connery – consummated the transition to the very marketable and commercially successful superstar. Lyndon Baines Johnson got his landmark Civil Rights Act passed in July, but the Gulf of Tonkin incident in August signalled the beginning of America's longest involvement in a war. North Vietnamese PT boats clashed with a US destroyer and carrier which lead to the initial US bombing of North Vietnam and the subsequent Gulf of Tonkin resolution passed by Congress, giving the president authority to use all necessary measures to help any member nation of SEATO (Southeast Asia Treaty Organisation). Though he would overwhelmingly defeat conservative Republican Barry Goldwater in November for the office of President, LBJ had laid the foundation for a decade of protest and social division – and for his own political demise.

In February 1965 in New York City, rival Black Muslims set the tone for the ensuing decades of violence among Afro-Americans: they gunned down Malcolm X, who had broken from the Black Muslims and founded the Black Nationalist movement. Meanwhile, Martin Luther King Jr continued to spearhead civil rights marches and demonstrations which led to violent confrontations and deaths of civil rights advocates, both black and white. The dream of a Great Society was coming at a nightmarish pace from out of the shadows of such technological wizardry like the opening of the Harris County Dome Stadium in Houston, Texas, for the 9 April home opener of the Houston baseball team. The arena would soon be renamed the Astrodome.

Bob Dylan shattered the haven many had sought in his music when he went "electric" on stage at the Newport Folk Festival in July. And what many consider the epitome of a rock song, the Rolling Stones' 'Satisfaction', crested the airwaves through the summer of 1965. The Mod Look became the garb of the emerging counter-culture: tight bell-bottom jeans and stylised long haircuts designed by Vidal Sassoon, a London-based hair dresser.

But the impoverished reality in America's own backyard of racial minorities would erupt with riots in many cities, notably several days of riots in August in Watts, a densely populated, mostly black section of Los Angeles. After white Californian state highway patrolmen stopped a 21-year-old black man who was driving while drunk, Watts exploded with riots of economic and social frustration that left 34 dead, over a thousand injured, and damage estimated at $200 million and revised down to $40 million. Despite the efforts and pleas of leaders like Dr Martin Luther King Jr, some 13,900 National Guardsmen were required to restore order as the smoggy skies of LA became grey with the smoke of the buildings burning in Watts.

During 1966 a more aggressive black power began organising. Though the purpose of 'black power', a slogan used in a June 1966 civil rights march in Mississippi by Stokely Carmichael, was to promote pride and organisation among the Negro community, outspoken blacks began sticking stark images into America's consciousness through the media. Using street-smart rhetoric and resolve which was sharply distinct to Martin Luther King Jr, Bobby Seale and Huey Newton (founders of the Black Panther Party), H Rap Brown ("Violence is as American as apple pie..."), Eldridge Cleaver and Carmichael cut at the well-worn white social fabric that was laggardly easing its resistance to the marches and demonstrations for civil rights. The black community was now quite aware of its inequality, but the promise of The Great Society hadn't relieved it. The US economy was booming, led by unprecedented federal government spending by on both domestic programs and the Vietnam War and powers-to-be in both government and business were not anxious to use restraint with the overheating economy. Medicare went into effect, and anti-war demonstrations began descending on the isolated policy makers in Washington DC.

Internationally, French President Charles De Gaulle, the general who was France's WW II hero, was undermining NATO's objectives by asserting French autonomy while the Soviets and Chinese continued to escalate the tension over who would lead the communist half of humanity's political world. The Great Proletarian Cultural Revolution in China to purge bourgeois ideology, though far more deadly, paralleled similar apprehension to the intellectual and artistic unrest in Western culture. Despite the Cold War tensions, within Russia there was appreciation, if not desire, for the former country's ties with Europe; ironic as it was then, a book was published titled, *The Soviets In NATO*. The Middle East continued to be a boiling cauldron with military actions justified by previous provocations. Though the world, like the US, simmered in polarising ideologies, life wasn't all that black-and-white.

By the fall season of 1966, almost all the prime-time programming on the three major US television networks (ABC, CBS and NBC) was in colour. Lee J Cobb's rivetting portrait of Willie in the television adaptation of Arthur Miller's *Death Of A Salesman* juxtaposed with the twice-a-week campness of *Batman* led by Adam West (Batman) and Burt Ward (Robin). *Star Trek*, the television series, debuted, while the season's half-hour comedies formed the foundation of syndicated shows for cable two decades later: *Andy Griffith Show, Bewitched, The Beverly Hillbillies, Get Smart, Gilligan's Island, Green Acres, I Dream Of Jeannie, The Lucy Show* and *That Girl*. And from the 1966 fall world of television came The Monkees, whose music would soon rule the sales charts leading up to the 1967's summer of love. Despite the overwhelming presence of The Monkees, popular music was filled with rock's political and social commentary – which was not beyond the Monkees (ie 'Pleasant Valley Sunday'). The swelling ranks of college-aged young people embodied a commixture of naive ideals and reactionary desires for change.

In the August of 1966, Charles Whitman barricaded himself in the tower on the University of Texas at Austin and began shooting and killing people until he himself was shot and killed. Truman Capote's *In Cold Blood*, a non-fiction account of the murder of a farm family in Holcomb, Kansas, became a best-selling book, along with Jacqueline Susann's elaborate and seedy harlequin novel, *Valley Of The Dolls*, whose film version would include the young actress Sharon Tate. Ralph Nader's book *Unsafe At Any Speed* challenged the automobile industry's apathetic attitude to safety, and the federal government quickly responded with legislation – change could happen, if it were politically expedient. Timothy Leary was proselytising about LSD, still legally sold, notably at head shops in California: "Turn on, tune in, and drop out."

A 55-year-old former film actor, Ronald Reagan, was elected governor of California in the November elections, and Walt Disney died in December of lung cancer. Aptly, the 8 April 1966 cover of *Time* magazine asked, "Is God Dead?" and spurned a slew of responses in other publications around the theme of "The Challenge Of God Being Dead." Notable was the 25 April cover of *US News* which proclaimed, "God Is Not 'Dead'" inside was the magazine's eight-page interview of affirmation with America's leading evangelist, Billy Graham.

"We live in an age of revolutionary transformation. We can seek to shape it or we can doom ourselves to irrelevance. We can accept the challenge to our creativity or we can resign ourselves to ineffectual bitterness. We can lose ourselves in passionate and paralysing controversy over technical aspects of individual problems, or we can, as I deeply believe we must, develop a more creative perspective – one which enables us to see the inner relationship of great issues and the larger framework within which they can be solved."

New York Governor Nelson A Rockefeller, *Policy And The People*, Foreign Affairs (January 1968 p231)

By the mid-1960s, artistic imagination had began turning toward social commentary because the social protest of the early Sixties – most conspicuous in the music of Bob Dylan, Joan Baez, Phil Ochs and others – had made its point: social protest didn't change the problems; it only made others, especially authority, more immutable. The Atlantis of folk rock, before sinking beneath the onrush of the next wave of the rock era, provided a brief but significant bridge from the Sixties folk music and the commercialisation of the rock 'n' roll of the late Fifties to the onrush of what has been called the Golden Age Of Rock. The Beatles and Bob Dylan consolidated the artistic potential of rock 'n' roll and then sent it scattering in infinite directions.

And with the advent of the cassette tape, pioneered and promoted by Philips, this explosion of creativity via music became accessible to anyone – both artist and listener. A portable, inexpensive tape deck could now both record and play music without the need for elaborate and expensive electronic equipment. From the West Coast came hippies, love children, flower power, and a music that was turning people on to more than just the endless summer of the Beach Boys and Jan And Dean.

President Johnson had escalated the war in Vietnam to proportions previously undreamed of while pushing his vision of The Great Society. America's youth were leery of being told not to stray from the path leading to materialistic success and college-age students were beginning to discover the power of sit-ins and marches. Despite Martin Luther King Jr's non-violent tactics, frustrated militant black leaders were mobilising a stifled black spirit. Detroit was about to erupt into a hot summer of riots and fires.

Lines were being drawn – for the American way of fitting into the system, or for the American spirit of freedom and revolution. Authority vs Youth. Them against Us. Establishment vs Pop culture. The rhetoric and attitudes of the Cold War were not limited to just the world's political stage.

The vision of brotherhood had not yet been shattered by the events of 1968 and 1969, by the reality of the political machinery of America, by Richard Nixon and Watergate, by the assassination of Bobby Kennedy and Martin Luther King Jr, by the killing of students at Kent State and Jackson State Universities, by the disaster at the Rolling Stone free concert at Altamont. There was a magical tension – and in 1965 in Los Angeles, an obscure rock group was formed named The Doors fronted by one Jim Morrison.

The Jekyll and Hyde nature of the times was evident in the works of many rock artists, notably The Doors, whose six-year history embodied such a dualistic nature. By 1966, The Doors consisted of John Densmore (21), drummer; Robby Krieger (20), guitarist; Ray Manzarek (27), keyboards; and Jim Morrison (22), vocals. The period from the summer of 1965 through late 1966 marks the group's often labelled acid fertility period, when the group played nightly gigs on the Los Angeles Sunset Strip. Free of commercial demands and constraints, the group worked out their songs during the gigs, filling in with old blues numbers. The bulk of these original compositions eventually provided the material for their first three albums. In late 1966, Elektra Records signed the group to a recording contract, and Paul Rothchild (30) was assigned as the group's producer. In January 1967, what many critics have labelled "the best debut album in rock 'n' roll," *The Doors*, was released.

At the top of the singles charts were The Monkees' 'I'm A Believer' and the Royal Guardsman's 'Snoopy Vs The Red Baron'. The Beach Boys' 'Good Vibrations' was on the way out and the Rolling Stones' 'Ruby Tuesday' was on the way up. The Beatles' were about to release the double single, 'Penny Lane'/'Strawberry Fields Forever'. The Monkees debut album was Number One on the album charts, ahead of the durable selling soundtracks for the 1966 film, *D. Zhivago* and the 1965 film, *The Sound Of Music*. Simon and Garfunkel's *Parsley, Sage, Rosemary and Thyme*, the Rolling Stones' *Got Live If You Want It* and *Aftermath*, and The Beatles' *Revolver* shared slots on the top-selling albums along with albums from The Mamas and The Papas, Eric Burdon and The Animals,

The Association, Lovin' Spoonful, Donovan, Herman's Hermits, Paul Revere and The Raiders, Lou Rawls, and five albums by Herb Albert and The Tijuana Brass. *The Doors* would steadily work its way up the chart of top selling albums in America, sitting behind The Beatles' *Sgt Pepper's Lonely Hearts Club Band*, The Rolling Stones' *Flowers* and The Monkees' *Headquarters*. Eventually The Doors' debut album reached Number Two behind *Sgt Pepper*, an interesting statement by The Beatles on the culture blossoming from and nurtured by their rock music.

The Doors found little comfort in either the established system or the emerging Pop culture. The American way clothed itself in arrogant, aggressive attire – a facade of plastic machismo, a costume Morrison felt little comfort in wearing. He perceived fitting in to the system as a subtle form of murder, as he explained to Lizze James: "When others demand that we become the people they want us to be, they force us to destroy the person we are."[3] As often portrayed in Doors songs, the American way of life was too mechanical, too self-enslaving for the soul. Nor did Morrison dress himself in the Pop culture's cloak of brotherly love. As Lester Bangs in *Creem* magazine observed, Morrison saw that "machismo equals bozo in the drag" and that rock stars were just "huge oafus cartoons, more gushers of American snake-oil."[4]

Reactions to The Doors – especially to Morrison – ranged from Nik Cohn's opinion in his book, *Rock From The Beginning*, that The Doors "are no great band" and a lot of Morrison's lyrics "come across as pure pretentious bullshit"[5] to underground newspaper *Los Angeles Free Press* writer Gene Youngblood's view that The Doors "reach for outer limits of inner space" and Morrison and The Doors "are a demonic and beautiful miracle that has risen like a shrieking Phoenix from the burning bush of the new music."[6] Somewhere between falls the review from *Disk Review* magazine which labelled The Doors' style as "hard rock with slippery, psychedelic overtones" and defined "Morrison therapy" as "to become more real, to be a better person, cut your ties to the establishment past, swim in your emotions, suffer symbolic death and rebirth; rebirth as a new man, psychologically cleansed."[7] Morrison therapy reveals a poetic perspective Jim rendered to express his view of life,

---

3 Lizze James *Lizze James Interview With Jim Morrison* printed in *The Doors: The Illustrated History* Danny Sugerman and Benjamin Edmonds (eds) (New York: William Morrow and Company, 1983) p65.
4 Lester Bangs *Jim Morrison, Oafus Laureate Creem* Special Edition: *The Doors*, Summer 1981 p29.
5 Nik Cohn *Rock From The Beginning* (New York: Stein and Day, 1969) p236.
6 Gene Youngblood *Doors Reaching For Outer Limits Of Inner Space, Los Angeles Free Press*, 1st December 1967 pp6 & 15.
7 Irwin Stambler *Encyclopedia Of Pop, Rock And Soul* (New York: St Martin's Press, 1974) p167.

just as other artists do, drawing from the paraphernalia of their times to create images that express these perspectives of the human condition. For rock 'n' roll, drugs and sex – and in the Sixties, violence and the Vietnam War – provided a fountain of imagery for artistic spirits to draw from. Like his contemporaries, Morrison sketched many pictures with imagery of sex, death, drugs, and the unknown to convey this Morrison therapy of self-realisation and rebirth. As John Densmore wrote in *Riders On The Storm*, Jim's poetry was "erotic, but not pornographic; mystical, but not pretentious."[8] Wallace Fowlie, in his comparative study of Jim Morrison and the French poet Morrison so admired, Arthur Rimbaud, wrote that Morrison's poetry "appears as a reflection of great poetry," a reflection that is "obsessive and subtle" and images in Jim's verses "spring up...like reflexes and answers to the subconscious law of chance and free association."[9] Shadowed with such bizarre and dark imagery, Morrison's poetic perspective reflects seemingly confusing renderings, leaving the impression of a negative portrait of the world of man. However, Morrison sought to reveal that some basic forces were being suppressed behind the facades of both the Western way of life and the romantic notions of this latest, newly born Pop culture, an offspring of rock 'n' roll.

The Sixties being a time of activism, The Doors as artists wanted people to react. Fred Powledge noted in an insightful article for *Life* that Morrison's lyrics "challenge you to try to interpret."[10] In an interview with Lizze James, Morrison said that the facades we live behind block "perceptions from coming in" and "feelings from coming out" and that he tried to shatter those facades in two ways: "one way is violence, pain," and "the other is eroticism."[11]

Short snatches of both poetic and musical imagery and themes from The Doors' artistic vision had a chance to take hold in the impressionable minds of either the youth or the media. Poetry built in the traditional sense upon a central theme within a well-defined format couldn't begin to get a foothold in a culture attuned for immediate, sensory impressions. These snatches of poetic images and themes are like fragments that piece together and ultimately form a coherent picture of The Doors' artistic perspective of life, a reflection that isn't always clear and

8 Densmore p129.
9 Wallace Fowlie *Rimbaud And Jim Morrison: The Rebel As Poet* (Durham, NC: Duke University Press, 1993; paperback edition 1994) p123
10 Fred Powledge *Wicked Go The Doors*, *Life*, 12th April 1968 p86B.
11 Lizze James *Jim Morrison: Ten Years Gone*, *Creem* Special Edition: *The Doors*, Summer 1981 p18.

can be described in many different ways.

The picture of life The Doors paint from this artistic perspective may appear to be puzzling and fragmentary, mostly because of Morrison's rich rendering with universal symbols rather than specific ones. And this was evident early. In the October 1968 issue of *Crawdaddy*, Robert Somma criticised the "supremacy of the banal" in The Doors' repetition of the elemental – like sun, moon, earth, fire, water, river, and sea. The Doors "dwell in the universe, probably because it is thus easier to pass from one century to another, to fornicate with the earth, to fuck the archetypes of the mind."[12] However, if an artist's works reflect the times, then The Doors' works, even in their copious universal imagery, echo the fragmentary nature of our society and the yearning for a connection to truths expelled from an artificial environment which has segmented the world into days, hours, minutes and seconds, into disjointed plastic images detached from life. And such fragmentation creates disquieting despair in even the most basic sanctuaries of a house or of love.

With the guidance of producer Paul Rothchild, the three albums drawing from this pool of songs generated during The Doors' formative years each reflect a well-composed portrait of their artistic imagination, a distinct artistic vision that emerged on each of the six albums. In producing The Doors' work, Rothchild explained to Paul Williams in an interview published in *Crawdaddy* that he focused upon his own perception that Morrison was saying that every trip we take brings a death "of concepts, of bullshit, a death of laughter and soft lies" and that we need to "kill the alien concepts" and return to "the beginning of personal concepts...to your *own* reality."[13] This theme of searching through death and self-realisation weaves together the first album, *The Doors*, which opens with a yearning for revelation in 'Break On Through' progresses through a series of songs which oscillate between pursuing the need both for the sanctuary of love and for the freedom to explore the unknown, and then arrives at a resolution with 'The End'.

> "The music is stark, brutal. Within the inner reaches of the barely suppressed consciousness, The Doors scream the cry of a twisted grotesque. A girl has disappeared and you are lying there, naked, cold, alone. Lost in a strange forest, with the last rays of light slipping away one is at the mercy of his hunters. The primeval ooze of the earth is damply sucking at your

12 Robert Somma *Banging Away At The Doors Of Convention, Crawdaddy*, October 1968 p20.
13 Paul Williams *Rothchild Speaks, Crawdaddy*, July/August 1967 pp20 & 21.

feet. Soon you will be absorbed.
"Far away a slight form huddles against the tree to keep from freezing.
"The music fascinates. Perhaps in us...a little...Doors, or...doors."
Ed Jilek, *Records* (his entire review of The Doors), *The Paper* (underground
newspaper) Michigan State University (East Lansing, MI), 9 May 1967, p12.

SIDE 1:
'Break On Through (To The Other Side)'
'Soul Kitchen'
'The Crystal Ship'
'Twentieth Century Fox'
'Alabama Song (Whisky Bar)'
'Light My Fire'

'Break On Through' opens the album and provides an overture that
etches out the message The Doors rendered on all six albums: they
probe life as something to be lived, yet always recognising that life is
mystical and made of many realities. The opening lines introduce The
Doors' artistic vision – that day destroys night and night ruptures day. A
light side; a dark side. Waking time; dream time. Things known; things
unknown. But the known destroys access to the unknown. And the
urgency of the music conveys an underlying tension. Morrison finds
refuge of an island in his lover's arms and tranquillity of country in her
eyes, yet those same arms chained and those same eyes lied. Life is dualistic, and Morrison does not trust what he feels is meaningful. Finding
refuge with love yields to a yearning to break through to the other side.

Inexperienced in the marketing of Top 40 singles, Elektra released
this song as The Doors' debut single, and the poignant and ambiguous
lyrics proved too cacophonic for Top 40 ears. The song hit Number 126
on the *Billboard* Hot 100 chart for 8 April 1967, and that was it. The
Number One song that week, for the third consecutive week, the
Turtles' 'Happy Together' was followed by The Mamas and The Papas'
'Dedicated To The One I Love' and Nancy and Frank Sinatra's
'Somethin' Stupid'. Densmore wrote he was worried the Brazilian-like
bossa nova beat he used was "too eccentric for the mass market".[14] So
the album and the group remained for awhile longer comfortable com-
modities for the heady underground.

14 Densmore p102.

Morrison finds refuge in the second song, 'Soul Kitchen'. Though the song was a tribute to Olivia's, a soul food restaurant Morrison frequented on Venice Beach in LA, Morrison doesn't miss the sexual metaphor of warming his head next to her oven as he wooingly urges to let him sleep in her soul kitchen and warm his mind near her gentle stove. Though *kitchen* and *stove* suggest a sanctuary, there is no asylum from time (the clock says it's closing time) or an urban scene with inhabitants in a state of resigned alienation and of cars crawling by, stuffed with eyes under the hollow glow of street lights. The dissonant, ominous mixture of images and sounds creates a disturbing impression of the shadow cast by LA's endless summer light. Morrison leaves 'Soul Kitchen' singing about learning to forget; it has been but a moment of sanctuary.

Morrison then seeks out the 'Crystal Ship'. His voice drifts in a sedate, drug-like tone, as if a fraction off-beat. He croons that before his lover slips into unconsciousness, he wants one more kiss, one more chance at bliss. Then he forsakes bliss for another chance to fly. The ambiguous duality of life: he'd rather fly than cry and be vulnerable. Youthful urgency has yet to understand the gentle rain of the rainman in 'L'America' on the sixth album. The song closes with enticing hyperbole – the crystal ship offers a thousand girls and thrills and a million ways to kill time. But Morrison understands the danger sailing on such a ship. This ship is *crystal* – expensive and fragile; hardly the type of sanctuary one seeks in life.

The Doors return to a love song, 'Twentieth Century Fox', regarded by many as one of Morrison's best lyrics. According to an article written in 1976 for *Crawdaddy* by Richard Blackburn, a fellow film student with Morrison at UCLA, Manzarek's long-term girl friend (and wife to be) Dorothy Fugikawa, inspired the lyrics to this song.[15] Manzarek, in his book *Light My Fire: My Life With The Doors*, indicated this song was for Dorothy.[16]

When set within the landscape of this debut album, the lyrics render a more expansive portrait. The twangy guitar of Krieger pans the opening portrait of a fashionably lean and fashionably late female who never breaks a date or ranks a scene. She's a Twentieth Century Fox – not a chick, not a lady, but, as Richard Goldstein wrote in his edited collection, *The Poetry of Rock*, a *fox*, "a liberated hunter on the prowl."[17] In his unprecedented book of critical analysis, *The Poetry of*

15 Richard Blackburn *Jim Morrison's School Days, Tripping through the College Jungle, Crawdaddy*, May 1976 p52.
16 Ray Manzarek *Light My Fire: My Life With The Doors* (New York: GP Putnam's Sons 1998) p5.
17 Richard Goldstein (ed) *The Poetry Of Rock* (New York: Bantam Books 1969) p81.

Rock: The Golden Years, David Pichaske considered the *fox* a "brilliant image", suggesting "sexual appetite, woman the huntress, the tinsel glamour of Twentieth Century Fox films" – and he noted Morrison's singing suggests a pun between *fox* and *fucks*.[18] But she's too twentieth century: no tears or fears or ruined years or clocks. The queen of cool displays no emotions. She may have life locked up in a plastic box, but this fox, as Richard Goldstein wrote in *Poetry Of Rock*, is "at home amid the plastic shrubbery because she herself is plastic, to the roots."[19] And she doesn't waste time with elementary talk, a basic building block of a relationship.

Having found scant sanctuary with the Twentieth Century Fox, Morrison, in the next song, turns to a traditional American drug – whisky. This song is a cover of 'Alabama Song', a song with English lyrics written in the 1920s by German Bertolt Brecht. The song was used in Brecht and Kurt Weill's 1930 German operetta, *Rise And Fall Of The City Of Mahagonny*. This song was on an album Manzarek's wife had of Brecht and Weill songs. Much like The Doors' artistic perspective, Brecht's lyrics and Weill's music paint a picture of how our modern capitalistic society crushes human choice. In the operetta, several prostitutes sing of needing to find the next whisky-bar, the next pretty boy and the next little dollar as they struggle to make it in a post-WWI world gone berserk in materialistic pursuits. Morrison sings for someone to show him the way to the next whisky bar and the next little girl. Effectively rendering a thirties Berlin cabaret tone to the song, The Doors transpose the theme of pre-Hitler Germany to the 1960s of America.

Then they return to one of the most intense sexual anthems in rock, 'Light My Fire', which became the group's signature song.

The heart of the song pulsates with solos of Manzarek and Krieger, whose interplay was inspired by that between John Coltrane's sax and McCoy Tyner's piano in their jazz rendition of 'My Favourite Things' from the Rogers and Hammerstein musical, *The Sound Of Music*. (The song became one of America's best known songs after Julie Andrews sang it in the film version.) Ray's weaving, spiralling organ solo dances with John's drumming, while Robby's guitar smoulders beneath as a gentle pulse. Then Robby rolls through a solo, Ray's organ quieting to a soothing ebbing with John easing into a steady back beat with occa-

18 David R Pichaske *The Poetry Of Rock: The Golden Years* (Peoria, IL: The Ellis Press 1981) p82.
19 Goldstein *The Poetry Of Rock* p81.

sional accent. After the foreplay of the two solos, the organ and guitar begin sputtering to a climax, John's drumming providing exclamations before a final lyrical statement. But it was the shortened version of 'Light My Fire' with the solos edited and trimmed for Top 40 radio airplay which catapulted The Doors and this debut album out of the underground and into the spotlight of mass consumption in the summer of 1967. According to Densmore, a local disc jockey in LA, Dave Diamond, "who spun records from the psychedelic depths of the Diamond Mine", showed Robby and John piles of letters requesting 'Light My Fire' and suggested editing the song down to the then-standard three minute format for radio.[20] Though Robby and John didn't like the idea of shortening the solos, they approached a less-than-excited Rothchild with the idea. John wrote that Paul grudgingly edited the song, but still believed the record didn't have a chance.[21] Eventually, on 29 July 1967, the song replaced the Association's 'Windy' as the number one selling song in America for the next three weeks before being displaced by The Beatles' 'All You Need Is Love' which was displaced by Bobbie Gentry's 'Ode to Billie Joe'.

> "Is there really any point in saying something like, 'The instrumental in 'Light My Fire' builds at the end into a truly visual orgasm in sound' when the reader can at any time put the album onto even the crummiest phonograph and experience that orgasm himself?"
> Paul Williams, *Rock Is Rock: A Discussion of a Doors Song*, *Crawdaddy* (May 1967) p43.

The song reflects the simple imagery of its creator, Robby Krieger. How much higher can we get than love? But the music's urgent rhythms behind Morrison's passionate plead for his baby to light his fire leaves a sense the song seeks a haven of lust, evident in the lyrics Morrison contributed about wallowing in the mire and only losing as love became a funeral pyre. This isn't a soothing love song seeking refuge in a trusting relationship. The plastic images of the pop culture's *free love* and the established Victorian attitude of sexuality melt under the pulsating rhythms of the song. To experience life's passions may require destroying sanctuaries of existing values which deny those passions.

20 Densmore p103.
21 Ibid.

SIDE 2
'Back Door Man'
'I Looked At You'
'End Of The Night'
'Take It As It Comes'
'The End'

Side two opens with one of The Doors' favourite blues numbers, Willie Dixon's 'Back Door Man'. Musically and lyrically a gutsy, earthy tune, this song juxtaposes nicely with the urgency of 'Light My Fire', the plasticity of 'Twentieth Century Fox', the elusive tone of the 'Crystal Ship' and the uneasiness of 'Soul Kitchen'. Morrison's vocals and the other three Doors' instrumentals droll through Dixon's bluesy love song.

Morrison interjects verses borrowed from Howlin' Wolf's version about eating pork and beans and more chicken than any man ever seen. Morrison isn't the hesitant lover in 'Soul Kitchen'. Nor the cynical lover in 'Twentieth Century Fox'. Nor the lustful lover in 'Light My Fire'. In this gutsy, earthy tune, Morrison grovels behind a brash mask of audacity, boasting that he is a back door man whom men don't know, but little girls understand. The lover who is in and out of back doors, leaving behind moments of sanctuary, of breaking through to the other side.

Interestingly, Morrison doesn't include lyrics Willie Dixon unassumingly slips into his laid back blues version of the song; lyrics depicting the Back Door Man being shot full of holes, being accused of first degree murder, being in six feet of ground. The risks of being a Back Door Man. Nonetheless, Morrison's youthful 'Back Door Man', tasting passions of love with the craftiness of a fox contrasts to the ensuing three songs' portrayal of his uneasiness of seeking sanctuary in relationships and his yearning for freedom.

This crafty 'Back Door Man' vanishes as Ray's swirling organ in 'I Looked At You' sweeps us into the passion of the moment: two lovers looked and smiled at each other, and now they're on their way. The Twentieth Century Fox and Stud don't waste time on elementary talk. The tempo is rapid and impulsive, Robby's guitar like a driven bass pushing heatedly onward with John's driving drum beat. But something isn't right, for the song closes with the lovers unable to turn back because it's too late. There has been no time for love to grow.

The rapid impulses of this relationship slow to a journey to 'End Of The Night'. Morrison opens the song singing about taking the highway to a mysterious destination, the end of the night, an image which Jim borrowed from the novel, *Journey To The End of the Night*, written by the French author, Louis-Ferdinand Ce'line. Morrison seeks the other side by trekking to the bright midnight and realms of bliss. And the musical interlude rendered by the organ and guitar conjures up a sensation of a surreal landscape. Though the imagery may suggest drugs, Morrison turns toward the mysterious. The journey into night leads to light and truth and to death and destruction. Though night is considered dark and ominous, Morrison sees a bright midnight illuminating life's realms of bliss.

The slow tempo of this song's invitation to journey to the other side contrasts sharply with the driving tempo of 'Break On Through'. Released as A/B sides of a 45 single, the two songs reflect life's dualistic nature: fast and slow. Both songs invite the same journey into the unknown to find bliss, the bright midnight, the other side.

Manzarek's spinning organ and Krieger's unrelenting bass-like guitar quicken the tempo in the song, 'Take It As It Comes'. But Morrison sings to this rapid beat to take it easy and not to move too fast so love will last. Two songs earlier, he sang about the hurried brevity of love. But if we ride the highway to the end of night, to the bright midnight, then we realise there is a time for everything. When we reach the other side, when the doors of perception, our senses, are cleansed and we see things as they are – infinite, then, as Jim sings, it's time to aim our arrows at the sun.

But living doesn't allow absolute freedom, and people constantly search for sanctuary. Since neither love nor traditional sanctuaries offer security, Morrison turns to 'The End' as his beautiful and only friend.

Richard Walls of *Creem* magazine wrote that 'The End' is "an audacious combination of impeccable musicianship, genuine poetry and psychedelic bullshit."[22] Before 'Light My Fire' hit Number One, Richard Goldstein had described 'The End' as "Joycean pop, with a stream of consciousness lyric" about travel, both physical and spiritual, that "builds to a realisation of mood rather than a sequence of events," opening with "visions of collapsing peace and harmony" and ending with "violent death."[23] Densmore wrote that the song "loosely based on classical

22 Richard Walls *The Doors* (record review) *Creem* Special Edition: *The Doors*, Summer 1981 p48.
23 Richard Goldstein, *The Doors Open Wide*, *New York Magazine*, reprinted in *The Doors: The Illustrated History* p21.

Indian ragas" built from the subdued first two-thirds of the "hypnotic droning sound" to a "musical orgasm" in the "turbulent finale".[24] And, in his review of the debut album for the *Los Angeles Times*, Pete Johnson summarily stated a common reaction, that 'The End' showed how bored Morrison "can sound as he recites singularly simple over-elaborated psychedelic non sequiturs and fallacies."[25] In a *Rolling Stone* interview with Jerry Hopkins, Morrison explained the song "just started out as a simple goodbye song," but added, "it's sufficiently complex and universal in its imagery that it could be almost anything you want it to be."[26]

Surrendering to a sense of hopelessness so artfully rendered in the song's opening, Morrison takes the hand of his only friend, *the end*. The imagery and music swirls as Morrison moves into journey motifs – seeking freedom, riding the King's highway, riding the snake to the ancient lake, going west, answering the call of the blue bus. Then the mood shifts to a calm, eerie look at the archetypal evil in humans as we take a journey with a killer down a hall in a place no longer a sanctuary – the home. Putting the killer's actions into a practical setting (awaking before dawn and putting boots on), Morrison then deviously makes the transition to the philosophical level with the human archetype of taking a face from the ancient gallery, an action that was literally done on the ancient Greek stage. But the calmness of the mask is shattered by the emotional release when the killer completes his journey: telling his father he wants to kill him and then confronting his mother with a good ol' Morrison orgasmic scream.

Producer Paul Rothchild repeatedly offered this interpretation of the Oedipal section of the song. Killing the father meant killing those things instilled in you but aren't of yourself, and sexually conquering the mother meant returning to your essence which can't lie to you – an end of alien concepts and a beginning of personal concepts, which are themes of the classic Oedipal story.

Then Morrison begins coaxing his baby to take a chance on the "blue bus," the colour suggestive of the blues tradition, a journey The Doors had only begun, evident in a response by a still quite young and not as reflective Densmore when asked what "blue bus" implied:

"I never even tried to think of what in the hell the "blue bus" means. It's just there. I can see where someone who wasn't familiar with this music

24 Densmore p122.
25 Pete Johnson *Popular Records: Latest Stones Album Best Yet, Los Angeles Times*, Calender section 26th February 1967 p30.
26 Jerry Hopkins *The Rolling Stone Interview: Jim Morrison, Rolling Stone*, 26th July 1969 p18.

would want to say, "Now what does that damned 'blue bus' thing mean?" You can tell them that if the guys in the band don't even know what it means, they don't have to worry about it."[27]

The music and Morrison move out on the tense edge of being alive, of taking a chance to ride the blue bus, but this isn't going to be an *easy ride*, evident in the disquieting cacophonic climax of music over Morrison's masked chanting of "kill, kill, kill, kill".

Just as 'The End' has built through a series of images and themes to a realisation, so has the album. In this initial flash of The Doors' artistic vision, modern life has destroyed the traditional sanctuaries of the home and of love and destroyed whatever gave life a sense of meaning. Morrison's message was *act* now, *search* later. Life is a journey, but any journey will be painful. Life is pain, love is pain, and fear prevents people from experiencing life, from accepting what The Doors ultimately come to realise, that we are all *riders on the storm*.

> "Oedipus, his father's murderer, his mother's lover, solver of the Sphinx's riddle! What is the meaning of this triple fate? It is as though the myth whispered to us that wisdom, and especially Dionysiac wisdom, is an unnatural crime and that whoever, in pride of knowledge, hurls nature into the abyss of destruction, must himself experience nature's disintegration."
> Friedrich Nietzsche, *The Birth Of Tragedy*

---

27 Powledge p90.

chapter 3

STRANGE DAYS IN THE SUMMER OF LOVE

"We were never really protagonists of the flower movement;
in fact, we were the complete opposite...love and peace and
everything's great – that was only half of the side of the coin.
We were providing a glimpse of the other side as well."
Robby Krieger, *No One Here Gets Out Alive: The Doors Story*, Jim Ladd's
radio special *The Inner View*

The Summer of Love. 1967. From the West Coast, the Summer of Love
had swept across the country, flower power and hippies spreading
seeds of a brotherhood of love, peace and harmony on the swirling
winds of a magical tension. Vietnam was polarising the political and
social climate of America, a tangible tip to the tension wrought by the
Cold War and the potentially high-stakes entanglement with conflicts
elsewhere in the world. The June six-day war in the Middle East where
Israeli made shambles of their Arab neighbours' military abilities was a
blood stain compared to the blood bath that would begin in July with
the civil war in Nigeria after the secession by Biafra, Nigeria's eastern
region. The destabilised governments of Nigeria and Congo, Africa's two
most populated nations, struggled with armed conflict – Nigeria, a civil
war; Congo, a regional revolt lead by white mercenaries. The internal
resolve to resist the military junta lead by Colonel George Papdopoulas
that seized control of Greece in an April coup, faded in December with
the flight of King Constantine II and his family to Rome. Tension
abounded throughout the world, though America had yet to taste how
the violence of frustration would draw blood in its heartland.
Nonetheless, the American youths' brotherhood of love had grown

alongside a bizarre accordance of dissident and macabre times. The utopian vision of a brotherhood of love and peace characterised by the Summer of Love in 1967, to blossom in its fullest at Woodstock two years later, was about to be cracked by harsh political realities of 1968 before being shattered by the closing of the Sixties.

Promoted as a Gathering of the Tribes, a quintessential hippie happening in the Polo Field of San Francisco's Golden Gate Park in January opened this magical year of 1967. Known as "The Human Be-In", the reporting press largely misses the pun on *human be-in* (*human being*), making the same word connection as the political *sit-in*, and the words *love-in* and *hippie* begin appearing with considerable regularity as labels to attach to this youth movement. For the 20 January edition of the underground newspaper, *The Berkeley BARB* (Berkeley is a suburb of San Francisco), Ed Denson wrote an article, *What Happened At The Hippening*, and, though he clearly liked the idea of all these folks gathering for a "Human Be-In," Denson kept repeating his theme of the irresponsibility of the organisers not knowing "how to organise on a scale that has 10,000 people anywhere doing anything." Yet to many the gathering of thousands became a bench mark of the emerging youth subculture that people could spontaneously gather and get along – and that anything was possible. However, the swearing in of Lester Maddox, also in January, as the new governor of Georgia indicated that certain parts of America still valued a man who, three years earlier in defiance of the Civil Acts Right of 1964, passed out axe handles to the white customers in his restaurant so they could resist any desegregation of his public place of business.

But the seeds of the times had taken root and sprouted, and the summer opened in mid-June with a three-day festival of music, love, flowers and people, known as the Monterey Pop Festival, just south of San Francisco. Many relatively unknown rock 'n' roll artists were featured: The Jimi Hendrix Experience, Jefferson Airplane, Big Brother And The Holding Company (with Janis Joplin), The Who, Otis Redding, Ravi Shankar, Hugh Masekela and others.[1]

---

1 'Light My Fire' would become the number one selling single in America the week of July 29th; in June, The Doors were just another one of many bands from Los Angeles and the West Coast and they didn't warrant any particular attention for the organisers of Monterey to recruit them. Bands that appeared at Monterey Pop Festival (June 16th-17th-18th 1967) included: The Association, Big Brother & The Holding Company (with Janis Joplin), The Blues Project, Booker T and the MG's with The Mar-Keys, Buffalo Springfield, The Byrds, Canned Heat, Country Joe and The Fish, The Electric Flag, Eric Burdon and The Animals, The Grateful Dead, Hugh Masekela, Jefferson Airplane, The Jimi Hendrix Experience, Laura Nyro, Lou Rawls, The Mamas and The Papas, Otis Redding, The Paul Butterfield Blues Band, Quicksilver Messenger Service, Ravi Shankar, Scott McKenzie, Simon and Garfunkel, The Steve Miller Blues Band and The Who.

The first festival of its kind, Monterey strengthened the growing sense of community among youth and the alternative subculture. But in July, violent riots in the black sections of Detroit and Newark erupted. The Beatles gave this flourishing rock culture widely acclaimed artistic authenticity with the release of their album, *Sgt Pepper's Lonely Hearts Club Band*. Arthur Penn followed with the release of his film, *Bonnie And Clyde*, starring Warren Beatty and Faye Dunaway as two ill-fated, searching young souls who are swept into a cinematic waltz of violence, bullets and blood. Marshall McLuhan delivered, *The Medium Is The Message*, a book which became the gospel of McLuhan's relentless preaching on how our newfangled technological communications impact society and Ira Levin's novel integrating the evil side of witchcraft, *Rosemary's Baby*, shocked an American public who made the book a bestseller and basis of a equally successful subsequent 1968 movie. On the first Monday in October, Thurgood Marshall began his tenure as a US Supreme Court justice, the first black to do so. The magazine that would embody and nurture the emerging youth subculture, *Rolling Stone*, first appeared in November. A 17-year-old British model, Twiggy, became the fashion image, an unrealistic blend of pencil-thinness and wide-eyed vacuousness. In December, Dr Christian Barnard performed the first successful human heart transplant in Cape Town, South Africa, though the patient died later that month.

Released during the all important Christmas movie season, Mike Nichols' film, *The Graduate*, showcased Dustin Hoffman as Benjamin Bradock, a confused, quietly rebellious college graduate whose rejection of getting a job with the college degree, adulterous affair with Mrs Robinson and subsequent obsessive attraction to Elaine, Mr and Mrs Robinson's daughter, undermine the credibility of what was the programmed American way of growing-up. The absolutely silent scenes of the tumultuous University of California campus at Berkeley underscore the closing scenes when Katharine Ross, as Elaine, before running off with Ben from her own wedding, tells Ann Bancroft, her mother, she won't make the same mistake mom made. The film closes with Elaine in her ruffled white wedding gown and the dishevelled Ben sitting in an uneasy quiet in the back of a city bus travelling a scheduled route. The soundtrack of Simon and Garfunkel songs (ie 'Sound Of Silence') further augments the theme that this spontaneous flow of desires and energy doesn't naturally head toward utopia.

The Doors' second album not only mirrors the strange days of the Sixties up to that Summer of Love in 1967, but also augurs the estranged times to follow. With expanded recording capabilities at Elektra studios (the advent of eight-track technology meant, as Ray exclaimed in *The Source* radio special, "We can overdub?!"), The Doors recorded their second album, *Strange Days*, which was released in October 1967. The material on this album also came from the repertoire of songs composed during the group's so-called acid fertility period when they were free from commercial demands and developed their material in front of a live audience. The complexity and quality of themes in *Strange Days* rival the artistic imagination with which the Beatles and their *Sgt Pepper's Lonely Hearts Club Band* had revolutionised the music world a few months before at the start of the Summer of Love. Before 1967 was over, Frank Zappa released his second album, *Absolutely Free*, and the Moody Blues re-emerged with *Days Of Future Past*, both, like *Sgt Pepper* and *Strange Days*, explicitly designed albums unified around an underlining theme of expressing what lay under the shadows of the flowering youthful ideals of change and an alternative culture.

Strange Days doesn't offer a cozy refuge of soothing ideals or of placid, complacent sensory comfort; The Doors portray a reality of alienated people and strange days. We have become chained to a mechanised world, segmented by the clock and an alien landscape, a world separated from unknown forces that no longer fit into the smoothly running machinery of the modern way of life. In the Sixties, personal identity started becoming focused and then fixed upon numbers: social security number, phone number, driver's licence, credit card numbers, insurance policy numbers, etc; and the list has continued to snowball. People hold onto chains – either of an established way or of a new vision – because those chains represent security and identity. But The Doors perceived either set of chains as false because neither confirmed the individual's existence or allowed passage to the "other side". Their artistic vision reflects little coherence in a culture building upon disquieting plastic images that are detached from the organic nature of life and that breed uneasy despair in even the most basic sanctuaries of life – the house and love.

Like a prism which refracts white light into a rainbow of colours, this album refracts a spectrum of the afflictions of the times. Within the album, underlying themes weave together to reflect the nature of *strange days*: the despairing effects of existing under the shadows of the confusion of the Vietnam War and the potential of a global holocaust; the despairing effects of being a rock group, of being artists, the harbingers of unwanted messages; the despairing effects of two lovers at odds with each other because trust cannot exist; and ultimately, the despairing effects of death – death of innocence, of trust, of love, of music, of sanctuary. This album tells a story of strangers meeting strangers in strange surroundings.

To Morrison, the values of the times offered attire only for acting out a role, evident in an interview with Lizze James. He explained people trade reality for a role and give up their "ability to feel, and in exchange, put on a mask."[2] Society molded individuals to be actors, the individual performing what was to be expected and acting out roles in attempts to find personal happiness. Hence, the album's cover picture which wraps around the front and the back, reflects this theme: a one-point perspective of carnival-like characters performing in a dreary enclosure of a side street walled in on three sides, with the fourth side sealed off by the eye of the camera.

> "Whereas the surrealist watches and waits for the unpredictable manifestation of the unconscious, Rimbaud violates his mind and ravishes the images as they form. His poetic secrets are the result of a spiritual rape and conquest. His art is the seizure of his own reality."
> Wallace Fowlie, *Rimbaud (A Critical Study)*, p75.

Why make such an album? An album – as Sugerman and Hopkins wrote in *No One Here Gets Out Alive* – not as strange as the first album but still quite a "catalogue of psychic jolts and pains."[3] In response to the question 'which album expressed best what The Doors were all about?' producer Rothchild replied that *Strange Days* was "bulls-eye"[4] – the album musically said everything they were trying to say and had some of Morrison's best poetry. Morrison told Michael Cuscuna of *Down Beat* that he was proud of this album because it told a story and that many people didn't realise what the group was doing, but that eventually this

2 James *Jim Morrison: Ten Years Gone* p21.
3 Jerry Hopkins and Danny Sugerman *No One Here Gets Out Alive* (New York: Warner Books, Inc, 1980) p130.
4 Vic Garbarini, *Blues For A Shaman: Doors' Producer Paul Rothschild* (sic) *Musician* August 1981 p56.

album would get the recognition it deserved.[5]

Reactions to the album did reflect a lack of understanding regarding the story The Doors tell in the album, as the album was buried by both comparisons to the fantastically successful first album and reactions to the group's, especially Morrison's, persona. A 1981 review in *Creem* offered this universal appraisal of the album in hindsight, stating that The Doors probably had too much to live up to: "Even without the instant-standard kiss of death of 'Light My Fire,' there was simply a lotta promise (or threats) inherent on the debut."[6]

There were those who did perceive the artistic imagination of The Doors. The same review in *Creem* also said the album's "most endearing (and enduring) qualities" were its ominous themes of people being "lost, strange, confused, alienated, friendless"…"The Doors were peering into the sin-filled souls of hippies everywhere and offering no comfort."[7] Eric Van Lustbader of *Circus* magazine recognised that the album's storyline of people "trying desperately to reach each other through the choking haze of drugs and artificial masks" builds upon the "images and characters in a series of vignettes"[8] the whole becoming more visible as the album's story unfolds.

By now the sound of The Doors had become distinct. In a review of this album, Steven Lowe of the classical music oriented *High Fidelity Magazine* wrote that "The Doors' 'sound' is unique in its relative freedom from overly distorted hurricanes of acoustical storms; they concentrate on producing a sort of undulating harmonic effect. Chords progress less by definite steps than by oozing in and out of focus."[9]

And so, the music of this second album expresses how strange times create unfocused lives and such is the whirlwind of strange days.

SIDE 1
'Strange Days'
'You're Lost Little Girl'
'Love Me Two Times'
'Unhappy Girl'
'Horse Latitudes'
'Moonlight Drive'

5 Michael Cuscuna, *Behind The Doors*, *Down Beat* 28th May 1970 p13.
6 J Kordosh *Strange Days* (record review) *Creem* Special Edition: *The Doors* Summer 1981 p48.
7 Ibid, p48.
8 Eric Van Lustbader, *Jim Morrison: Riding Out The Final Storm*, *Circus* September 1971 p37.
9 Steven Lowe, *The Lighter Side*, *High Fidelity Magazine*, January 1968 p98.

The opening song, 'Strange Days', swirls into a mood of strangeness as Manzarek drapes a musical backdrop with the Moog synthesiser, one of its earliest uses in rock. The electronic twang which accents the hard syllables in Morrison's vocals effectively colours the opening image that strange days have tracked us down. The *day* is when things are visible and known – but not these days, not these times. There are strange rooms filled with strange eyes, and strange days create despair, as Morrison sings about people lingering alone with bodies confused and memories misused.

The suppressed unknown returns to track us down, and confusion pervades these strange days that create "strange hours" – a recurrent theme in many Doors lyrics of the chains the clock imposes upon us. Our deep psychic past is becoming muddled, memories with no sincere structure through which one generation can transmit to the next the knowledge of what it means being human. And we rapidly drift from strange days to an equally strange night of stone. How can we find safety in love if bodies are confused? Or in our past if memories are misused? Or in the mysterious, if the night is made of stone or if being stoned delivers us to a state as strange as the one from which we are running?

In such strange times, trust is difficult, if not impossible and the song, 'You're Lost Little Girl', begins a story that transcends two estranged lovers. With a sense of high-handed compassion, this Krieger song creates a melancholic yet cynical tone, a loneliness intensified by minor-mode verses. Morrison peers into the soul of the Twentieth Century Fox and asks a confused and lost child if she can tell him who she is. Having lost her identity, she is as estranged as the society in which she lives. But the way to find herself remains within her, a theme in The Doors' artistic vision that everyone has the power within to break out of strange days. Though she may say, "Impossible", Morrison sings she knows what to do.

As a way to find oneself, rock 'n' roll and The Doors invoke not only music, but also love. So in 'Love Me Two Times' Jim urgently sings to the lost little girl to love him two times to last him all through the week. Krieger's song pulsates with his commanding guitar hook and Densmore's frenzied drumming. But how much refuge has this love? Jim weaves through Robby's lyric for his lover to love him two times because he is going away. Although Morrison drops the '*s*' on '*times*' to make the lyric sound like "love me two time", he sings of his need to be loved twice, once for tomorrow and once for today. Love today for tomorrow because the future is uncertain, so characteristic of the shallow relationships, personal and non-personal, of strange days. The pulsating music and urgent lyrics create an undercurrent of brief sexual gratification as a way to stay afloat in the ocean of strange days. Accused of being written strictly for pure pop (and hence, commercial) reasons, the urgent and pulsating song breaks the album's solemn tone, yet it doesn't skip a beat in its message: in strange times, sanctuary isn't easily found in love.

'Unhappy Girl' continues the story of the lost little girl, the song's oozing tones portraying an alienated soul. Manzarek played the song backward, and Densmore created a soft-suck rhythm sound by playing backward high-hat. The unhappy girl has retreated to a prison of her own making, where she is playing warden to her young soul. In sequential verses, Morrison sings of her being *locked*, *caught* and *dying* in this prison of her own device. Past tense to progressive: locked, caught, dying…but not yet dead. Morrison challenges her to tear away the web she has woven, to saw through bars and melt her self-made prison of limitations. Refusing to be locked in this prison, Morrison then invites her to swim in mystery – the moonlight drive.

'Horse Latitudes' leads into 'Moonlight Drive'. The common story is that Jim penned this poem in his high school days after seeing a paperback cover of horses being tossed overboard from a Spanish galleon into the Sargasso Sea.[10] The Sargasso Sea is in the north Atlantic Ocean (Horse Latitudes in this part of the northern hemisphere are located within this area). The various ocean currents that rotate around this region, notably the Gulf Stream on the west and south, make the Sargasso Sea waters relatively still and clear. If ships sailing to the New World faltered in these waters, cargo was jettisoned to lighten the ship. The area is also abundant with brown gulfweed, a sort of seaweed that clusters in huge patches resembling meadows on the water. These peculiarities gave rise to the legends from the tales brought back by New World sailors that the Sargasso Sea was where galleons could become entangled in a snare of thickly matted islands of seaweed, which were inhabited by huge monsters of the deep.

Though objectivity of experience now explains the Sargasso Sea,

10 Hopkins and Sugerman, p19.

Morrison taps into that sea of imagination that ebbs through humans in his rendition of life's becalmed waters.

The opening lyrics and swelling electronic confusion conjure a not so tranquil setting on the sea. The ocean of life's currents has been stilled by strange times, becoming sullen and aborted, void and dead in the eyes and minds of the sailors. Yet the calm waters are alive and threatening, breeding tiny monsters. Meaningful life – true sailing – is dead. The crystal ship has become more fragile than blissful. But man must try to go on, in sailing and life; thus sacrifices are made in hopes to appease the tiny monsters and to lighten the ship and take advantage of what wind there is. With poetic precision, Morrison describes the awkward instant of the agony of drowning as he screams the words till they are drowned in emotional disorder and electronic feedback. The progression of adjectives and verbs mirrors the sealing over of souls by the still sea: first the horses bob up and gulp for air, they become poised for a delicate moment, and then they consent to submerging, to being sealed over by the sea. If life gets out of sync, man breeds a few of his own tiny monsters.

Morrison then wooingly urges his lost, unhappy girl to swim in mystery on a 'Moonlight Drive' down by the ocean where horses have just drowned. How more appropriately to end side one of the album than with a cozy tryst on the beach under the moonlight, even as Krieger's sinisterly laughing guitar draws us into a rather disquieting love song. Richard Riegel wrote that one of the "finest heart-stops in recorded rock" is when the "gloomily romantic, itchy-crotch 'Moonlight Drive' suddenly slithers out of the choked raucousness of 'Horse Latitudes'."[11] In a 1972 interview by John Tobler with the three surviving Doors, Manzarek said this song was the first song they recorded as The Doors, "but it was also the weakest" and they left it off the first album.[12] In a subsequent interview with Pete Fornatale of *Musician* magazine, Manzarek further explained that the song was a "funkier, bluesier kind of song" at first, like a James Brown or Otis Redding song; but while recording it for the second album, the group "fooled around for awhile" before Ray said, "I got it – we're gonna do a tango...a *rock tango.*"[13]

Morrison sings of being out of the back seat of a car, or the refuge of a bedroom and taking a 'Moonlight Drive' to the darker mysteries: to step

11 Richard Riegel, *Tongues Of Knowledge In The Feathered Night (The Blue Bus Is Double Parked): The Doors On Record*, Creem Special Edition: The Doors, summer 1981, p10.
12 John Tobler, *The Doors In A Nutshell: 64 Quick Questions*, ZigZag September 1972 p28.
13 Pete Fornatale, *Strange Days: Doors' Organist Ray Manzarek*, Musician, August 1981, p48.

into a river of sensations and surrender to those waiting worlds that will be lapping at their sides. The night for the 'Moonlight Drive" is alive. But Morrison croons that when she reaches out to hold him once they begin swimming in this mystery, he can't be her guide. Don't expect trust when relationships are based on lust and lies. As they swim up to the moon and fall through wet forests, Morrison breaks through to the other side, and his tone becomes seductively sinister, wooing her to go for a little ride down to the ocean side where they can get real close and real tight and drown tonight. Though they have broken through, the bodies are still confused, the memories are still misused, and the times are still strange.

SIDE 2
'People Are Strange'
'My Eyes Have Seen You'
'I Can't See Your Face In My Mind'
'When The Music's Over'

'People Are Strange' restates the theme of alienation. In 'Strange Days' Manzarek's Moog synthesiser provides the restrained, uneasy backdrop. In this song, Krieger's guitar moans and slithers around the lyrical portrait of estrangement. During a time guided by the visions of JFK's New Frontier, of LBJ's Great Society, and of the Woodstock Nation's brotherhood of love, Morrison sang of a painful reality that when you are a stranger, *people are strange*. His phrasing of the first stanza effectively pauses on disquieting words. When people can't trust relationships and feel alone, then everyone seems threatening. Faces that come out of the estranged rain offer no sense of familiarity. And people don't remember your name, the stamp of alienation – loss of identity.

In 'My Eyes Have Seen You', Morrison probes the loss of identity of the unhappy girl, now seeing her free from her disguise. The lyrics are simple and direct, and Manzarek replaces the haunting organ with the crispness of a piano. The invitation in the first stanza to stand in her door and to show him some more isn't the same invitation Morrison croons in 'Moonlight Drive'. He has discovered there is more to be seen in the lost, little girl. The images of photographing her soul and memorising her alleys suggest the alley has become part of her soul – be it a refuge of the dark side of the urban landscape or a place void of the life of the streets. We aren't down by oceanside anymore as Morrison realises the photographs of her soul could be part of an endless roll.

The empathetic music of this song shifts to a melancholic sound in 'I Can't See Your Face In My Mind'. Again, Jim keeps the images short, and the pregnant pauses after each stanza add to the song's haunting tone. Having seen the lost, little girl free from disguise, Jim discovers he can't picture her face in his mind. Has she returned to her "disguise," to a prison of her own device? In strange times, intimate relationships become void of any sort of union other than the very basic physical one which underlies the themes in 'Love Me Two Times' and 'Moonlight Drive'. If love merely fulfils a physical need of sex and not a desire to share and trust, what is there to remember? The lines of any memory are erased as the song oozes along to the sandpaper sound of the maracas in the background.

The Doors' love songs often portray the inability of love to provide sanctuary if people lack trust. In 'Unhappy Girl', her unhappiness touches Jim; but now that he has seen her free of disguise, he cowers from any emotional attachment. He doesn't want to face those eyes and sings that he can't find the right lie. The ironic end of this estranged relationship concludes the song as Jim croons for his baby not to cry and he won't need her picture till they say goodbye. To remind him who she was, Morrison will take a photograph which can only capture the outer disguise – the plastic memory of film.

With sanctuary in a relationship disillusioned by strange days, The Doors turn to a refuge which is the cornerstone of Pop culture: music. But what happens "When The Music's Over"? When society has estranged the rhythms which appeal directly to the soul, then you can turn out the lights. When a relationship is going smoothly, troubles seem so far away, as Paul McCartney sings in 'Yesterday'. But when things go sour the music stops playing, and it seems as if someone has turned out the lights.

Like music, the invocation that begins the song evokes one to *dance on fire*. In a broad sense, *fire* represents being alive, experiencing forbidden and mysterious aspects of life. Unable to find fire in love, Morrison wails that music is our only friend till the end, and a distorted guitar solo and cacophony of disorder follow.

Morrison rejects the promise of the great banquet, wanting to cancel his "subscription to the Resurrection", the reward of the hard work and sacrifice ethic of either the American economic-social system or the Christian after-life. Instead he wants his "credentials" sent to the "house of detention". The "house of detention" recalls the earlier prison image of one's own device, except this is society's prison – or rather house of sanctuary for those who don't fit in, who have sinned.

As the song builds through a series of moods, the music tightens with the tension of impatience, of hanging and waiting around. Then an angry mood follows, accusations that *they* have ravaged and plundered the earth – sticking knives in the side of her dawn and tying her with fences and dragging her down. As the music fades to the calm of only a steady *bum-bump* heartbeat of Manzarek's organ, the anger explodes into a demand of retribution that we want the world now.

After the anguishing bellow of *"now!"*, Morrison cries to Jesus and the mysterious Persian nights, to see the night lights Jesus saw. The song has drawn the desolate imagery of the "strange night of stone" in 'Strange Days' through the sinisterly seductive evening in 'Moonlight Drive' to the bright midnight of Persian nights. Then The Doors return to the opening dirge of turning out the lights when the music is over, but close with an empathetic chorus to "dance on fire" until "the end!" as if to go out with a last spark of life.

The story The Doors tell in *Strange Days* reflects the struggle of living during strange times. When a culture cocoons itself into an environment detached from the natural fluxes of the world and when the cocooned soul traps the screaming butterfly, not even the most basic sanctuaries of life can be trusted. There is little sanctuary in love if relationships are void of trust. Friendship is elusive when people are strange. Security and meaning, so essential for peace of mind, become as estranged as the people groping in silence for each other. There is little safety in pursuing self-realisation when there are no guides into the unknown. Just as it was in the Summer of Love in 1967, this album remains a vivid reflection of modern society.

> "Music is distinguished from all the other arts by the fact that it is not a copy of...the adequate objectivity of the will, but is the direct copy of the will itself... We might, therefore, just as well call the world embodied music as embodied will."
> Friedrich Nietzsche, *The Birth Of Tragedy*

chapter 4

WAITING FOR THE MUSE, WAITING FOR THE DOORS, WAITING FOR THE SUN

"Jim Morrison has grown to be the sex-Death, Acid-Evangelist of Rock,
a sort of Hell's Angel on the groin. Journalistic accuracy tends to
depend on expediency, but the case of the Doors stretches
the mass media's credibility gap to almost impossible lengths."
Mike Jahn, *Jim Morrison And The Doors* (pp8, 11)

The Sixties were ascending to the fruition of the seeds planted in the late 1950s and early 1960s: Woodstock, Altamont, Vietnam and the war protest, the killing of college students, the ecological movement, the assassination of leaders who had dreams of brotherhood, the political reality of American democracy, and ultimately the deaths of rock stars burning their life flames out on the edge.

Events on the larger world stage provided background for the irrevocable path of these forces. The spirit of violence and confrontation had intensified across the planet. The Middle East seethed under a tenuous equilibrium in the aftermath of the 1967 Six-Day War, as commando raids, artillery shelling and air strikes accompanied public reprisals and threats. The brutal civil war in Nigeria that would last till January 1970 forced into the rest of the world's sensibilities the stark visual images of starving Biafran refugees – mostly innocent children. A substantial threat, at least socially, to the hard-line dictates of the power mongrels in Moscow emerged with the succession of Alexander Dubcek, a progressive Communist, as President of Czechoslovakia in January 1968. After suspending censorship, the Czech government began a liberalisation of political rights which Western Europe and America took for granted. In August, Soviet Union forces with support from other Warsaw Pact countries (Bulgaria, East Germany, Hungary and Poland) invaded

Czechoslovakia to suppress "dangerous counter-revolutionary forces." This Soviet invasion of Czechoslovakia to squash this movement toward a more liberal and freer society and to re-establish the status quo did little to deter the growing impatience of the American establishment to quell the rising anti-war protests and calls for social equality. As a reminder of America's other unresolved "war", the Korean Conflict of the 1950s, North Korea's seizure of the Pueblo, a US Navy intelligence ship, in January took eleven months of tense negotiations before the harshly treated 82-man crew (one had been killed by the boarding party) were released just before Christmas.

During that interval, a seemingly iron-clad Presidency fell in the March New Hampshire primary to the flickering hope of presidential candidate Minnesota Senator Eugene McCarthy. Though McCarthy would try, in vain, to sell peace as a political policy, it was Bobby Kennedy who, for a brief period, inflamed the sputtering fires of idealism before being snuffed out in June as Martin Luther King Jr was in April. George Wallace, the former governor of Alabama, organised a third party, the American Independent Party, and ran for President on a platform that revived the South's strong states' rights attitude to return jurisdiction to state and local governments. In this way they could resolve their own regional and local issues like crime, property rights, voter eligibility, public school systems and other issues – notably those being affected by federal civil rights legislation. Eventually, Richard Nixon would rise like a phoenix from the ashes of his own political expiration. His approach of moderation could do little to alter the course of the swirling forces, and a restoring of the conservative status quo, with Ronald Reagan's ascension in 1981, would wait until after recovering from the Watergate fiasco.

As 1968 began, at the top of the album charts sat The Beatles' *Magical Mystery Tour*, The Rolling Stones' *Their Satanic Majesties Request* and The Monkees' *Pisces, Aquarius, Capricorn And Jones, Ltd.* By summer the charts and airwaves were filled with the sounds of Simon and Garfunkel, riding the crest of success of the soundtrack to the movie, *The Graduate*. And in 1968, bubblegum pop music became big business through Buddah Records: Super K Productions, the independent production arm of Kasenetz-Katz Associates, recorded gross retail sales of $25 million bolstered by 25 charting singles, six of them gold records. The sweetness flows from such saccharine groups as 1910

Fruitgum Company, Ohio Express and Lemon Pipers.

Stanley Kubrick's film *2001: A Space Odyssey* offered a sci-fi psyche-delic voyage – though arduously threatened by the ominous computer HAL – toward humanity's next phase in evolution, while Rod Sterling's co-written *Planet Of The Apes* offered a more prosaic allegory with Kim Hunter and Roddy McDowall in costumes that were as technically realistic as the opening scenes of early ape-man in *2001*. Due to its unexpected commercial success in American movie theatres, *Blow-Up* elevated the stature of Italian film director Michelangelo Antonioni beyond the world of artsy film houses. Francis Ford Coppola, considered one of the upcoming talents still under the age of 30, hired as an assistant George Lucas, fresh from University of Southern California's film school. Besides the *Godfather* films, Coppola would also direct *Apocalypse Now* and use 'The End' to open the scenes of the Vietnam War in this 1979 movie. George Lucas would create something known as *Star Wars*.

On American television during the 1967-68 season, the upstart and irreverent Smothers Brothers (premiered in February 1967) did the unthinkable – beat the top rated show on television, *Bonanza*. This long running American icon incorporated much of what is endearing in the American myth: the American West of the late 1800s, a tight-knit Cartwright family, and resolve to meet any challenge to their kingdom – the Ponderosa. However, constant squabbles with higher-ups at CBS lead to the demise of the *Smother Brothers' Comedy Hour* (the brothers were fired in April 1969), and the established *Bonanza* would survive at its 9.00pm Sunday time slot through the 1971-72 season – the end of the Sixties.

The Pepsi generation was replacing the Geritol crowd; their innovative voices had revolutionised the arts, their numbers and pocketbooks were revolutionising the market place, but political clout was still a couple of decades away.

Underneath this tangible turmoil, the politically implemented "New Economics" was being tested. The canon of New Economics established a national goal of sustained economic growth that creates and maintains high employment, strong production, good paycheques and increasing profits while keeping prices reasonably stable. We just needed to constantly adjust the combination of fiscal and monetary policies – a mantra of tax-spending-credit. When the economy was overheating, impose constraints to slow the expanding by increasing and/or legislating taxes to curb spending and postpone investing, tightening government spending and making credit more expensive to limit borrowing. When the economy was sputtering, introduce incentives to stimulate the rate of growth by cutting and/or legislating taxes to encourage spending and investing, increasing government spending and making credit easy and inexpensive to stimulate borrowing. And when the culturally appropriate rate of growth is reached, moderate all these polices. Modern life was a machine; we just needed to know how to fine tune it – and from which ideology to forge the tools. Furthermore, Atlantic Richfield (ARCO) and Standard Oil of New Jersey announced in 1968 that they had discovered oil underneath the North Slope of Alaska. This would keep the engine of the machine running and would fuel the heightening debate of how to define our relationship to our dwindling natural resources.

The whirlwind of forces was spiralling in heightened anticipation of its destined final fling of energies before subsiding to a gentle breeze, to a period of recollecting energies. In this whirlwind, The Doors found themselves inside a vacuum: they were a vital source of energy swirling the whirlwind of forces, yet they were cut off from them.

With meteoric success comes also the inevitable conflict – if not cession – of maintaining contact with the creative and social forces upon which the artist draws. At first, The Doors' self-imposed aloofness from society had fuelled their creative flames. But now, the whirlwind of success had swept the group from their roots, isolating them and all but crushing the muse. It is not coincidental that the third and especially the fourth albums drew upon as a creative source the very whirlwind of success – the idioms of the Pop culture, a shallow source of creativity compared to what had fuelled the artistic output on the first two albums.

Hence, shaped by both imposed and self-imposed influences, the third and fourth albums were not as strong conceptually as the first two. Since the summer of 1967, The Doors found themselves on a mission to deliver their artistic vision now in mass demand. They had become public property to fill the demands of deliverance *en masse* to people living in strange days. But the shamanic spirit cannot be packaged and sold as snake oil to the grasping reach of a public stumbling in neon groves. Pop could provide a quick, enticing fix for the spiritually deprived masses, eagerly receptive to any stimulus which puts them in contact with their feelings and lets them feel the momentary pulse of life's unseen forces. As Lester Bangs continually pointed out, it was all just the latest snake oil/con man scam to tantalise the American public. Though the group may have sold out so they could rattle the masses in hopes of reaching a few, the artistic vision of The Doors doesn't offer any such quick doses of soothing assurance.

Plans for this third album had begun as grandiose with one side devoted to a twenty minute-plus version of a Morrison piece entitled 'The Celebration Of The Lizard'. But it wasn't to be, as evident in Richard Goldstein's recollection of a recording session when a roughly recorded dub of the track was played back: Ray, "gently, almost apologetically" told Jim the piece was "too diffuse, too mangy," and "Jim's face sinks".[1] Without a studio version of 'Lizard', The Doors suddenly found that a lot of music was needed to fill this third album.

Yet they had lacked any time to develop songs with the night-after-night tension of an intimate club audience, nor had Jim had any quiet time to allow songs to flow to him. Having been regulated to playing the standard cuts off the albums and other favourites from their original repertoire of songs, the group had cornered themselves, allowing public success to stifle the messages they had initially wanted to express. When it came time under contract to provide another album, The Doors had to produce, using a creative process foreign to their normal rhythm of creating. Ray said in an interview in *Musician* magazine that they couldn't "fool around and goof off" while waiting for their muse to arrive, but had to "call the lady down" with a plead of, "come on, give us a hand here!"[2]

But the artistic vision of The Doors appeared less lucid. Though the pieces still fit in the puzzle, the overall resultant picture framed by the third album seemed hazier than the more lucid portraits rendered by the first two albums. Perhaps tired by the touring and catering to the public, The Doors might have been saying, "We have things to say, but we're tired of trying to spell them out to you, so take our half-hearted offering and make what you want from it." Perhaps the swirling forces had made them a bit dizzy...

Waiting For The Sun evoked the typical wide range of immediate reactions. Rich Mangelsdorff asked in the Milwaukee underground newspaper, *Kaleidoscope*: "Has someone discovered that with a little printing The Doors albums can sell real big? Someone standing

1 Richard Goldstein *The Shaman As Superstar*, *New York Magazine*, reprinted in *The Doors: The Illustrated History*, pp75-76.
2 *Fornatale* p49.

pat?"[3] Yet Pete Johnson wrote in *The Philadelphia Inquirer* that since this album contained "the smallest amount of self-indulgent mysticism" of the group's first three albums, The Doors had "traded terror for beauty" and the "success of the swap" was a tribute to the band's "talent and originality."[4] In retrospect, most reviews years later reiterated the same belief: the album was uninspired and as Lillian Roxon wrote, "strengthened dreadful suspicion that the Doors were in it just for the money."[5]

The contrast of this third album with the first two is one of paradoxes. The music of the first two was studio ready when the recording began. For this third album, as Hopkins and Sugerman wrote, almost every song, mostly due to blunders by Jim, needed at least twenty takes and 'The Unknown Soldier' required 130 starts.[6] Allegedly, 'The End' and 'When The Music's Over' each had taken two takes. Starting in January 1968, The Doors finished recording the album in May. Whereas the debut album had smouldered in the charts for half a year before soaring to the top with the release of the abbreviated 45 version of 'Light My Fire', this third album had advance orders of nearly half a million and sold 750,000 copies within ten weeks of release.

The album changed titles from *American Nights* (a lengthy poem which later appeared in several publications) to *The Celebration Of The Lizard* (Morrison wanted the album cover to be in imitation lizard skin) to *Waiting For The Sun* (the title of a song left off the album, inevitably to emerge on *Morrison Hotel*). And Jim had wanted, as Hopkins and Sugerman noted, to recite some of his poetry between songs (a posthumous reality with *An American Prayer*). Instead, printed inside the album sleeve was *The Celebration Of The Lizard*, a Morrison poem that "had refused to be wedded to music".[7]

The Celebration Of The Lizard complicates any critical rendering of this third album. As a printed insert, the piece stands as a vivid part of the album and a reflection of Morrison's artistic vision. Yet this piece failed to be composed onto vinyl or into The Doors' artistic vision save for one or two well-executed live performances. *The Celebration Of The Lizard* remains an attached aside, a metaphor for the frustrated muse denied the creative input of an intimate audience every night. Mitchell

---

3 Rich Mangelsdorff *Doors Stuck?*, *Kaleidoscope* (Milwaukee underground newspaper), 23rd August – 12th September 1968 p6.
4 Pete Johnson *Waiting For The Sun*, *The Inquirer* (Philadelphia newspaper) reprinted in *The Doors: The Illustrated History* p100.
5 Lillian Roxon *Rock Encyclopaedia* (New York: Grosset and Dunlop) 1969 p152.
6 Hopkins and Sugerman p179.
7 Ibid, p191.

Cohen wrote that the piece "in black and white, seemed silly, an unstructured *tour-de-force* by a mediocre poet."[8] Morrison told Hank Zevallos in an interview printed in the March 1970 issue of *Poppin* that 'The Celebration Of The Lizard' was built upon the central image of a "band of youths who leave the city and venture into the desert" where each night, for pleasure and to cultivate the "group spirit," the youths "tell stories and sing around a fire."[9] In an interview with Bob Chorush published in the *Los Angeles Free Press* in January 1971, Morrison said that since we identify the lizard and snake with the unconscious and forces of evil, 'The Celebration Of The Lizard' was "kind of an invitation to the dark forces" but it was "all done tongue in cheek".[10]

Because even Doors songs that could be considered light have some purpose, usually to make fun of people who don't even realise it, the inclusion of 'Celebration' could be an apology, or a gasp for breath from under the rampaging Pop culture. It is dubious whether Morrison intended 'Celebration' to be a joke – this prolonged piece has coherent structure and theme. Morrison starts at the heart of a city with lions roaming the streets, rabid dogs foaming and in heat and a caged beast. He quickly leaves and heads south, across "the border", to begin a journey of exile that pauses in a "green hotel" where he wakes up to find a "strange creature groaning" beside him. Morrison then continues the journey to a place inside his brain, back past pain, back to a little game called "go insane". Then he and his lover are on the run, from and through a mosaic of conspicuous images. Eventually, Morrison pronounces at the end of the piece that he has lived seven years in the "loose palace of exile" but now, as night arrives, he prepares to reenter the town of his birth. Nevertheless, this elongated poetic escapade never had the chance to be creatively developed in the typical Doors' manner, nor was it taken very seriously artistically by Morrison.

> "And the media weren't about to be allowed to treat the Doors as Top Forty morons, even if Jim did look like jean-creaming pin-up material. 'We're erotic politicians' – that gave 'em something to think about. The alternative press – now, they were different. They wanted to understand. The Doors' message that the end of the world was nigh was right."
> Ian Whitcomb, *Rock Odyssey: A Musician's Chronicle Of The 60s* (p341)

8 Mitchell Cohen *Remembering Morrison, Fusion* June 1974 p19.
9 Zevallos p47.
10 Bob Chorush *The Lizard King Reforms: Taking The Snake And Wearing It – An Interview With Jim Morrison, Los Angeles Free Press*, 15th January 1971 p24.

Moreover, Morrison was no longer taking Morrison seriously. Jim was basking in the contemporary Americanised image of the Dionysus: allowing an ever-changing crowd of groupies to pander to him, frivolously spending money on senseless things and indulging merrily with the great American elixir: alcohol. Tales of turmoil in recording this album abounded, evident in these two recollections. Hopkins and Sugerman wrote that during the rehearsal and recording of this third album, there were "wall-to-wall hangers-on" and events like the night every guy who wanted "had a poke" at a fat girl who had no panties on and had passed out in the vocal booth with her dress pulled above her waist or when John quit in disgust as Jim laid collapsed on the studio floor in a spreading stain of his own urine.[11]

In an article for *The Saturday Evening Post*, Joan Didion described waiting for Morrison to arrive at a recording session. When he finally did, no one acknowledged Jim "by so much as a flicker of an eye," and after an hour or so, no one had spoken to him. After some whispered conversation of frivolous suggestions between Morrison and Manzarek, silence returned to the studio. Didion wrote that Morrison lit a match and then slowly and deliberately lowered the flame to "the fly of his black vinyl pants", leaving the feeling no one would "leave the room, ever".[12] This is the essence of the Morrison outlook on existence: moments suspended in time often twisted in subtle yet bizarre ways to remind us that things are never entirely what we perceive them to be.

But the tension and challenges that Morrison was presenting, not only to himself but the group and others, weren't much different than the typical American way of doing things. The problem could be recognised, maybe it was discussed, maybe it wasn't, but nobody knew how to resolve it…yet everyone optimistically figured that everything would work out.

Years later, writers continued the paradoxical reactions in retrospective reviews. Lester Bangs wrote that "the whole nightmare easily translated into parody" with Morrison becoming a "true clown" and wearing his Lizard King cartoon like "a bib to keep the drunk drool" from staining his shirt and that when *Waiting For The Sun* was released, the band's worth had fallen to "just this side of bubblegum".[13] In contrast, David Dalton and Lenny Kaye in *Rock 100* reflected that the album expressed

11 Hopkins and Sugerman pp172, 174. Also see pp161-64 in *Riders On The Storm: My Life With Jim Morrison And The Doors* (New York: Delacorte Press 1990) for John Densmore's account of this tumultuous time of recording.
12 Joan Didion *Waiting For Morrison, The Saturday Evening Post*, 9th March 1968 p16.

"a rite of natural fertility". The music "gained texture and ornamentation" and Morrison "scooped deeper into his fantasies, rich and loamy" suggesting that his struggle was an inner one, a rebelling by the "pretensions of a pop star" against the "pretensions of an artist".[14]

Whether playing the tragic clown parodying the latest snake oil selling con man or the pretentious pop star duelling with the pretentiousness of the artist, neither Morrison alone nor The Doors as a unit gave any clear indication what was to be the next act on their newfound stage in life. With just a few pieces left from the earlier repertoire of songs, The Doors and producer Paul Rothchild sketched out the third album with snatches of The Doors' artistic vision. The album isn't necessarily less valid than the previous two, for it reflects The Doors' state of existence at the time. People grow and expand in many different directions throughout their lives, and art is a reflection of being human. We cannot expect an artist to maintain the same style and concepts forever. Labelling a personality type creates conflict because labels imply rigidity of existence, when actually everyone is made up of different facets interacting continually. Labels imply expected outlooks and behaviours, which create internal conflicts – and negative album reviews.

Both sides of the album continue portraying the attempt to find momentary sanctuary in the embrace of love or the freedom of breaking through, but each side ends with artistic indictments: side one with 'The Unknown Soldier', a ritualistic purging of war, and side two with 'Five To One', a dark portrait of the swirling forces of the times.

SIDE 1
'Hello, I Love You'
'Love Street'
'Not To Touch The Earth'
'Summer's Almost Gone'
'Wintertime Love'
'The Unknown Soldier'

'Hello, I Love You' opens the album. On the radio special, *History Of Rock 'n' Roll*, Manzarek described how the song originated when he and Jim saw a particular black girl walking along the beach who had "a dusky,

13 Lester Bangs *The Doors, The Rolling Stone Illustrated History Of Rock 'n' Roll*, Jim Miller, ed (New York: Rolling Stone Press 1976) p262.
14 David Dalton and Lenny Kaye *Rock 100* (New York: Grosset and Dunlap, publishers 1977) p166.

dark complexion" and was "just a little jewel, walking by" and that night Jim wrote a song about walking up to a girl he didn't know and saying, "Hello, I love you".[15] The song, one of the six cuts on the original demo the group recorded before Robby Krieger joined, echoes the passionate urgency of love portrayed in the first two albums. What is more natural than the spontaneous feeling on seeing someone who evokes a passionate greeting of "I love you" and asking your name?

The song shot to Number One and was the target of sharp criticism. Richard Walls labelled the song "psychedelic bubblegum",[16] and typical was Terry Rompers' critical blast that the song was "the most blatant sell-out single of the year" and was "such a crass Top 40 (AM!) single" that many fans gave up and went looking for "more committed anti-establishment groups".[17] *Harbinger*, a Toronto underground newspaper, was a little more sensitive in its August 1968 review: the song gains "immeasurably from being heard within the context of the album, as opposed to being sandwiched between a Clearasil commercial and the weather on your favourite Top 40 station."[18]

Many accused The Doors of cloning Ray Davies and the Kinks' 'All Day And All Of The Night'. In an interview over ten years later, Manzarek commented on the alleged Kinks derivative, saying that the group initially thought the song was "a *lot* like a Kinks song" but added, "It's all rock and roll, we're all family, we're not stealing anything from them, we're sort of... (hums melody) ...Yes it *is* a lot like it, isn't it? Sorry, Ray."[19]

The simple lyrics and Krieger's pulsating, stifled guitar resound the frustrated sensual urgency for this queen of the angels. Morrison then shifts perspective from the throbbing sensations of a longing lover to an emotionally detached third person observer. He watches this dusky jewel walk down the street blind to all the eyes she entices as she walks by and, like a statue, holding her head and attitude high. She won't expose vulnerability. The throbbing urgency swells to drown Jim's description that she has wicked arms and long legs and she makes his brain scream out this song, followed by Manzarek's organ swooping down and back up. By the end, the tone is more urgent, if not more sarcastic, as Morrison sings about the sidewalk crouching at her feet like a

15 *History Of Rock 'n' Roll*, aired 29th April 1978, WOWO Radio (1190 AM) Fort Wayne, IN.
16 Richard C Walls *Waiting For The Sun* (review) *Creem* Special Edition: *The Doors*, Summer 1981 p51.
17 Terry Rompers *Looking Through The Doors, Trouser Press*, September/October 1980 p2.
18 *The Doors* (record review of *Waiting For The Sun*) Harbinger (Toronto underground newspaper) August 1968 p21.
19 Fornatale p49.

begging dog (a petty god? or perhaps a modern Greek god?) and asks if anyone really hopes to "to pluck" such a "dusky jewel". This queen of angels, no less an allusion to the city of Los Angeles also, is no longer a Twentieth Century Fox in the sky, but a dusky jewel – hard and cold to the touch – to be plucked, rhetorically close enough to what a lover really wants to do. Yet, the frustrated and longing lover is drowning in both his desire and his foolishness for even thinking she would look at anyone, much less him. The song closes with Morrison crooning the eternal Top 40 triad of "I want you, I need you, I love you."

Just as silence often says more than words, simplicity can imply complexity. The sarcasm is made even more powerful, instead of being diminished, by the accompanying bubblegum music. Here, to walk up to someone and say, "Hello, I love you" signifies pure and simple lust – and presents quite an enticing contrast to the wicked woman imagery of 'People Are Strange'. Perhaps labelled as blatant Top 40/bubblegum sellout, the song, nevertheless restates previous themes of love: short and urgent, but don't expect anything lasting or meaningful.

Recapitulating the theme that life is dualistic, the flip side to the 45 release of 'Hello, I Love You' was the ensuing song, 'Love Street'. The girl on Love Street has a house and garden, a traditional symbol of sanctuary that offers a more reposing refuge in contrast to the sidewalk cruised by the queen of angels. Rather than luring with lust, this Twentieth Century Fox is more sophisticated and appeals to the deeper lure of mystery. Sensual urgency subsides as a relaxing piano replaces the passionate organ of the previous song. The long vowels and consonances that roll off Jim's tongue combine with the playful renderings by Robby's guitar and Ray's piano to create a lazy-dazy tone. A summer Sunday afternoon on Love Street – quite a contrast to a Moonlight Drive down by the oceanside. The song slows as Morrison speaks the last stanza of lyrics, creating a tone in stark contrast to the passionate urgency of previous love songs. The tone is mellow. Easy going. Jim leaves the song cruising into mellow oblivion with, "La-la-la La-la-la-la" carried along by John's soft back beat and gentle rapping of a cymbal. Yet the song's imagery renders the disquieting sense that Jim, though enticed by Love Street, won't surrender to such sanctuary.

Static images of 'Love Street' dissolve into swirling images of nature in 'Not To Touch The Earth', a song salvaged from 'The Celebration Of The

Lizard'. Krieger's leering guitar churns with Manzarek's tersely repetitive organ to shift from the casual pursuit of love to frenzied fleeing from comforts in the house upon the hill. The guitar, organ and the hard edge of the drum beat and persistent cymbal crescendo with each repeated chorus of "Run with me" as Morrison, his lover and the listener move deeper into a portrait of disturbing images – to the edge of lawlessness, of drowning, of breaking through. We reenter Eden to find the minister's daughter is in love with Christianity's symbolic adversary, the snake, in this song the archetypal image of both creativity and the forbidden side.

The structured imagery yields to Morrison's primal chanting to forces of life. Manzarek's organ and Krieger's guitar swirl around and down through the crescendoing chant, Densmore's drums punctuating the dissonance of the swirling forces. Finally, Morrison breaks through and states he is the "Lizard King" and can do anything. Calling upon the forces around him, the Lizard King emerges in control, without being at the mercy of lust – quite an opposite to the persona in the opening two songs.

The music is especially effective. There is not only the urgency of the lovers to flee, but also the feeling somebody or something is chasing them. The eerie and threatening tone of the music heightens the disturbing images rendered by the lyrics as The Doors switch moods with each new idea, becoming more dissonant as the journey progresses – so different from the nice music before and after this song.

The flash of organ that vapourises the cacophonic moment of breaking through at the end of 'Not To Touch The Earth' dissolves into the reticent love song, 'Summer's Almost Gone'. The ominous mood yields to Krieger's gentle, grinning guitar, Manzarek's soft and slightly inebriated piano and Densmore's softly stroked cymbals. After waning through the opening, Jim asks where they, as lovers, will be when summer is gone. The swoon of wanting to light a fire or going down on a moonlight drive has yielded to mature compassion. Instead of drowning in a sea of passion, Jim is swimming in a laughing sea. There is now the awareness that though the summer is only a brief season, it still means something to enjoy basic human experiences like compassion and basking in the sun. Instead of the lover playing the fool like a dog begging for something sweet, Morrison sings of romanticised moments, of their "good times". The tone and imagery reflect little if any quenching of passionate urgency. Yet there lingers the sad sense winter is coming. Near the end, the music pauses after Jim asks where they will be when summer is over, punctuating the question as we contemplate the answer.

Summer's carefree love yields to winter winds in Robby's song, 'Wintertime Love', and Jim answers the question in the previous song: he hopes to be falling in love. Since love needs contact, needs warmth, the waltz tone is so appropriate. Jim's crooning for his dear to come dance with him is more compassionate than the panting urgency of previous love songs. Though a wintertime waltz provides warm refuge, the song's images are cold and wintry as are the crisp, tingling sounds of Ray's keyboards, creating undertones of bittersweet love that won't last. There is the realisation that winter will be cold no matter how warm the lover; sometimes there are periods in life where things can't or don't happen, where love is lost.

Such a winter period in American politics was occurring with the war in Vietnam, as the urgency of the shamanic-artist surfaces in a song of political unrest to close what had been side one of the vinyl album. 'The Unknown Soldier' took its name from the national monument and, according to Manzarek, was not another Vietnam War protest song, but a song about war. Morrison, quoted in *Rolling Stone*, labelled 'The Unknown Soldier' a love song "about sexual intercourse," that the violence and firing squad were just metaphors "for what's going on".[20] Sure – a regimented approach to sex climaxed with an eruption of gunfire as bullets and lover unite. Manzarek offered a more even-keeled explanation in a radio special produced by *The Source*: Jim said, "Let's do a war song." I said, "Everybody's doing a Vietnam song." And he said, "Nah, nah, this isn't a Vietnam song. This is just a song about war."[21]

Hopkins and Sugerman recalled the song began in October of 1967 and was developed on the road; in two or three months "the dirge became a celebration" with a rhythm "both military (metronomic) and carnivalesque."[22] Producer Rothchild stated in an 1981 interview in *Musician* that "Unknown Soldier" was a "programmatic concept" of Jim's with so many different sections it required an "enormous amount of time to record."[23] Shown at concerts, a short film of the song presented Morrison being executed with simulated vomiting and a political montage. Released as a single in March 1968, the song was subsequently banned by several radio chains.

20 Jonathan Cott *Doors, Airplane In Middle Earth, Rolling Stone*, 26th October 1968 p12.
21 *The Source: The Doors Special Encore* (3-hour radio special) Show NBC 82-23 (New York: NBC Radio's Young Adult Network) aired 2-4th July 1982. In his book *The Lizard King: The Essential Jim Morrison*, Jerry Hopkins wrote 'Unknown Soldier' was from Morrison's writings when he lived in Venice Beach during the summer of 1965, right after graduating from UCLA (pp93, 95).
22 Hopkins and Sugerman pp149-50.

The song opens with Morrison softly singing to wait till the war is over and we are a little older. With time, war fades in memory. But the lull is shattered as the music and Morrison, in a very sarcastic nasal twinge, belt out that breakfast is where we read the news. In the morning we consume news, which in 1968 consisted of large dosages of the Vietnam War. And the fruition of children who are television fed is the paradoxical image of the *unborn living, living dead*, mentally and spiritually dead people who have yet to be born into living. The middle of the song acts out a ritual in the ancient tradition of the shaman (The Doors probably weren't too conscious of this parallel). Morrison, the artist incarnate of the shamanic spirit, sacrifices himself in a ritual – one of military execution, the firing squad – to purge us of the burden of war. Then he softly invites us to make a grave for all this death. The song recants the breakfast and television fed images, but Jim doesn't repeat *unborn living, living dead*, allowing the listener to fill in that hollow space before the bullet hits the helmet's head and The Doors close by chanting that the war is over.

Although this chorus fuelled the growing social chorus to end the Vietnam War, Morrison's chanting also underscores the reality that war will not fade away. It couldn't, not with a generation having been breakfast and television fed with vivid images the Vietnam War portrayed.

SIDE 2
'Spanish Caravan'
'My Wild Love'
'We Could Be So Good Together'
'Yes, The River Knows'
'Five To One'

Robby's flamenco guitar introduction sweeps us away on a journey in 'Spanish Caravan'. Instead of urgent flight toward something unknown, there is willful yielding to this desire to escape to a place not as dangerous. Jim has faith the caravan will carry and take him to Portugal and Spain. Rather than the repetitive urgency of *Let's run*, "An-da-lu-si-a" rolls off Jim's tongue, and Robby's flamenco guitar carries us off toward this exotic land in southern Spain bordering on the Atlantic Ocean and the Mediterranean Sea, an image as exotic as the girl on Love Street.

23 Garbarini p54.

The song pauses; then the journey swirls into a realisation that there might be danger as Krieger's guitar transforms into a driving electronic six-stringer cutting across the swirling rhythms of Manzarek's organ with Densmore's drumming swelling with every spin of the emerging vortex, and Morrison sings that the ocean winds find galleons lost on the high seas, alluding to the recurring image of a ship lost at sea, so vividly rendered in 'Horse Latitudes'. Though Jim croons about silver and gold in the distant mountains of Spain, recalling the image of digging for treasures in 'Break On Through', he sings he needs to see his lover again and again, suggesting the treasure he really wants is to attain love or happiness. Pursuit requires energy against the currents of life, so Morrison needs to see once in awhile the treasure he seeks in order to keep going on. A rather touching moment on Jim's part as he usually spends so much time running from life. In sharp contrast to the urgent pursuing of his repeated imagery of "Let's run", Jim has faith that the Spanish Caravan will take him there.

Morrison returns to love in the song, 'Wild Love'. He is removed from the lover's trance – neither a dog begging for something sweet, nor a lazy-dazy lover laid back on 'Love Street'; neither the carefree golden boy in the summer noon sun, nor the embraced dancer in the wintertime waltz. He sees his lover as he sees his own quest for life, in terms of audacious adventure. Accompanied by primal tones of a group chant with hand clapping and harmonic moans, Jim mixes images of confronting the devil, of the devil wising up to repent, of destinations seemingly with no connections. More complex than the dusky jewel strolling down the sidewalk and more worldly than the vamp on Love Street, this wild love is crazy and very enticing.

The song echoes the theme of a lengthy journey to reenter a town portrayed in 'The Celebration Of The Lizard', only this has been a journey by Jim's "wild love." Morrison has been on a Spanish Caravan and now he longs for their reunion in the next song, 'We Could Be So Good Together'.

There could be little doubt of Morrison's intent in the opening line that he and his lover could be good together. The deliciously latent image of the world that the two lovers could invent, a wanton world without any lament (Jim cleverly plays on the word, *wanton*, evoking both the noun and the verb, *wanting*), envisions a sensual world without limits.

The four nouns *enterprise*, *expedition*, *invitation* and *invention* frame an enticing picture, but there is something uneasy in the static nature of nouns. Nouns are labels and labels don't stick forever because things change. Moreover, the image of an angel reappears – of angels who fight and cry, of angels who die. Angels are vulnerable. How powerful the ramifications if ethereal angels are no better than humans, if being human is one of the best deals available in the universe.

Though Jim repeatedly sings a chorus of telling her lies – wicked lies, the song closes with the hypocritical, upbeat lyric that they could be good together. If existence requires lying to yourself to create an illusion of sanctuary, what happens when that sanctuary is shattered?

Wanton desire dissolves into Robby's melodic song, 'Yes, The River Knows'. The mellow sound and drawn-out vowels and consonances lull the lover and listener into Jim's gentle plea for his love to believe that the river very softly told him she should hold him. As Jim draws us in with the image of the free fall flow of the river, Ray's supple piano and Robby's percolating guitar lap at the listener floating on the rapping of John's soft back beat. One has to be quiet and accepting to yield to the free flowing river of life and its freedom and peacefulness. And if his lover doesn't need him, Jim promises to drown himself in *mystic heated wine*, a stark contrast to the spirits of whisky in 'Alabama Song'. Though the song closes with the image of breathing under water till the end, evoking a sense of drowning, the tone is more receptive, not the angst portrayed in previous songs. The end of the song slides into a crescendo, swelling to drown the singer in a gentle wave of music.

Flowing on the river of life brings understanding, and The Doors emerge to deliver a social indictment. The daze of mystic heated wine and allure of being so good together vanish beneath the drums and steady bass beat that open 'Five To One'. The poignant cry that no one gets out of here alive captures the understood but unspoken essence of life. Morrison's guttural, unrelenting sexual come on is a voice beyond the earlier lustful desires or casual yearnings. A brazen statement of political reality ensues of taking over – of the old becoming old and the young becoming stronger, of *they* may have the guns but *we* have the numbers. Morrison sings with an urgency no longer being denied, sneering that the young take over, even if the older generation isn't giving way easily – the "Us versus Them" ideology of the Cold War, of the Sixties. Yet Morrison parodies youth alluding to the growing numbers of hippies who carried flowers and said no one understands, but who panhandled outside concert halls for a handful of dimes.

Morrison concludes the song with a deviously drawled out portrait of drugs and free love. He moans at his honey to go home and wait because he has to go to a car with some people and, not clearly on the studio album but evident on bootleg concert recordings, "get fucked up". As the band drones on with the chorus about getting together one more time, Morrison snarls about his carnal intent. The popish, almost innocent 'Hello, I Love You' opening is gone; The Doors leave a menacing impression of what such casual access to love and drugs brings.

For some, 'Five To One' finally brought out The Doors' sound which they felt had been buried in the ballady melodies of the previous songs. A reviewer in the underground newspaper, *Harbinger*, wrote: "If Morrison isn't a demon on 'Five To One' then what is he? This is Doors distilled and concentrated-spine arching music. Who'll be the first to bludgeon his parents? Pull down all the walls and ball in the smoking ruins. Bass and drums drive, guitar pierces. Morrison sings like he had a spike through his throat. Maniacal, brutal, unrelenting. Insane laugh. Jesus, what a song."[24]

The title? 'Five To One' is, as Hopkins and Sugerman wrote, a statistic that Morrison never explained.[25] Jim offered an explanation to Hank Zevallos in an 1970 interview published in *Poppin*; the song, which Morrison said he didn't think of as political, was an idea he got while waiting in the audience before starting a concert at San Jose, California: "It was one of those big ballroom places and the kids were milling around and I just got an idea for a song."[26] (On 19 November 1967, The Doors performed at the San Jose Continental Ballroom in San Jose, California.)

The song isn't explicit and doesn't present a neat, tidy statement; it leaves space to think, to react – typical of Doors songs. 'Five To One' ends the album on a note of anger and confrontation, of conflict evident in The Doors both outside and inside their music that would climax in the Miami concert on 1 March 1969 and in the transformation of their sound which would begin in the fourth album.

The boys – the group, the sound, the artistic vision – were maturing.

For many, this third album diverged unexpectedly from the sound rendered so vividly in the first two albums. But it reveals that The Doors were realising they would have to live with the swirling whirlwind of the

24 Harbinger p21.
25 Hopkins and Sugerman p152.
26 Zevallos p50.

times. The passionate and frustrated urgencies to find love or freedom became muted to tones of being patient, of experiencing the pain and joy of living without fighting life. The album, though considered one of the weakest and least focused of all the albums, frames a well-rendered landscape from The Doors' artistic vision.

"Like a mighty titan, the tragic hero shoulders the whole Dionysiac world and removes the burden from us. At the same time, tragic myth, through the figure of the hero, delivers us from our avid thirst for earthly satisfaction and reminds us of another existence and a higher delight. For this delight the hero readies himself, not through his victories but through his undoing."
Friedrich Nietzsche, *The Birth Of Tragedy*

chapter 5

SOFT ASYLUM, SOFT PARADE

"The narcissism of adolescence…continues in the making of
lyric poets who are eternal adolescents, eternally unadaptable,
forever incapable of fixing themselves into a pattern of life.
The essentially romantic trait of narcissism is its
inevitable obsession with the indefinite and the unlimited."
Wallace Fowlie, *Rimbaud (A Critical Study)*, p239.

The Sixties were beginning the slide to a dramatic end by the early
1970s. Leaders were being assassinated: Martin Luther King Jr in
April of 1968; Bobby Kennedy in the June of the same year. The political realities of America steamrolled over the flower power of the youth.
At the 1968 Democratic convention, Chicago Mayor Richard Daley
demonstrated police army – Gestapo – tactics to maintain democratic
principles. Though both were destined to resign in shame and scandal,
Richard Nixon and Spiro Agnew were elected President and Vice
President in November. American involvement in Vietnam in terms of
troop numbers peaked in January 1969. Half a planet away, in China, the
violent turmoil of the "Cultural Revolution" continued to rip apart the
fabric of the aging Maoist regime with bloodshed as the Chinese communist way of life, like the Western capitalist way of life, was confronted
by disgruntled youth, artists and intellectuals.

Forcible vanquishing of student demonstrations disrupted many
American college campuses. In April 1968, police cleared all buildings
occupied by a student sit-in at the Ivy League Columbia University; and
in May 1969, the police and the National Guard used shotguns, tear gas
and a helicopter to drop a stinging chemical powder on students, faculty and area residents who were occupying their self-made People's Park
on the University of California campus at Berkeley. Similar student
unrest confronted almost every European capital, notably the 19-day
eruption in Paris in May. An unpopular disciplinary action by university

officials triggered student riots that led to confrontations with police. The national student union advocated more demonstrations, and the national teachers' union demanded a faculty strike. Confrontations escalated, labour unions called for a general strike, and soon other organised labour joined the general strike, which paralysed President Charles de Gaulle's government, cut France off from the rest of the world and nearly resurrected the French Revolution ghosts of anarchy and civil war. The confidently dogmatic de Gaulle survived, but a year later in April of 1969, the WW II general and hero would resign after defeat in a referendum on his proposed constitutional reforms.

During 1968, riots in American cities continued to violently express this whirlwind of swirling forces: riots over Martin Luther King Jr's assassination, a riot in Miami's black section during the midsummer heat, and the riot with the Chicago heat during the Democratic convention in August – probably the largest and most confrontational riot in American history.

After King's assassination, much more attention was given the report issued by the National Advisory Commission on Civil Disorders which had been appointed by President Johnson in 1967. Headed by Otto Kerner, then governor of Illinois, the investigatory panel issued a 250,000-word report on 29 February 1968. Two of the conclusions the commission reached were that the disorders usually involved blacks reacting against symbols of white American society and not white people and that those who were rioting were seeking greater participation in the American system, not rejecting it. And the report's core tenet emphasised an axiom of racism: white racism digs and maintains the ghetto trench for the prejudicially suppressed black race.

At the 1968 summer Olympics in Mexico, Tommie Smith and John Carlos, two black American athletes, won the gold (in world record time) and bronze medals in the 200-meter dash. The two stood on the awards stand with black knee-length stockings, received their medals, turned to watch the raising of one Australian and two United States flags (the flags of the three medal winners), and, as the US national anthem was played, lowered their heads and raised clenched fists (Smith his right, Carlos his left) inside black gloves. It was a bold and defiant statement of both black power ("We shall overcome") and America's disregarded impoverishment. Although they had the freedom to express such a sensational statement, Smith and Carlos were immediately suspended from the Olympic team at the insistence of the International Olympic Committee.

On American prime-time television, *The Mod Squad* presented three rehabilitated street-wise young people – one white male, one white female, one black male – as undercover cops; they were mod, yet part of the system – marketable to television viewers, but politically correct. Showcasing a prancing and bouncing, robust Barbara Eden, *I Dream Of Jeannie* led into the 1968 fall season premiere of *Rowan And Martin's Laugh-In* which offered a weekly hour of comedy in an edited melange perfect for the medium.

But before the fall season had premiered, the news departments of the three major networks covered the Democratic National Convention in Chicago where Hubert Humphrey was nominated as the presidential candidate. The live broadcast of clashes between Chicago's police and the predominantly youthful demonstrators evoked a huge cry from the public. They claimed television had helped conspire this unnerving assault on authority, and the networks were left defending what they thought had been objective recording of what really happened. The viewing public, President Nixon's so-called *silent majority*, was upset with what they perceived as networks broadcasting only bad news – riots, lootings, killings and the Vietnam War. Where was the good news? It was being broadcast, but storms of mayhem and blood leave more lasting impressions (and attract bigger audiences) than tranquil sunsets and sunrises. Earlier in May, French television had been a target of the mass demonstrations because it had focused only on good news, in a sense, betraying the public with a foolish picture of their state of affairs. At Chicago, the anti-war demonstrators had the potential "no" march Washington DC had had: the presence of television, in this case, the complete focus of the three national networks news departments. It was a demonstration to an unsuspecting American public – and the television industry – of one distinctive power of this particular medium.

The "tribal love-rock musical," *Hair!*, made it to Broadway in late April, premiering at the Biltmore Theatre in New York City. Without a significant plot, the musical presented a vibrant, innovative and entertaining version of turning on, tuning in and dropping out. The emergence of the Theatre of Involvement followed a more brazen format akin to the reactionary artistic tradition of shocking the bourgeoisie (in the 1960s, the middle class). Though the energetic and often aggressive writers, actors and actresses laid bare the issues of the day, the anger they would predictably evoke shut down any dialogue or debate by audiences after the play. The Theatre of Involvement offered no endearing works that could survive beyond the swirling forces of the times, but when the avant-garde Living Theatre group performed in late February of 1969 at the University of Southern California in Los Angeles, Jim Morrison planted himself in the audience. The seeds of inspiration brought quick fruition at the 1 March concert at Miami.

By 1969, one of the first waves of *The Best of...* albums from groups of the Sixties hit the *Billboard* charts – the Association, The Bee Gees, Buffalo Springfield, Cream, Donovan, The Mamas and The Papas, Rascals and Diana Ross and the Supremes. While The Fifth Dimension's 'Aquarius/Let the Sunshine In' and songs by Creedence Clearwater Revival were being played repeatedly over radio airwaves, the tugging undercurrent of the times surfaced in two very poignant Top 40 war protest songs: 'Galveston' and 'Rudy, Don't Take Your Love To Town'. The Who unleashed *Tommy* while the fictitious and plastic Archies made millions of dollars. Led Zeppelin released their first album, a young Bob Seger was climbing the charts with 'Ramblin' Gamblin' Man', and The Beatles' *White Album* revealed what many had suspected: a fragmenting into individuals of the once-cohesive Beatles.

And in 1969 the first wave of rock culture heroes began dying off: author Jack Kerouac in April and Brian Jones of The Rolling Stones in July.

This phase of the rock culture, the Sixties, was about to end.

The forces and issues upon which the youth had honed their creative energies were peaking and dissipating. Not only that, it was damn difficult to keep sharpening a keen creative edge against a culture of which many of the counter-culture had become a successful part. With both commercial and limited social success, the revolutionary – if not just the reactionary – edge of the counter-culture didn't have that hard stone of resistance upon which to sharpen its edge. How could millionaire musicians like The Doors sing about the hypocrisy of a plastic, materialistic society detached from the roots of life?

Moreover, The Doors were no longer one of the influencing, let alone, controlling forces of the whirlwind they had helped swirl into its urgent and passionate pace in the Sixties. They had become detached from their own roots, no longer firmly grounded in any rich humus of creativity.

72

Instead, having kept pace with a swirling tour schedule, they were swept into the very plastic world so vividly rendered in their first two albums and less so in the third. In retrospect, Morrison wrote in one of his many note-books he had "ploughed" his seed through the heart of America, and like a "germ" in the nation's "psychic blood vein" he now embraced the "poet-ry of business" and became for a while a "prince of industry".[1]

Obligated to fulfil a recording contract, The Doors found themselves needing to create music for this fourth album. There were no new songs from gigging before an intimate night club audience; there were no new songs flowing to Morrison while idling away time on a rooftop or a beach. This was to be a period of transition. And after the Miami concert on 1 March 1969, The Doors, now freed of touring commitments, were clearly in transition.

Recording the fourth album began in late 1968, but the album wasn't completed until June 1969, though a string of singles were released, begin-ning in late December 1968 with the commercially successful 'Touch Me'.

Part of this transition was that *The Soft Parade* would include separate writing credits for individual songs. Krieger said Morrison wanted separate credits because, among other reasons, he thought the lyrics in Robby's song 'Tell All The People' were too political.[2] In a radio special produced by *The Source*, Ray offered this paraphrasing of Jim: "I ain't saying that: 'Can't you see me growing/get your guns/follow me down'."[3]

Jim told Jerry Hopkins in an 1969 *Rolling Stone* interview that initially the group did things in the interest of unity, but since the unity wasn't "that much in jeopardy," people should know "who was saying what" because he and Robby had very different visions of reality.[4] For many, it didn't mat-ter who was saying what; the album was panned as a *sell-out*. And the growing erratic behaviour of Morrison provided an easy target at which to aim – and make stick – such criticism. The consensus opinion was that dur-ing this period Morrison was basically a disinterested, drunken asshole, a view Jim seemed to share. In a passage from one of his notebooks, he wrote that being drunk was a "good disguise" and that he drank so he could talk with "assholes" which included himself.[5]

---

1 Morrison *Wilderness, Volume I* p206.
2 Robert Mathen *Through The Doors Again: Manzarek, Krieger And Densmore Today, Creem* Special Edition: *The Doors,* Summer 1981 p59. In his book *The Lizard King: The Essential Jim Morrison* Jerry Hopkins wrote that Morrison didn't want people to think he wanted others to follow him because he neither trusted leaders nor want to be a leader (p120).
3 *The Source: The Doors Special Encore* (3-hour radio special).
4 Hopkins *The Rolling Stone Interview: Jim Morrison,* p17.
5 Morrison *Wilderness, Volume 1* p207. Compare this poem by Morrison to Wallace Folwie's translation of Arthur Rimbaud's poem *Evening Prayer* [Oraison du soir] p89.

In a *Rolling Stone* article about the making of the Morrison myth, Mikal Gilmore summarised what has been repeatedly written about Jim at this time: Morrison had gone from being one the "smartest, scariest and sexiest heroes" in rock 'n' roll to a "heart-rending alcoholic and clownish jerk."[6] The impression that The Doors no longer appeared in control of their work and that no one was taking them serious anymore seemed quite apparent after the bawdy 1 March concert in Miami's Dinner Key Auditorium which brought warrants for Jim's arrest on charges of "lewd and lascivious behaviour in public by exposing his private parts and by simulating masturbation and oral copulation." The Lizard King, a self-proclaimed erotic politician, was about to meet the hard, cutting edge of judicial – and political – reality.

With the release of *The Soft Parade*, reviewers had more than just the music tempering their perspectives of this latest Doors album. Though writing for *Creem* in the summer of 1981, Richard Riegel encapsulated the general reaction, writing that, if *Waiting For The Sun* had made many older hippies question their view of The Doors "as Avatars of the avant garde", then *The Soft Parade* had finished any interest in the group.[7]

Lester Bangs was less cordial, proclaiming The Doors' "artistic stock had hit an all-time low," the group had abandoned their "original promise", and they – especially Morrison – had "turned what they represented into a joke."[8]

In an 1981 interview with *Musician*, Manzarek said the group was ready to move on to their next phase and to do something different, like recording with horns and strings.[9] The use of strings from the Los Angeles Philharmonic and horns of local jazz musicians generated a swell of critical response. In the underground newspaper, *Northwest Passage*, Rob Cline wrote: "The Doors, while trying to explore new musical horizons, fell flat on their asses. Does a rock 'n' roll group really need violins and trombones? The Doors are the best when getting it on straight and hard as witness their first two albums."[10]

David Walley in *The East Village Other* took direct aim, stating that the album was "badly messed up by the syrupy arrangements of Paul Rothchild" and could be retitled "The Rothchild Strings Play The

6 Mikal Gilmore The *Legacy Of Jim Morrison And The Doors, Rolling Stone*, 4th April 1991 p33.
7 Riegel p12.
8 Bangs *The Doors, The Rolling Stone Illustrated History Of Rock And Roll* p262.
9 Fornatale p50.
10 Rob Cline *Record Reviews, Northwest Passage* (Bellingham, WA underground newspaper) 19th August 1969 p20.

Doors."[11] Miller Francis Jr, in the underground newspaper, *The Great Speckled Bird*, felt "that a misfire in poetic 'Art Rock' like *The Soft Parade* comes on so fucking pretentious, like something written rather than something sung."[12]

Many in the underground felt betrayed, yet there were those who had hated the first albums but insisted this fourth one marked the maturity of the group away from teenybopdom. A reviewer in the Ottawa underground newspaper, *Octopus*, wrote that: "I always hated the Doors and Jim Morrison and found their previous albums boring. This time it is different. The sensual, animal, back to the hills, down on it sound is emphasised by the light use of strings and horns... [The Doors] have progressed, this album is not just for the teen queens to get horny over, it is an interesting, tough and important album."[13]

> "Nothing can kill the revolutionary potential of rock more than crass commercialisation."
> Robert G Pielke, *You Say You Want A Revolution: Rock Music in American Culture* p14.

Did they *sell out*? In an 1981 interview, the person some accused of gumming up the lucid Doors sound with the syrupy resonance of strings and horns, Paul Rothchild, said that the intention of this album was "to hit the mass, *mass* market, with horns, strings, the full orchestra treatment," but they consciously recorded "in an attempt to explore all the idioms available," although he agreed that "Touch Me" was a compromise which alienated part of The Doors' original audience while gaining "an enormous number of new fans."[14]

He also said in another interview that Morrison became "really rebellious" for the recording sessions to prove to the band they "weren't shit without him."[15] Ray, years later in a radio special produced by *The Source*, said that in retrospect using horns and strings "probably wasn't the best idea we ever had, but we enjoyed doing it."[16] In an interview

11 David Walley *The Elektra Company, Or How One Learns To Love the Bombs, The East Village Other* (New York underground newspaper) 10 September 1969 p12.
12 Miller Francis Jr *Callin' On The Gods, The Great Speckled Bird* (Atlanta underground newspaper) 20th October 1969 p18.
13 KT *Records* (review of *The Soft Parade*) *Octopus* (Ottawa, Canada, underground newspaper) vol 2-11 (1969) p26.
14 Garbarini p56.
15 Blair Jackson *Paul Rothchild: The Doors' Producer Recalls The Agony And The Ecstasy Of Working With The Doors, BAM,* 3rd July 1981 p19.
16 *The Source: The Doors' Special Encore* (3-hour radio special).

with *Guitar World* in 1994, Robby said he didn't "really like orchestrating the songs" on this album and would never have done it – it had been Rothchild's idea.[17]

Without much of a repertoire of songs from which to draw, The Doors and Rothchild could produce, at best, a fuzzy sketch of The Doors' artistic vision on the fourth album. If on the album cover the group seemed a distant image behind the camera stationed on the tripod, their music seemed just as distant, the album a collection of seemingly unrelated still life portraits. The Doors' artistic vision in the previous albums was more active and pervasive; this time, the vision wasn't as focused on society and remained behind the camera for the next photographic opportunity. The Doors and Rothchild rendered a hastily drawn portrait of the very pop idioms of which they were so critical. The songs are technically simple, unimaginative snatches seemingly covered in the blues, like the cover of the album.

Trying to impose a critical rendering that some sort of thematic structure underlies *The Soft Parade* isn't fair to The Doors' artistic vision. The cohesive artistic rendering in this fourth album was the idiomatic exploration of Pop. The Doors and Rothchild produced an album that would sell – a definite sell-out in terms of artistic vision and creative value.

Bangs, perhaps the most critical and appraising writer of Jim Morrison, reflected in an 1981 article for *Creem* titled, *Jim Morrison, Oafus Laureate*, that the "bubblegum/parody" of the third and fourth albums may have been "entirely intentional, premeditated; one juncture in a vast strategy" to reveal that "machismo equals bozo in the drag" that rock stars were just "huge oafus cartoons" and that Morrison's games of "poet" and "shaman" were "two more gushers of American snake-oil."[18] Yet Dave DiMartino offered a retrospective appraisal that Morrison "never dealt with specifics" and gave answers that were neither true nor false "because they were abstract and primitive simultaneously" – abstract because the lyrics dealt "with 'soft parades,' words that fit together nicely but meant little" and primitive because the lyrics dealt "with the basest of emotions and never taking them to their logical conclusions."[19]

The Doors, and especially Morrison, could paint lucid portraits with mere impressions which were musically and lyrically drawn from the

17 Alan Paul *Strange Days* (interview with Krieger) *Guitar World* March 1994 p112.
18 Bangs *Jim Morrison, Oafus Laureate* p29.
19 Dave DiMartino *Morrison In Miami: Flesh And Memories, Creem* Special Edition: *The Doors*, Summer 1981 p31.

vast and complex matrix of metaphors our culture uses to define reality. Such impressions touch what everyone suspects but doesn't know how to express in concrete terms. For people understand easier the subconscious metaphors which circumvent prejudices imposed upon the conscious mind by the environment. And Riegel hinted at such a realisation when he noted that the album marked Morrison's changing to a "newer rock 'n' roll persona", that Jim was finally seeing life from a "musician's eye viewpoint" and was "mutating into a bluesman."[20] It is not difficult to slide such an artistic persona under the term, *shaman*, or as some critics wrote, *shamanic bluesman*.

By this album, the overtones and poetic imagery of the artistic vision are far less introspective and self-enclosing, less urgent and less angry. In short, more melancholy. There are few answers, if any, and the outward trappings and confusion of this society aren't going to change. But one gets the impression that these shamanic spirits have approached a truce with mortality: "Life kind of sucks, society is screwed up, and that's the way things are going to be, but I don't care because I'm enjoying some of the simple pleasures of being alive; I'm feeling okay about things, so the futility can just wait until I have enough energy to define it in my mind." Artistically, then, *The Soft Parade* is an ambiguous transformation to the blues outlook, evoking undefined feelings without striving to be one thing in particular. Lyrically, Morrison is into this transformation, but musically, the others haven't caught up. This album, musically different to the style of the other five, becomes a compilation of musical cliches and rip-offs.

The seriousness of the lyrics of these songs, especially of those written by Morrison, is hard to determine. The words probably would have been much more effective with music that had organically grown with the lyrics, but they lose a lot of impact in this setting. To say that this discrepancy adds more tension to the message gives credit that is undeserved, given that this album wasn't really planned. When the music's good, enjoy it and when the words are good, enjoy them, but trying to link the two together isn't necessarily valid. This album wasn't created to be interpreted in that way. It was a creation painstakingly pieced together by Rothchild. Morrison told John Tobler in an interview at the Isle of Wight Festival in England that the album "kinda got out of control" and took too long to make and that an album, like a book of stories strung together, should have "some kind of unified feeling and

20 Riegel p12.

style," but that *The Soft Parade* lacks that.[21]

However, patterns and relationships do emerge which render a transition in The Doors' artistic vision. The rebellious cries for action are mellowing into the acceptance of the way life is. The cries of social anguish are becoming more reflective, more mirror-like in their renderings. The rush of the anxious, uninhibited lover who has transcended through the passive, detached lover is transforming into a shamanic bluesman. Beginning to understand his own feelings and limitations as a human, the youthful shaman has become closer to other people, at least on the most basic levels. The artistic vision, which before had rejected plastic people and society, now becomes more accepting. Life is becoming a "soft parade" – well, compared to the previous albums, a softer parade – of shamanic insights and artistic renderings.

SIDE 1
'Tell All The People'
'Touch Me'
'Shaman's Blues'
'Do It'
'Easy Ride'

'Tell All The People' opens the album with a full blast of horns proclaiming alternative leadership. Reactions to the song ranged from Francis writing that the song "is night club shuck"[22] to Mitch Kapor writing in the *View From The Bottom*, a New Haven underground newspaper, that the same song "is our great synthesis of erotic politician with Christ image martyr rock."[23] Penned by Krieger, the song reflects his style of simple and ambiguous textures as Morrison sings for people to follow him down, even though the music scales upward with the horns. There flows an undercurrent of uncertainty about this erotic politician crooning to follow him across the sea and promising he can set people free. The lyric urging us to take his hand and bury troubles in the sand may suggest the easy removal of problems from sight, yet the lyric also sketches an image of the ostrich-with-its-head-in-the-sand way of dealing with troubles. *Bury* can suggest death, and

---

21 From John Tobler's interview with Jim Morrison at Isle of Wight Festival 1970, on *Opening The Doors Of Perception* ("over one hour of rare and intriguing dialogue") CD. (Transcript of interview is printed in Jerry Hopkin's *The Lizard King: The Essential Jim Morrison*, see p235.
22 Francis p18.
23 Mitch Kapor *Soft Parade, A View From The Bottom* (New Haven, CT underground newspaper) 7th August 1969 p13.

the ensuing call to get our guns doesn't reassure that this journey will be peaceful. New awareness destroys old preconceptions, but also may cause death and destruction. And so can voluntary blindness and denial. To get to this promised land requires crossing the sea, a place where there has been more than one unnerving breaking through to the unknown, as in 'Moonlight Drive' and 'Horse Latitudes'. The portrait The Doors paint of breaking through to a promised land is hazier than previous depictions, for what they are running from isn't as clearly defined.

The Doors then render a portrait of love in Krieger's song, 'Touch Me'. In an interview with Robert Matheu in 1981, Robby explained the song originally was 'Hit Me', not 'Touch Me', but Jim wouldn't sing that lyric.[24] Densmore expounded on this, writing that Robby had written, "Come on, come on, come on, now, *hit* me, babe!", from one of the many rumoured domestic squabbles between him and his girlfriend, but had offered no resistance when Jim suggested the change to "*touch* me."[25] A mellowing Morrison wanted to tone the lyric down a little to "touch me", a line he had used in previous live performances of 'When The Music's Over' as recorded on bootlegs: "Something wrong, something not quite right/Touch me baby/All through the night."

This song evoked probably The Doors' most popish expression of love, with sweet strings of violins swelling as a background for Morrison's crooning. The single was panned by many critics as a sell-out. Bob (Turk) Nirkind in a Detroit underground newspaper, *The South End*, offered a typical reaction: with strings and horns replacing the raw power of The Doors, 'Touch Me' loses the forcefulness the group had demonstrated in the past, and "the words do zero for the image" established by The Doors.[26]

Francis was more blatant about The Doors' sell-out, rhetorically asking if 'Touch Me' could "be sung with a straight face in a super-elegant night club to a drunk set of plastic middle-aged Muzak-lovers, *with identically the same sound?*"[27] But why not enjoy good feelings when they happen, even syrupy ones like loving someone till the stars fall? How long can you survive trying to outfox Twentieth Century

---

24 Matheu p59.
25 Densmore p190.
26 Bob (Turk) Nirkind *The Doors – Follow Them Down*, *The South End* (Wayne State University, Detroit, underground newspaper) 21 August 1969 p8.
27 Francis p18.

Foxes? Beneath the horns and strings, The Doors generate a controlled frenzy of sound along with the Krieger-esque lyrics before Curtis Amy's jazz solo on sax rises above the frenzy. The entire triad of sound and lyrics comes to a blunt end with the gang-chanted, "Stronger than dirt!" – the then-popular TV commercial slogan of Ajax household cleaner.

The popish love theme of 'Touch Me' slides into the enigmatic and fragmented imagery of Morrison's 'Shaman Blues'. As for 'Shaman Blues' fitting-in to mainstream Top 40, forget it. Our present daily existence isn't framed by values, metaphors, or an outlook that can comprehend or appreciate the landscape that the shamanic spirit (or for that matter, the artistic spirit) moves through. You have to be able to economically shape and market your art if you want to survive on our modern landscape. Thus, the shamanic world is difficult to communicate in modern languages or thoughts which have diminished the capacity and ability to represent such realities. And Morrison was more unconscious than conscious of the shamanic landscape from which he spoke.

Instead of a smart-ass persona taunting with cynicism, Morrison evokes a more sensitive honesty as he sings about his lover and wanting to be with her. His voice is quite human as he sings about there never being someone else like her or someone who does the things she can do. He then croons for an invitation to get back together, if she has an evening she could "lend". A much softer yearning than the taunting and demanding lover of earlier songs.

Yet the undercurrent of uncertainty surfaces like waves upon the shores of our ears with Morrison's spattering of disturbing images. Within his weaving of fragmented impressions, he brings an abrupt shift to an allusion of frenzied flight with images of stopping, wondering and remembering.

It is the blues – one lover pleading for the other not to forget, not to make mistakes. Running from yourself goes in circles. The path to breaking through comes with honest self-awareness, from stopping and reflecting. Having broken through to the meadow, to the other side, the shaman finds he hasn't left behind all that makes him human. The disquieting spoken coda which ends the song was created by mixing ad-lib bits from vocal takes of Jim's before it slides into a wicked laugh which opens the next song.

In 'Do It', perhaps the child-like chanting by the boys which precedes Morrison's wicked laugh is a subtle way of saying the song was all in fun. Besides, the bubblegum pop fits the repeated calling to the "children" in the song...until you hear the song effectively rendered in concert by one of the Doors tribute bands (The Doors never performed the song live). And then the power of the music hits you. The erotic politician is no longer preaching that ultimate revolution is wanting the world *now*, or that one can leave the world behind by breaking through to the other side. No; Morrison sings repeatedly for children to listen to him because they eventually will rule the world.

The album opens with Krieger's calling for people to take a journey, and what had been side one of the original album closes with Morrison's return to the journey image, recanting the *carpe diem* theme to a lover to seize the day and take an 'Easy Ride'. Robby's laughing guitar, Ray's prancing organ, and John's upbeat drumming create a simple and carefree texture and Jim's light and crisp vocals are dominated by long vowels and rolling consonants. The Doors may be rendering the appearance of a light-hearted trip through love, but there emerges the impression of something deeper than an "easy ride".

Instead of enjoying the moment, Jim returns to a campy, sarcastic portrait. He knows what will get a reaction and will explore the mask she wears. The Doors frequently portray masks covering deeper emotions and her costume of control yields to unfolding passion. Morrison closes with the *carpe diem* theme of seizing the day resounded in full passionate resonance. The pride which vaguely had fought the unfolding joy can now seize the power of summer. The seasons have been absorbed by the lovers, instead of marking the passage of love through a summertime love into a wintertime waltz as they did in the album, *Waiting For The Sun*. Hand clapping through this lyric amplifies the upbeat tone of the guitar, organ and drums – and unabashed, Morrison rides the calculated excitement of passion. But it has been but a momentary delight as a laughing guitar carries this *easy ride* into a fade out.

SIDE 2
'Wild Child'

'Runnin' Blue'
'Wishful Sinful'
'The Soft Parade'

What had been side one closes with Morrison almost laughing an upbeat "all right", and the next song opens with a very different "all right". The pulsating, deliberate deliverance of Densmore's drumming, Manzarek's organ and Krieger's guitar in Morrison's 'Wild Child' marks a dramatic change from the tightly composed orchestrated opening of the album and the upbeat tone of 'Easy Ride'. The wild child is full of grace that isn't the calculated coolness or costume of control of previous Twentieth Century Foxes. Her cool face reveals a mask balanced with wisdom previous vamps have yet to learn. Free from disguise, she has become, as portrayed on Waiting For The Sun, the "wild love" who has eluded Morrison.

The wild child is free to face her fears and not cower in hesitancy, to experience the journey of living, which The Doors often expressed with a return to primal intuitions and urges. And she does so full of grace. The "wild child", not chained to anything, is free to experience life, dancing on her knees with a "Pirate Prince" by her side. Not necessarily the Prince of Darkness, Morrison draws upon the dualistic image of Prince Charming as a pirate, capable of taking her on a "Spanish Caravan". For many critics, annoyed with the cliche-ridden earlier songs, in this song, Morrison sang his revolutionary rhetoric, finally evoking his usual – and expectant – apocalyptic images.

Morrison's image-laden 'Wild Child' dissipates in Krieger's upbeat, simpler 'Runnin' Blue', with Robby's vocal debut on the chorus. Offering homage to the recently deceased Otis Redding, Morrison sang the opening lyrics of this song in 'When The Music's Over' during a three-day engagement at Winterland in San Francisco in late December 1967 (he sang these lyrics just before the final refrain of 'When The Music's Over'). Redding died in a plane crash on 10 December 1967 and had been scheduled to perform at Winterland with The Doors.

The crisp confidence expressed in the previous songs has evaporated as The Doors sing about stopping, backing down, turning around slowly, and remembering – but life doesn't slow down because of the runnin' blues. Like Otis looking for that dock in the bay, The Doors conjure up a vision of looking for sanctuary, maybe back in LA. But the running in this song, unlike the urgent fleeing in previous songs, seems to be in circles, toward a past that always returns to the present. And this exposes vulnerability, of running scared, of going so fast and wondering what to do. The cost of not retracing your steps to find where you lost yourself is to become permanently vulnerable and battered by life.

The jazzy rhythm of 'Runnin' Blue' dissolves into the meditative allure rendered in 'Wishful, Sinful'. Ironically, the violins swell, musically rendering a popish remorse of longing for a lost love; but the sexual pun on *came* in the closing line of the stanza doesn't elude the crooning Morrison. Yet as he gazes into the sea, he can't escape the *blue* – of the water or the feeling of being separated from his lover. The allusion to drowning is a powerful one, reinforced by the paradoxical image of rising magic while both the sun beneath the sea and the background of soft woodwinds tow gently at us to sink into that sea. The "moonlight drive" Jim had urgently used to woo his lover in *Strange Days* has been reversed.

The 45 single of 'Wishful, Sinful' had the typical antithetical B-side song, 'Who Scared You', which sounded like a studio-blues concoction that badly emulated Blood, Sweat and Tears and was strained through lyrics whose ambiguity and piece-meal nature probably contributed to keeping the song off the album.

As in previous albums, The Doors end with a resolution, the song 'The Soft Parade'. Some critics stated the song was juvenile and contained atrocious poetry typical of a college writing class. Others argued it reflected musical constancy and a sense of humour. In a 1981 interview with *BAM*, producer Rothchild stated that a lot of the song was composed with poetic bits from Jim's notebooks which they thought fit rhythmically and conceptually.[28] And loose connections do piece together to render an artistic vision The Doors were trying to express.

'The Soft Parade' begins with what opened the album, an allusion to a saviour. Morrison oratorically recites a time in seminary school when a person preached we could petition the Lord with prayer and then Jim screams that we can't.

Brash and arrogant in his rebellious stance, Morrison pronounces his

28 Jackson *BAM*, 3rd July 1981 p19.

freedom from schooling he believes has betrayed him and finds he has broken through to the realisation that what he has always been led to believe to be security isn't – and that he is now adrift. Plaintively Morrison laments for *sanctuary* and for *soft asylum*. Just when The Doors render a picture that gets your head and blood pounding with anger against the soft lies of society, they plunge you into the depths of personal vulnerability and fear.

Then the song becomes upbeat as Morrison draws quick sketches of images, snatches of life (reminiscent of scenes from the Venice Beach area of LA), fragments which piece together in a disconcerting tone with the paradoxical backdrop of soft brushing of the drums by Densmore. As the other three Doors musically wind into the heart of the song, Morrison underscores them with a rap about this being the *best part* of the song's trip. The trip Morrison is about to paint isn't from a hallucinogenic drug, but from the drug The Doors believe to be the most deceiving and destructive of all drugs.

In previous albums, The Doors have rendered a picture of a world separated from life's unknown forces that don't fit into the smoothly running machinery of our contemporary life. 'The Soft Parade' reveals a less acrimonious attitude and a reluctant acceptance that everything must be like this.

The tone in the imagery Morrison paints is quite a shift from his scream in 'When The Music's Over' that we want the world *now*. But acceptance of the soft parade doesn't mean that accolades would replace the disquieting tone of The Doors' artistic vision, evident in the subsequent image of listening to the engines of the soft parade hum. Passive resignation to the way everything must be, to the easy ride of successful hills, doesn't change the mechanised reality of modern life; it just makes for a smoother, quieter running engine, a soft parade. But engines can chew you up or run you over. The Doors depict an organic, yet mechanical machine that gives the illusion of humming, for it is really a disjointed conglomeration of disquieting images.

Morrison then slides into imagery of primal Nature, imagery not from the soft parade of successful hills, of suburbia sprawled under the neon grooves, of fields of asphalt that never die. Again, The Doors render an artistic vision of facing the primal past which lies beneath the soft parade. But this return to our primal past begins to end with lights becoming brighter and with the interjection of the pulse of our modern world – the moaning radio. Though the pathways to this primal land-scape are becoming dimmer, there is an acceptance that the soft parade must be this way.

Morrison brings this fragmentary trip through the soft parade to a close as three overlays of lyrics weave a cacophony of confusion. (The recording of this song The Doors made for the NET [National Education Television] special, *Critique*, in 1969 doesn't have the over-lays of vocals and offers a clearer rendition of this coda, though it is not exactly what Morrison vocalised for the studio recording.) The cacophony of confusion is underscored by the repeated lyric, "calling to the dogs". For Morrison, *dog* was a reverse pun of *god*, and this is evident in the closing chanting chorus of "Calling on the dogs...Calling on the gods."

Jim croons to meet him at "the crossroads" on the "edge of town" under the "evening sky". The soft parade, the moaning radio and the brightness of the neon grove yield to the darkness the wild child found so liberating, to the evening sky – a softer image of the bright midnight Morrison had so urgently sought in the debut album or of the sensu-ously sinister moonlight drive of *Strange Days*. But the guns of libera-tion/death in the album's opening song return when Morrison cries to "bring your gun". If we are to wrestle with lions in the night, come pre-pared. And then the spoken ending stirs one last ripple through the imagery of water and soft resignation rendered so prominently through-out the album.

The intensity of the ending manages to be compelling without the anger, escapist without the fear or frustration, urgent without the danger.

The Doors frame the album upon a pattern quite consistent with the previous albums, but a more mellowed tone has heightened the pic-tures they were drawing. Moreover, their artistic vision is revealing that they are coming to terms with their own individual vulnerability and are more at peace with it, now both susceptible and ready for *love*, for tak-ing the risk of trusting someone with his deepest secrets. And the next album, *Morrison Hotel*, expresses the ascension into what the blues often embrace – the fulfilment of love.

"To understand tragic myth we must see it as Dionysiac wisdom made concrete through Apollonian artifice. In that myth the world of appearance is pushed to its limits, where it denies itself and seeks to escape back into the world of primordial reality."

Friedrich Nietzsche, *The Birth Of Tragedy*

chapter 6

THE HARD ROCK CAFE
AND MORRISON HOTEL

"Certain roads one took emotionally also appeared on the map of the
heart as travelling away from the centre and ultimately leading to exile."
Anais Nin, *The Spy In The House Of Love*, p60

The meteoric success of 'Light My Fire' in the heated Summer of Love
had rocketed The Doors out of night club gigging into a swirling
schedule which came to a crashing halt after the raucous Miami Dinner
Key concert. After baring their souls and delivering their message
through the unseen rhythms of the electric heart of rock 'n' roll, The
Doors were yearning – and needing – to return those souls to some
earthy roots.

But 1969 was hardly a reposing period. On 20 July, America answered
the challenge issued by President John F Kennedy: Neil Armstrong and
Buzz Aldrin took the first human steps on the moon. Technology had
made the 'Moonlight Drive'. On 20 November, the federal government
conceded some of the dangers of this moonlight drive with technology:
federal legislation outlawed DDT and initiated a two-year phase-out of the
once hailed miracle chemical designed to eradicate unwanted insect pests.

By the end of the year, otherwise significant events would emerge in
the monetary spotlight from behind the mid-summer shadow of
Armstrong's and Aldrin's walks on the moon. On a farm in upstate New
York in August, removed from mainstream America, the Woodstock
Festival brought to fruition the seeds of flower power which blossomed
over the overt mass drug usage at the gathering before the chill of The
Rolling Stones' free Altamont festival held in California in December
brought a killer frost to those pastoral ideals. The gruesome Tate and

LaBianca murders in Los Angeles in August eventually led to the arrest of Charles Manson and members of his "family". Hoping the courtroom would rectify the unruly display at the Democratic National Convention, the American justice system began the trial of the Chicago eight in September. As the initial test of the criminal offence of intent to incite a riot as defined in the 1968 Civil Rights Act, the trial would become both a farce and insult to America's sense of impartiality. With the conviction of Black Panther leader Bobby Seale for contempt of court, the "eight" were reduced to the Chicago seven.

Meanwhile, a rather quiet scientific event was engineered by a group of young Harvard University Medical School scientists: they isolated from a living organism, for the first time, a gene, the basic building block of life. Landing on the moon and isolating a gene from a living organism, science had broken on through to the other side. Now that we were there, what was next?

In October, the New York Mets, since their first year of existence in 1962 probably the worst team ever in American baseball, won the World Series. But after the St Louis Cardinals traded outfielder Curt Flood, he did the inconceivable – sued America's pastime, Major League Baseball. Flood challenged the traditional view that major league baseball was like a large company with divisions in each major city whose owners could shuffle players as they wished under the "reserve clause"; he contested that by not allowing him to work where he wanted, just like any other worker in America, Major League Baseball was violating federal antitrust laws. Though Flood would lose in court, the sport of baseball, with the subsequent emergence of free agency and very lucrative television contracts, would become the big business of entertainment.

Fears of "runaway inflation" followed by recession shaped governmental economic policy which hoped to deter rising unemployment and higher costs to borrow money. As Congress pondered how to re-tune this New Economics engine, the Banking Committee of the House of Representatives examined the plausible adverse effects on the housing industry caused by the prime lending rate's jump from 7.5% to 8.5%. In some still distant future quietly slumbered the double digit figures of the late 1970s, which would pale these figures of the 1960s.

Repeatedly serious commentators of American society were pointing that never before had so many Americans had it so good economically, but the presence of television unabashedly presented to the impoverished the stark contrast between their day-to-day world and the images of advertising. The resultant frustration was further fuelled by television also displaying to the *have's* how the *have not's* lived. Vietnam wasn't the only source of agitation coming into the American living room every evening.

Troops were actually being withdrawn from South Vietnam – by both sides – as the Nixon administration pursued "peace with honour" at the laggard peace talks in Paris. On 3 September, Ho Chi Minh, the president of North Vietnam, died at age 79. In November, news reports of a civilian massacre by American soldiers at the South Vietnam village of My Lai in March 1968 prompted charges to be eventually brought against Lt William Calley, who was in charge of the unit at that time.

In the film *True Grit*, John Wayne's one-eyed, hard drinking Rooster Cogburn depicted Old West Americana ideals of dogmatically administrating justice with his gun while aiding a feisty, independent young woman's determination to bring her father's murderer to justice. Meanwhile, Paul Newman and Robert Redford delighted millions with their charming, rebellious portrayal of Old West outlaws in *Butch Cassidy And The Sundance Kid*. Portraying a young Texan spirit who rides into New York City with idealistic ambitions of making it, Jon Voight joined Dustin Hoffman to tell the story of two lost youthful souls, Joe Buck and Ratzo Rizzo, who ride out the alienation of America's modern urban landscape by learning how to trust each other and share compassion in *Midnight Cowboy*. Though the public was somewhat misled by the film's title which is a term for "male hustler" and equally surprised by the film's ruthless realism, the movie became a box office hit despite its "X" rating (regarded as a commercial handicap back then) and then received the Oscar for Best Picture. Barbara Streisand made her big screen debut (an Oscar winner) in the lively *Funny Girl* film adaptation of the Broadway musical. But the line between what had been considered mainstream Hollywood films and pornography was blurring with the importation of such films as the Swedish *I Am Curious (Yellow)* and *Fanny Hill* and subsequent forgettable releases by Hollywood film studios themselves.

The pre-eminent doctrinc of the marketplace now focused on youth and sex.

In July, the movie *Easy Rider* opened and ominously, Capt America tells Billy, "We blew it."

In the fall of 1969, public television premiered a children's show called, *Sesame Street*. And thus began the debate over its presenting the rudiments of American education and values in commercial-like formats – snippets and snatches of images that would capture the pre-schooler's attention. On television the edited rhythm is natural to the medium – as it is on the concert stage or in the sports arena; in the classroom or living room of life, the rhythm isn't as fluid.

In June of 1969 The Doors had begun playing concerts again that were...well...concerts. They included gigs in Mexico City (28 June-1 July), two concerts at the Aquarius Theatre in Los Angeles (21 July), and a performance at the Seattle Pop Festival (25-27 July). In September they headlined the Toronto Rock 'n' Roll Revival festival which featured the last-minute addition of the Plastic Ono Band fronted by John Lennon and Yoko Ono with guest guitarist Eric Clapton. A NET TV special focused on The Doors, allowing a slightly pouchy and heavily bearded, cigar-toking Jim Morrison to introduce songs from *The Soft Parade* and poetry from his just privately published *The Lords* and *The New Creatures*. And the 26 July issue of *Rolling Stone* featured the articulate interview that Jerry Hopkins had with Jim Morrison and that ended with a printing of Morrison's poem, *An American Prayer*.

In that interview, Hopkins asked Morrison if he believed rock was dead. Jim replied that what was called *rock and roll* "got decadent" and was revived by the British, became "articulate" and finally "became self-conscious, involuted and kind of incestuous" which marks "the death of any moment" when the energy or belief dissipates.[1]

So a similar judgment could be cast upon The Doors, for they were reflecting, as always, in part, the larger forces of the culture around them. In 1970, with successive releases of the last three Beatles albums, *Abbey Road*, *Hey Jude* and *Let It Be*, the articulate phase to which Jim had referred was about to shift to the even more self-conscious focus of rock as a business from the early 1970s on. The Doors needed a return to some roots, to reaffirm their own beliefs.

The group, especially Morrison, had more than once alluded to a yearning to do gigs again at the Whisky, in the tight, sweaty atmosphere of a club. In the excitement and electricity of the mass hysteria of a con-

---

1 Hopkins *The Rolling Stone Interview: Jim Morrison* p16.

cert, as Morrison told Hopkins, with so many people gathered together, what you do doesn't matter that much.[2] Lizze James indicated from her interviews with Jim during this period that he had "talked excitedly" about doing a TV special on the history of the blues.[3]

Moreover, pressures to showcase Morrison were building. Morrison's film, *HIWAY* (or *HWY*), was the focal point of the *Jim Morrison Film Festival* at the Queen Elizabeth Theatre in Vancouver (27 March 1970); the film festival included the showing of The Doors' self-produced documentary *Feast Of Friends*, which had been shown in several *artsy* movie houses.

In May 1970, *Billboard* magazine reports that MGM Records president Mike Curb had signed Jim Morrison to a pact calling for the recording of individual albums and to develop a script for the film *Adopt*.[4] This report further fuelled the speculation of Jim going solo for recording and movies. An heir to the swashbuckling image of Douglas Fairbanks – which didn't quite fit the pouchy, mellowed, cigar-toking, bearded beat poet on the NET TV special recorded a year ago.

Added to all this, Elektra Records wanted another album, hopefully, as Sugerman and Hopkins pointed out, a live album in time for the Christmas season of 1969, less than six months after the release of *The Soft Parade*.[5] And the depressing aftermath of the Miami fiasco was slowly hardening into the reality of the energy and time needed for judicial defence. But what The Doors had been missing for the preparation of the third and fourth albums wasn't for this fifth album: time to work on sculpturing and rendering portraits from their artistic vision.

According to Sugerman and Hopkins, the band began rehearsing in September of 1969 and started recording tracks in November.[6] Three days after *Morrison Hotel* was released in February 1970, The Doors achieved, as the 4 March issue of *Variety* reported, a first for an American rock group – a fifth straight gold (million dollar selling) album.[7] *Morrison Hotel* quickly climbed *Billboard*'s top LPs chart, stopping behind Simon and Garfunkel's *Bridge Over Troubled Water*, the Beatles' *Abbey Road* and *Hey Jude*, *Led Zeppelin II*, and Crosby Stills Nash And Young's *Deja Vu*. The album stayed only 27 weeks in the charts.

Besides the pronounced presence of *Bridge Over Troubled Water* and

2 Hopkins *The Rolling Stone Interview: Jim Morrison* p15.
3 James *Jim Morrison: Ten Years Gone*, p18.
4 *Curb Inks Morrison In New Now Artist-To-Film Movie*, Billboard 2nd May 1970 p3.
5 Hopkins and Sugerman p269.
6 Hopkins and Sugerman p269.
7 *Archies' 'Jingle, Jingle' Wins 'Em A Gold Disk; Doors Cop 5th Straight*, Variety, 4th March 1970 p43.

the Beatles' last three albums, Chicago was beginning to toot their horns, Creedence Clearwater Revival was delivering a distinct sound, and young Michael Jackson was leading the Jackson 5 into the charts. It was as simple as "ABC". Into these calming waters of "letting it be" and being a "bridge over troubled water," Elektra released the single 'You Make Me Real'. *Billboard* billed the song a "rousing rocker" and "perfect discotheque item that's loaded with sales appeal" that would quickly find a "high spot" on their Hot 100 chart.[8] The song charted at Number 97 on *Billboard*'s top 100 for 11 April, peaking at Number 50 on 7 May before slipping out of the hottest hundred tunes in America two weeks later.

Like the diminished chart performance, the heated anticipation of the reviewers for the second, third and even fourth albums had cooled for the reception of this fifth album. Kind of. Lester Bangs, in his review of the album for *Rolling Stone*, thought it might have been a "fine album" but couldn't judge it apart from the previous ones and concluded that so much of its music came from the "same extremely worn cloth" as the music on the other albums and that The Doors' artistic "well of resources" had become a standing lake that was slowly drying up.[9]

A reviewer in the lesser read underground newspaper from Tallahassee, *Amazing Grace*, drew the same comparison, writing that the album was "the same basic Doors sound…you've been hearing for three years" and stating "had this been their second or third LP, it would have been a smasher."[10] Patricia Kennely, writing for *Jazz And Pop*, stated *Morrison Hotel* would have been a "great second album", but musically was neither inspired nor dazzling, just "competent, very workmanlike rock": the album had "good polyfuckrhythms, but sad to say, some pretty faggy-sounding piano work" and it had a "Fanny Farmer Valentine quality that is not only lacy but craven."[11] In the context of the rest of The Doors' work, the sound may be the same worn cloth, but the music is never exactly the same colour or pattern.

More than one reviewer celebrated the absence of strings and horns, the music now stripped down to what many perceived as the hard, churning driving sound the group excelled at on their own – but this time with guest bassists Ray Neopolitan and Lonnie Mack and John Sebastian (late of The Lovin' Spoonful) on harmonica. *Fusion*, then an

8 *Spotlight Singles: Top 60 Pop Spotlight* (Doors – 'You Make Me Real') *Billboard* 4th April 1970 p60.
9 Bangs *Morrison Hotel, Rolling Stone*, 30th April 1970 p53.
10 *Morrison Hotel, Amazing Grace* (Tallahassee, FL underground newspaper) vol 1 no 5 (1970) p12.
11 Patricia Kennely *Pop Record Reviews: The Doors, Morrison Hotel, Jazz And Pop* May 1970 pp54-55.

underground publication out of Boston, in a January 1971 issue retrospective of 1970, labelled *Morrison Hotel* "Drinking man's album of the year."[12] An earlier review of the album in a May 1970 issue offered a more introspective assessment that the album presented a "continual shifting of Morrisonian blues off of musically dark poetics" portraying the "assertive density, the graveyard, strep-throat vocals and the existential abrasiveness" that was expected from The Doors.[13]

Dave Marsh, though somewhat harsh towards some of the album, wrote in *Creem* that The Doors were "truly the most American rock 'n' roll band" he had ever heard: "like this country, when they're good, they're unbeatable, when they're awful, they're horrifying. And sometimes, they're horrifyingly good."[14] In probably the most comprehensive review of any Doors' album at the time, Chris Reabur (a pseudonym for Bruce Harris) in *Jazz And Pop* levelled his critical review to a more even keeled assessment, writing that at the core of Morrison's song writing was a "basic sense of order" and that it was dubious Jim tolerated "blank visions of empty chaos in his lyrics." Having faith in Morrison's integrity as an artist, Reabur wrote that Jim "does not throw words around in his work but rather tends to be simplistic, direct and painfully concise."[15]

The subtitles of side one and side two of the album underscore Reabur's point. Reabur noted that *Hard Rock Cafe* (side one) denotes a kind of house, that *Morrison Hotel* (side two) is "the hotel of Jim Morrison's mind" and that this *hotel* (the album) is a house with "many visitors, many different views and ways of life."[16] Cruise to the Hard Rock Cafe roadhouse before checking into Morrison Hotel. Hopkins and Sugerman recollected that Ray and his wife found in LA's skid-row district a real Morrison Hotel with rooms for $2.50 a night.[17]

Maybe the boys couldn't return to the Whisky, but they still could rub elbows with good ol' folks, the blue-collared people, the ones rooted to life's realities. More than one critic took a stab at this image portrayed by the front and back cover photos of *Morrison Hotel* and *Hard Rock Cafe* respectively, and by the inner sleeve picture. Kennely, whose

12 *Records 70, Fusion* (Boston underground publication) 22nd January 1971 p24.
13 *Albums* (review of *Morrison Hotel*), *Fusion* (Boston underground publication) 1st May 1970 p20.
14 Dave Marsh *Morrison Hotel – The Doors, Creem* (Detroit) vol 2 no 10 (February 1970) p25.
15 Chris Reabur *Morrison Hotel Revisited, Jazz And Pop,* September 1970 p22. "Chris Reabur" was a pseudonym for Bruce Harris.
16 Chris Reabur *Morrison Hotel Revisited, Jazz And Pop,* September 1970 p23.
17 Hopkins and Sugerman p270. For a detailed account of the photograph session with Henry Deitz at Morrison Hotel and Hard Rock Cafe see Densmore's account in *Riders On The Storm* p244.

THE ULTIMATE DOORS COMPANION

relationship with Morrison, according to Hopkins and Sugerman, had soured, wrote with a sharp edge: "Oh fie. Where are the *Doors*; those musical brats?" before she answered "certainly not on the jacket" nor on the inside foldout photo of the "scummy bar" with The Doors trying to look "equally scummy and not making it by a country mile" and with Morrison looking like "he just missed the urinal."[18] With preliminary pronouncements that The Doors (notably Morrison) were returning to their earlier sound, Kennely echoed how many reacted – that she had "expected more from Dionysus."[19]

Morrison was too intellectual to be simply rock, but too rock to be purely intellectual. Jim's relationship to his listeners seemed similar to kids watching an adult movie: they laugh when the adults laugh, even though they don't understand the humour, and they identify with the raw emotion portrayed, even though they don't understand how or why it is really affecting them. Thus, Jim's popularity started to drop when the kids finally got bored. Some of the grown-up critics and fans gave up too, embarrassed by the overdramatic display of personal emotion by Jim which made them feel like voyeurs. And some just may have resolved The Doors were mainly portraying a personal struggle and emotional evolution that couldn't carry anyone else along.

According to Reabur, the "best way to discover" The Doors is through those who dislike them the most because such attempts to prove what is wrong with The Doors always point out what makes them so great: "The best picture of The Doors' brand of insanity is best drawn by the sane man who hates them."[20] Like maybe Stephen Halpert writing in his article, titled 'Get Back: The Doors Are Closed' in the 20 March 1970 issue of *Fusion*:

> "For years we suffered from [Morrison's] oedipal hang-ups and some of us even ate it up. For years we listened to his poetry, as trite and meaningless as the language could produce… With the release of *Morrison Hotel* we've finally crashed; the past albums and style rejected and what do you think they're trying to tell us, that Morrison's finally gotten into rock and playing us funky roadhouse blues? But Morrison's grovelling – his cracked, whisky voice milking it out, freaking around in stupidity, perpetrating a shallow legend. Morrison was the product of a frantic, confused decade… He

18 Kennely p55.
19 Kennely p55.
20 Reabur p22.

was our most subjective rock performer, substituting musical ability for psychological release. [He] is full of upper class torment and
anger. He is an actor of the grotesque, the Lizard King of the Doors,
very much part of hallucinogens, an ambiguous poet and not much
of a performer. Who needs it?"[21]

Marsh countered that Jim "doesn't bother trying to justify his mental
voyeurism" but "simply writes a song about it" and the other Doors
"back him perfectly".[22] Reabur expanded this view writing that Morrison
was always "more a prophet than a pied piper" and that though Jim
couldn't show us how to live, he could show us "how *not* to live";
"*Morrison Hotel*, for all its flurries of autobiography, is really more
directly an album about America, about you and me only by infer-
ence."[23] Furthermore, Reabur framed his review upon the perception
that the album was built on two central image patterns of roads and
houses and this imagery portrayed "a vision of America in all its savage
splendour and awesome beauty."[24]

> "The great mark of the genius is to reveal to each critic what he is look-
> ing for." Wallace Fowlie, *Rimbaud (A Critical Study)*, p127

The same basic Doors pattern emerges, tempered by the realisations
the blues bring. This is no longer the reckless, freedom pursuing lover
of the first album trying to find an island in his lover's arms and country
in her eyes or seeking a soul kitchen to warm his mind by. Nor is this the
detached lover singing to an unhappy girl locked in a self-made prison
to join him and swim in mystery. Nor the passive lover of Love Street,
content to wait and see what will happen. This is a shamanic bluesman,
more aware and mature of what being human and being sensual means.
Jim removed the personal sanctuary of the beard, and a more relaxed
Doors sound drew a portrait rendered in the tones of the blues.

Musically, it can be called blues, but the entire picture rendered by
the album doesn't demonstrate the birth of full-fledged bluesmen, lyrically or musically. A tentative attitude and approach to the blues tint the
album. In the real world of jazz blues, one of the most important underlying feelings is reverence for age, a respect for experience, knowledge

---

21 Stephen Halpert *Get Back: The Doors Are Closed, Fusion* (Boston underground publication) 20th March
   1970 p38.
22 Marsh p52.
23 Reabur p22.
24 Reabur p22.

and wisdom you can only attain after a whole lifetime of playing and learning – of experiencing life at all stages. The greatest emphasis is on the sharing of knowledge between generations, because people need a structure of knowledge to understand what they feel. We experience emotion from the day we are born and we can play our music and evoke the spectrum of being human, but nobody *understands* life until they have experienced and learned all of its twists and turns. The blues are about the lifelong struggle to come to peace with oneself – a struggle that The Doors experienced, but that never really reached a true fruition. They perform all the technical aspects and are in touch with the underlying emotional currents of life as they render the blues, but they aren't truly bluesmen at this stage of their artistic lives.

In this album, the pop idiomatic production of *The Soft Parade* aside, The Doors seem caught between being their old psychedelic, poetically ambiguous selves or all-out bluesmen. What results is old Doors images being forced into an incongruous musical framework. They are trying to return to some kind of roots, but cannot reconcile this search with their artistic evolution toward mature blues – which they are beginning to truly feel, beginning to break through to. True blues, although tempered by age to the point that their nuances seem almost imperceptibly subtle, still pack a strong emotional punch. It is a punch The Doors as a group would never learn how to deliver, as the swirling whirlwind of the Sixties would rock its own punch on Morrison.

Hard Rock Cafe
SIDE 1
'Roadhouse Blues'
'Waiting For The Sun'
'You Make Me Real'
'Peace Frog'
'Blue Sunday'
'Ship Of Fools'

Hard Rock Cafe opens with a trip to the 'Roadhouse Blues', a song many felt was a blast to The Doors' earlier sound, garnering such critical adjectives as *raunchy, sweaty, dirty, funky*, and so on. The song paints a picture based upon, as Reabur pointed out, the two central images of the album – roads and houses.[25] The Doors render another portrait of the journey motif, only we are not on a crystal ship, nor are we drifting or running down a highway to wherever. We have some control, if we keep our eyes on the road and a hand on the wheel.

According to Sugerman and Hopkins, the opening lines Jim had said to his perpetually on-and-off again girlfriend, Pamela, as she drove to a cottage Jim had bought behind a country bar and club in Topanga Canyon, located just northwest of LA.[26] You better keep your eyes on the road and a hand on the wheel after you leave the free-wheeling interstate highways of LA and drive on the tightly curved Topanga Canyon road winding through the mountains north of Malibu. Like all journeys The Doors take you on, this one offers risk and danger – a risk willingly taken not only to go to some place but also, as Reabur noted, to leave something.

The roadhouse offers a real good time, and the bungalows provide refuge from the soft parade of masks and soft lies. The tightness of the song's rocking blues rhythm is musically a real good time, rolling and bouncing along with Jim's rhythmical lyrics. The minor mode tone of taking the highway to the end of the night has been transformed into a rhythmical blues of going down slow in a bungalow all night long, driven along by the steady, pulsating bottom of the bass guitar.

Paul McCartney would sing "let it be" in an anthem the Beatles would soon release, but for Jim life rolls, as he repeatedly sings in the chorus, "Let it roll". He sings about waking up in the morning and getting a beer because the future is always uncertain and the end is constantly near. But sometimes you have to keep your eyes on the road and hand on the wheel to get to the next roadhouse because each house is only temporary. Death may be the next stop down the road, inevitably some next moment, for as we roll down the road of life, we draw nearer to that end.

The Doors pause and reflect in the next song, 'Waiting For The Sun', a leftover from the third album. We race down to the ocean's edge, but instead of the darker, urgent tones of 'Moonlight Drive' Jim renders an image of dawning light and innocence as the urgent running becomes *standing* on the shore. But the sun is *scattered*: the light of innocence, of freedom, of love, of trust, of security – scattered. Eden hasn't been destroyed, just fragmented and scattered in these strange days. Yet we have to live on and part of that living is waiting, though Morrison sings

25 Reabur p23.
26 Hopkins and Sugerman p271. See also Hopkins *The Lizard King: The Essential Jim Morrison* p129.

this is the *strangest life* he has ever known.

Then, in the ensuing song 'You Make Me Real', Jim portrays a *real* good time. He opens with the first two laments of the standard pop triad: he wants and needs his lover. He sings of being free of the past, of the old securities and insecurities. And this relationship does what waiting on freedom's shore didn't, what being in island of her arms didn't, what hanging around Love Street didn't, what cruising on a crystal ship or down a highway to the bright midnight didn't. This relationship makes Jim free because it makes him real. The haughty, urgent arrogance or passive hesitancy or ambivalent sarcasm in other love songs has become confident self-assuredness. The focus is still on what *I* can get, but there has been a recognition that love, though temporal, isn't trite. Love isn't as plastic as the people who play with it.

But life rolls, and The Doors roll us through a journey in the song 'Peace Frog'. According to Densmore, Krieger had a great rhythm guitar lick, but Morrison didn't have any lyrics to go with it; eventually though, Rothchild had Jim record two poems on top of each other – one poem as a metaphor of Jim's life, the other of Pam, Jim's long-time girlfriend.[27] Alluding to both national and personal confrontations of a violent, if not bloody nature, Morrison yanks away the blanket of peace and security America snuggles under and portrays a scene of blood in the streets and blood rising to follow him. A litany of water and blood imagery flows through the song with a rhythm and tone minus The Doors' usual acrimonious electronic bitterness.

Reabur explained that some of that blood in the streets results from accidents caused by careless travellers "who don't keep their eyes on the road and their hands upon the wheel" and that on the highway of the dawn of America, we find a dead Indian: the birth of our nation (careless travellers from the Old World?) brought blood and, as Reabur wrote, "blood is the rose of her flag which sometimes is striped red, red and red."[28] Though there is some serious pain being inflicted on a personal and national level, we remember – and find sanctuary in – moments of loving, trusting intimacy, in momentary pauses on the road of life with someone who can make or has made us feel real.

Instead of a journey to the other side, to escape, to seek sanctuary, 'Peace Frog' portrays a journey to reflect on personal and national

---

27 Densmore pp244-45. In his book *The Lizard King: The Essential Jim Morrison* Jerry Hopkins wrote that, in one of Morrison's notebooks, Manzarek found 'Abortion Stories', which included the litany of blood sung in 'Peace Frog' p129.
28 Reabur p23.

events, be it the riotous 1968 Democratic Convention in Chicago to Morrison's stage bust at New Haven in December of 1968 to his early childhood memory of an accident Morrison's family came upon involving Indians on the highways of America. Interestingly, and probably legally intelligent, there was no allusion to the Miami fiasco.

The barrelhouse rhythms of this opening set at Hard Rock Cafe comes to a reposing moment in 'Blue Sunday'. The song is simple, content with finding true love on a blue Sunday and having her look at him and tell him he is the only one. The Doors have come a long way since the hectic, intransigent pace characterised by songs on the first album. They are admitting, without necessarily a bitter tone, one's vulnerabilities. Instead of fleeing from moments of sanctuary in a lover's arms, Morrison sings he has found a sincere refuge with his girl. The passionate desire to light her fire has been complemented by the comfort that she waits for him in tender times. Morrison's drifting off in his *la-la-la-ing* at the end recalls the same ending to 'Love Street', but this feels more comfortable, less reluctant to yield to the vulnerabilities of life, to the blues.

Just as 'You Make Me Real' is followed by an apocalyptic portrait of America, so is 'Blue Sunday' – 'Ship Of Fools' depicts the American trip. The image of the *ship of fools* became part of America's consciousness when Katherine Anne Porter's first novel *Ship Of Fools* was published in 1962. Best know for her short stories, Porter (1890-1980) weaves together a rich tapestry of threads that detail and intertwine the fascinating and the mundane of the novel's spectrum of characters in this drifting micro-world of humanity.

The novel, which took her twenty years to write, is about the voyage of a German ship from Mexico to Germany in 1931 just before the rise of Hitler. The movie version of Porter's story was a box office hit in 1965. And after the photographs from the Apollo moon flights came back, especially the earthrise photographs, many readily perceived the image that earth was just an shimmering island, a vibrant spaceship in the vast sea of the universe.

In this song, Morrison opens with the apocalyptic image of humanity dying out. For The Doors, modern life is on the ultimate drug trip to oblivion. We're hooked on a drug called technology. The same magic that put us on the moon generates the smog that will kill us. The technology which can take us to other worlds is destroying our own world, just as the abuse of any drug destroys an individual. The imagery alludes to a drug trip, an unsteady and a dangerous one at that, given the fragility of our only ship, Earth. But The Doors accept that this is our only ship; there won't be any saviour, any Mister Good Trips who will bring us a new ship. So we better climb on board and make the best of going home, a home that, as a ship of fools, is not too enticing.

Morrison's lyrics sweep an undertow of uneasiness beneath the rolling, bouncy rhythm of the music, as he repeats the first stanza fading with the call to climb on board. The lyrics deliver a similar apocalyptic image as 'When The Music's Over', but the musical rendering is far different. Maybe the music isn't over and it isn't time to turn out the lights at the Hard Rock Cafe. The blues means embracing and celebrating life's pains and joys. The Doors close the set at Hard Rock Cafe and check into Morrison Hotel.

Morrison Hotel
SIDE 2
'Land Ho!'
'The Spy'
'Queen Of The Highway'
'Indian Summer'
'Maggie M'Gill'

Just as side one opens rolling down the road to find a real good time, side two of the album opens with 'Land Ho!' and a portrait of a sailor itchy to sail the seas and to walk in foreign lands. The pace of this old man is more mature, attuned more to the rolling, natural rhythms of the simple pleasures this voyager of the world enjoys. Although there is usual imagery of risk and danger, the seas aren't so strange: this old one has sailed them. This old sailor has travelled to other sides; still, he is graceful, returning with *silver* in his smile, rather than *gold* from the mountains of Spain. This isn't quite the same grace the wild child in *The Soft Parade* was full of.

Morrison closes the song with the rollicking acceptance of letting life roll. He sings that if he gets back home and feels all right, then he will love his baby – an expression of passion and sincerity that a similar closing refrain to 'Five-To-One' lacked. There is no need to get *fucked up* first before coming home to make love to his lover. Then the rollicking, rhythmical 'Land Ho!' slows to the deliberate, foreboding tone of 'The Spy'. Jim opens the song almost moaning that he is a spy in the house of love. More mature and accepting of the limitations and more intricate dynamics of love, Jim is willing to be a spy, rather than a conquering Lizard King. Such understanding diminishes the once so cynical tone. Jim knows how to sooth with the word his lover longs to hear, but doesn't indicate how he will use that word. He stealthily moves through the song, and his comfortable knowledge and smug awareness leaves the uncomfortable sensation of what will he do with that knowledge and awareness. Despite Densmore's soft brush drumbeat, how safe is *this* house of love? This bungalow where the lovers go down slow? This room in Morrison Hotel?

The imagery of this lyric may well have been borrowed from Anais Nin's 1954 novel, *A Spy In The House Of Love*. Nin (1903-1977) uses a kaleidoscope of organic and inorganic imagery to portray the main character Sabina's psychological and sensual pursuit to impale her sense of trapped obligation and to feel, if only momentarily, freedom – yet all the while seeking that illusive sanctuary of love. Like the lyrics of The Doors and particularly Morrison, Nin offers the reader more than a lifting of the veil for the voyeur's eyes: the swirling imagery that portrays Sabina's variation of being a "back door man" occasionally mingles with the emotional and psychological comets and shooting stars that grace the internal universe of being human.

Whether or not Morrison actually read this novel, he certainly shared Nin's artistic perspective. From interviews with and articles by Nin (especially a 1973 interview[29]) printed in *A Woman Speaks: The Lectures, Seminars, and Interviews of Anais Nin* (1975), Nin uses language quite kindred to ideas Morrison expressed, notably in his interviews with Lizze James between 1968-70. Both talk about how the individual inherits his or her cultural concept of morality and how guilt is induced by religion, family and whoever has had prestige over an individual; how people willingly trade in freedom and play roles and wear masks; and how each individual needs to rid himself or herself of those things that are not genuine to them.

29 Anais Nin, *A Woman Speaks: The Lectures, Seminars, And Interviews Of Anais Nin* edited by Evelyn J Hinz (Chicago: The Swallow Press Inc 1975) pp255-56. Compare Nin's ideas to Morrison's responses in Lizze James's interviews as used in her article *Jim Morrison: Ten Years Gone, Creem* Special Edition: *The Doors* Summer 1981 pp6-23 and as reprinted in *The Doors: The Illustrated History* – see *Part I: Lizze James Interview With Jim Morrison* pp64-67 and Part II: *Lizze James Interview With Jim Morrison* pp122-24.

The Doors have clearly depicted such social role playing and trading in of freedom with the meticulously arranged second album, *Strange Days* – a follow up to the themes rendered in 'The End' which closed the debut album.

As portrayed in both the works of The Doors and Nin, to confront alien concepts and search for personal ones, invites the start of a journey of adventure. Nin stated that this sense of adventure is "tremendously necessary" for us to transcend the sense of tragedy and loss we experience in life and that once we accept that experience can be painful, that relationships end, and that we will be challenged – that "as long as we have a place that says this is our life and it's going to go on, then we won't have any of this tremendous pessimism or suicidal impulses."[30]

The music of The Doors, quite evident in the lyrics of Morrison, was reflecting such awareness that modern life wasn't just a sequence of apocalyptic experiences whirling toward some decisive, unavoidable finale. Life is a process, and know where the roadhouses are, as life rolls on...

Leaving the sedated, uneasy tone of 'The Spy' The Doors pick up the beat to musically render Jim's portrait of his 'Queen Of The Highway'. Ray said this song was a great song about Jim and Pam – "an American Frontier Indian swirl, a love dance, a mating ritual."[31] The queen of the highway is the wild love but tempered. Just as America brings together a patchwork of vivid images, the ensuing fragments of vivid images are held together by the relationship of the two lovers. Life brings the roaming lovers, the angry tiger and his restless princess, back to innocence, to trust in love and in each other, and to starting the cycle of life again. The final stanza reiterates that life is a cycle, that this innocence, this dancing formless in the midnight whirlpool doesn't last. But it's a moment Jim hopes will last a little while longer, because eventually the moment shifts.

Seasons also shift, and The Doors render a portrait of a season they hadn't before – of autumn in 'Indian Summer'. There had been summertime loves and wintertime waltzes, but the peacefulness of the autumn of love had eluded them. A time to reflect, to harvest the fruits of a summer love, rather than to lament the wintry absence of its warmth or to hop off in pursuit of the next sultry sanctuary of lust. The music slows, the lyrics rendering simple brush strokes of what Jim realis-

30 Nin, *A Woman Speaks*, p220.
31 Fornatale, p50.

es; he loves her the *best* and *better* than all the others. But things, like Indian summer, don't remain calm. And the opening riffs of 'Maggie M'Gill' sweep away the tranquillity.

But the song isn't as settling as its tone might suggest. 'Indian summer' harks back to the scattered Indians on dawn's highway. And Jim sings he loves her better than the rest he had met in the summer, but things, like summer, aren't going to remain this calm. And the opening riffs of 'Maggie M'Gill' sweep away this Indian summer's soft tranquillity.

In 'Roadhouse Blues' we leave town for the hills; in 'Maggie M'Gill' we return from the hills to town, to roadhouses and bungalows in the back. We have gone through the Hard Rock Cafe and arrived at Morrison Hotel. Maggie has to leave the refuge of home and goes down to Tangie Town, and this isn't Love Street. No longer depicting existence with harsh hypocritical tones, The Doors offer a portrait rendered with a more compassionate tone.

The repetition of the word *down* and the raucous music of this song have brought down the previous ethereal high renderings of love. Maggie isn't another lover in the alternating questing for sanctuary The Doors have been portraying; rather, they render a portrait of another soul who also has been singing the blues, lovingly sketched out in the penultimate stanza.

The Doors seem more grounded in the realities of life, more accepting of the roadhouses, the crystal ship of fools, the Blue Sundays and Indian summers, the Maggie M'Gills; they now are able to sit at the Hard Rock Cafe and drink that mug of understanding with Maggie M'Gill. The theme which had begun emerging in the album, *Waiting for the Sun*, and was so resoundingly stated in 'Roadhouse Blues' closes the set in Morrison Hotel as Morrison sings for Maggie to roll on. Let it roll. You don't need crystal ships or stores on Love Street or highways to a bright midnight. Life will take you on journeys and to sanctuaries if you just let it roll.

"Dionysiac art, too, wishes to convince us of the eternal delight of existence, but it...makes us realise that everything that is generated must be prepared to face its painful dissolution. It forces us to gaze into the horror of individual existence, yet without being turned to

stone by the vision: a metaphysical solace momentarily lifts us above
the whirl of shifting phenomena."
Friedrich Nietzsche, *The Birth Of Tragedy*.

chapter 7
LA WOMAN, CITY OF NIGHT

"'Nietzsche killed Jim Morrison,' I had once said rather
melodramatically to some startled friends in Berkeley."
John Densmore, *Riders On The Storm: My Life With Jim Morrison And
The Doors*, p3.

The Sixties were about to close: peace accords to end the Vietnam War
"with honour" were finalised in January 1973, nine months before the
US Senate formed a committee to investigate something known as the
"Watergate Break-In". With the resignation of President Richard Nixon,
the United States was ready to be driven by a Ford, rather than a Lincoln.
The resurgence of the status-quo would wait another decade.

But the painful ending of the Sixties continued as the spring of 1970
brought the murdering of American youth on the college campus of
Kent State (Ohio) and Jackson State (Mississippi). On 4 May, Ohio
National Guard opened fire and killed four people during an anti-war
demonstration at Kent State University who had nothing to do with the
demonstrating. On 15 May, state highway patrolmen opened fire at
Jackson State College and killed two. These killings were followed by
the autumn drug-overdose deaths of rock music idols Jimi Hendrix (18
September) and Janis Joplin (4 October).

As the downspin began of the whirlwind of forces that had swirled
through the Sixties, the country was weary from what seemed to be a
nightmarish onslaught on the American Dream. In January 1970, the
jury convicted five of the Chicago seven on crossing state lines with
intent to promote riots, but acquitted them of conspiring to actually
cause riots. The Weathermen, a radical underground militant group, was
making noises with actual bombs and acts of terrorism, notably explod-

ing a bomb in 1971 in the Senate wing of the Capital Building in Washington DC. Somewhat lethargic to another manned-moon flight, the nation became rivetted with the unscripted drama of the Apollo 13 mission in April 1970 as NASA performed perhaps its greatest feat during its finest hour – rather than conquering a new world, safely returning home the crew on board a crippled ship. While the nation was still recovering from the three-man crew's dramatic and successful return to Earth, President Richard Nixon carefully explained why the US had launched an "incursion" into Cambodia on 29 April, and there followed massive anti-war demonstrations highlighted by the presence of many Vietnam veterans.

The August killing of Judge Harold Haley and three of his four kidnappers during an escape attempt at one of the last monuments by architect Frank Lloyd Wright, the Marin County Civic Centre in California, led to the nationwide manhunt for college-educated, streetwise, ex-UCLA philosophy instructor, Black Panther activist, Angela Davis (a physical manifestation of the long-legged "dusky jewel" in 'Hello, I Love You'). She would be acquitted in 1972 by an all-white jury of charges of murder, kidnap and criminal conspiracy. In September, the Presidential Commission on Campus Unrest concluded that the gap between the youth and the establishment posed a threat to American stability; Vice-President Agnew denounced the commission's findings, and President Nixon did nothing to acknowledge them.

In November, the court-martial of Lt William Calley, for the massacre of Vietnamese civilians at My Lai, began. In December, the Supreme Court ruled constitutional the federal law lowering the voting age to 18 and the Twenty-sixth Amendment to the US Constitution became law when the 38th state, ironically Ohio, finally ratified it on 30 June 1971 – small consolation to the average aged soldier of 19 years old fighting in Vietnam.

In January 1971, Charles Manson and three women accomplices were found guilty of the Sharon Tate and LaBianca murders; and in March, Lt Calley was likewise found guilty of the premeditated murder of 22 people at My Lai while his superiors were exonerated. By May, several weeks of anti-war protesting in Washington DC culminated with mass arrests which reached 12,000.

The clear-cut political labels of "hawk" and "dove" continued both to intensify and blur as America grappled with the growing confusion stirred by the images and issues of Vietnam. This ambiguous public view seemed mirrored in two movies which depicted differing views of war which were box office hits in 1970: in an Oscar-winning role, George C. Scott recreated the enigmatic WW II American hero, General George S Patton Jr in *Patton*, which also won the Oscar for Best Picture; and Robert Altman's *M*A*S*H* used the Korean War to make a satiric, irreverent statement about both the Vietnam conflict and war itself.

Besides the Vietnam War, a faltering American economy of rising inflation and joblessness also confronted President Nixon, who countered with fiscal austerity while promoting federal legislation to clean up the environmental mess America was stewing in. His first act for the new decade, on 1 January 1970, Nixon signed into law the National Environmental Quality Improvement Act. On 22 April, the first "Earth Day" took place as a nationwide teach-in on environmental awareness and responsibility. On 3 June, the Endangered Species Conservation Act became law. And in December, the Environmental Protection Agency (EPA) was established by merging several federal agencies overseeing environmental issues. The political and legislative actions of 1970's "Year of the Environment" would radically alter the *laissez faire* way people had conducted business at the exploitation of America's natural resources. We no longer could just wantonly stab the Earth in the side of the dawn and drag her down with fences; at least the American compartment of this ship of fools would try to clean up the smog before it got us.

It was a time of juggling principles and aspirations. Political and social administrating could no longer just merely tinker with the cursory worn-out seams of the economic fabric that tied society together or just replace standard parts of what had been a durable engine of economic success with which to drive a society. The automobile companies, the standard American industrial barometer, were struggling due to a major strike, slipping sales and the assault by imported smaller cars. Detroit responded with what had been unthinkable for American highways – subcompacts; American Motors introduced the Gremlin, and Ford soon followed with the Pinto. Forces far larger than patching thread-bare social fashions or fine tuning a sputtering economic/political engine were overtaking the languishing status quo.

On the evening of 12 January 1971, the world of American television changed: Norman Lear's *All In The Family* premiered, and Carroll O'Connor's Archie Bunker ushered in a real-life irreverence never before seen on American public prime-time television. While two other prime-time family shows, *The Brady Bunch* and *The Partridge Family*, are forever affixed to that early 1970s aura with their 1950s sitcom demeanour, *All In The Family* portrayed relationships – the bickering, the prejudices, the frailties, the warts, the humour of a squabbling low-income family – that transcend the times. Based on the British television show *Till Death Do Us Part*, the Bunker household was not the Ponderosa of *Bonanza*, and viewers responded favourably to what they saw. The stalwart *Ed Sullivan Show* was gone by the start of the fall season of 1971, and *Bonanza* by the start of the fall of 1972.

Even in the world of rock 'n' roll, things were falling apart. The imminent demise of The Beatles was all but done with the release of solo albums by McCartney, Lennon and Harrison before the summer of 1971. The feuding and dissension among The Beatles, the complacency of successful groups from the Sixties, and The Doors themselves underscored the events of the last couple of years, signalling that the times were a-changing.

The LA and San Francisco sounds were withering back into the social humus of change, as the blossoming of a new sound began unfolding. Social commentary was yielding to the pleasantries of Pop. Rock was becoming calculated showmanship; the Lizard King was yielding to the snake-oil artist of a young Alice Cooper. In June 1971, Bill Graham closed what had been an energetic forum for early rock 'n' roll bands – his Fillmore East (New York City) and Fillmore West (San Francisco). Graham said rock musicians were becoming too greedy and wanted more lucrative venues, like sports arenas.

The rock scene pulsed with the music of the Jackson Five, fronted by a pre-pubescent Michael Jackson; the Osmonds, fronted by a pre-pubescent Donny Osmond; and the Partridge Family, fronted by an adolescent David Cassidy. Then there was John Denver, James Taylor, Carole King, Carly Simon, Cat Stevens, The Carpenters, Three Dog Night, Grand Funk Railroad, Black Sabbath (with a young Ozzy Osbourne), Chicago, Jethro Tull, Santana, and Elton John. Rob Houghton, in a March 1971 review of this last Doors album, made a comment about the

band's sound, yet his off-the-cuff sarcasm was such a prognostic statement of what rock music would do. He wrote that if Pabst Blue Ribbon,
a beer company, were smart, they would contract The Doors for a bunch
of commercials: "They would increase sales by as much as a hundred
percent mostly by me."[1]

There was one last burst of creative expression in this so-called
"Golden Age of Rock" before the recording industry finally formulated a
rock sound and rock 'n' roll became the ever self-conscious business of
rock music. And before 1971 was over, the unassuming but ubiquitous
Smiley face had conquered the market place.

As Morrison's trial for "lewd and lascivious behaviour" in Miami
unfolded, Elektra released two albums after *Morrison Hotel*: a double live
album, *Absolutely Live*, in July 1970 and a compilation of hits, *13*, in
November 1970 for the Christmas sales season. Disillusioned as he was to
be dragged through the very real experience of the American judicial
process, Morrison was no longer the boisterous lion in the night, but he
could still rattle off the quotable snips, like the one Danny Sugerman para-
phrased: "First Janis, now Jimi; you're drinking with number three."[2]
Bearded again, Morrison also was rounded at the edges – physically, mentally and emotionally. Ageing had done to Dionysus what nothing else
had: grounded him to the reality of being human on Earth, a grounding
that would bury him as Jim's heart ceased on 3 July 1971, three months
after the release of the sixth original Doors album, *LA Woman*.

This album had become a long awaited enterprise for The Doors, for
it would fulfil their contract with Elektra, an obligation which had
become increasing burdensome, especially for Morrison, who never
learned to accept such imposed limitations. Jim had become a prisoner
of not only his own devices but also forces he couldn't begin to control.
He had repeatedly expressed his desire to escape the frustration of ful-
filing what was expected of Jim Morrison, lead singer of The Doors, also
evident in a writing from his notebooks where Jim wondered which of
his "cellves" would be remembered.[3] Moreover, all of The Doors open-
ly had expressed the desire to return to where they felt they had originally derived their music – the blues.

But those weren't the blues spun from the souls of slaves adrift in a
strange land with no roots save the humanity of their own people. The
blues with which The Doors rendered their artistic vision came from the

1 Rob Houghton *LA Woman* (record review) *Creem* Special Edition: *The Doors* Summer 1981 p54.
2 *The Doors: A Tribute To Jim Morrison* (Burbank, CA: Warner Home Video Inc 1982).
3 Morrison *Wilderness, Volume I* p209.

souls of struggling artistic spirits adrift in their own culture and land. In the hands of The Doors, that blues evoked a rather chilling impression. Though separate from the trends of pop and rock music, The Doors, since their beginning, had been mirrors, and their lives and music – their artistic vision – had reflected the whirlwind of forces swirling in the 1960s and early 1970s. And they continued to reflect the times in their final album as a foursome.

Bruce Harris, in *University Review*, wrote what was a consensus opinion of The Doors, that the group was "never much involved in the mainstream of rock music" and was "always more of a monument than an influence", "unaffected by trends and fads, they are simply making music."[4] As if to underscore this aloofness, The Doors cut their last album in their own rehearsal studio at 8512 Santa Monica Boulevard, the corner of La Cienega and Santa Monica across the street from Elektra. Ray said they knew the sound quality in that studio: "We had that room down; we would make it sound really good."[5]

But the group didn't perform up to producer Paul Rothchild's expectations which even Ray admitted. In an 1981 interview, Rothchild recollected that there were two good songs, 'Riders On The Storm' and 'LA Woman' but the rest of the album was "dogmeat" with no heart in the music. He stated that he had his "head down on the console for the first time in my career", the group was "very lethargic", and nobody was listening to anybody's ideas. He resolved the only way the group would unify to make this record was "if they lost me as a whipping master."[6]

So The Doors moved a jukebox, pinball machine and sofa into the downstairs of their rehearsal studio. Engineer and now co-producer Bruce Botnick moved a recording console and portable eight-track machines into group manager Bill Siddons' office upstairs and then strung cables down to the first floor through the windows. And Elvis Presley's bassist Jerry Scheff and rhythm guitarist Marc Benno were hired to play. On the decision to use eight-track rather than sixteen-track recording machines, Densmore wrote that this move backward in technology forced the group to record "only genuinely great material...like our first album: raw and simple."[7]

These changes in instrumentation affected the interplay between the usual parts. Though still a Doors sound and style, the roles of the

4 Bruce Harris *LA Woman: The Doors*, University Review, reprinted in *The Doors: The Illustrated History* p173
5 Fornatal p50.
6 Garbarini p57.
7 Densmore p256.

different instruments became more distinct. Whereas Ray and Robby had woven all the lines between themselves before, interchanging melody and bass lines, etc, these lines no longer were so intimately woven together. The bass always played the bass lines, the rhythm guitar always played block chords, Robby played snatches of counter-melodies and melodic accents, and Ray became more or less a lead/rhythm player, filling in with more sophisticated harmonies and occasional melodies. There was a lot of good music that couldn't have been done before because, with more players, individual lines could be technically more involved. The result was that the sound was fuller, but the texture wasn't as deep nor nearly as intimately tied to the hearts of the artists as it was before. The boys and their music were maturing.

The reviews of the album split into the usual established viewpoints. Nick Tosches in *Fusion* offered an insightful perspective encompassing more than just the album:

"With *LA Woman*, The Doors' aesthetic hovers on (over?) the brink of *fin de vie*…no one else could validly commit either the theatricality of 'Love Her Madly' or that of the words/music to the refrain of 'The WASP' without producing some kind of laughable poo-poo. The Doors, on the other hand, create, in these two songs, works of total raunch by the very fact of their exaggerated heavy-handedness. Anybody can be subtle with a profundity but it takes some kind of a medicine man to be pushy with a vacuity."[8]

To say Morrison was consciously being a shaman or, as the modern mind generally synonymises, a medicine man, is to give Jim undue credit; he was more unconscious than conscious of the landscapes he was travelling beyond the profane, the so-called *real world*. That doesn't mean Jim wasn't a shamanic spirit, nor does that diminish the power of Jim's poetic vision. Jim's relationship with the creative spirit allowed him to tap into some very deep impressions that as a whole reflected a significant portrait of our society.

Especially in this last album, the lyrics seem to be more like a free-association outburst of poetic images as they crossed Jim's mind. Though these poetic images don't necessarily shape the same coherent work of art portrayed by the piecing together of the earlier poetic images, they remain emotionally provocative. The dissociated quality creates a subtle,

8 Nick Tosches *The Doors*, *Fusion* (Boston underground publication), 25 June 1971 p49.

but still powerful impact because you are never quite sure what is going to hit you next or how it will affect you. The images are vacuous, but substantial, leaving room to interpret them differently every time you hear them. This is a significant point of maturity when the artist can manipulate the images in a way that doesn't diminish their impact.

One of the starkest images from the album was on the yellow sleeve jacket over the record: a figure of a woman crucified to a utility pole, her head bowed below the dingy sky of LA, bowed below the wires carrying one of the invisible forces which we bow to and which fuels the world of electronic music. Eden, Eve, the source of fertility, our saviour – nailed to a modern tree. This theme, a consistent one in The Doors' artistic vision, emerges in a stark visual image. And Andrew Lloyd Webber and Tim Rice's *Jesus Christ Superstar* had become a rock opera (pumping new life into what had became in the hands of modern religious organisations a rather lifeless spirit) as 1970 yielded to 1971. It was a time for a resurrection, for the Sixties to become the Seventies, for Mr Mojo to get rising.

SIDE 1
'The Changeling'
'Love Her Madly'
'Been Down So Long'
'Cars Hiss By My Window'
'LA Woman'

The album opens with Morrison's personification as a *changeling* and the music renders a rich texture to Jim's short, concise images in 'The Changeling'. According to Hopkins and Sugerman, the lyric for this song was written in 1968, and the images within do reflect the rich artistic rendering so inherent in the first three albums.[9]

The term, *changeling*, derives from two meanings of the root, *change*. From the folklore of Northern European, usually the birth of a handicapped or other exceptionally abnormal child was explained away with the story of a changeling – a fairy substituted for a human baby. The substituted fairy could have been a fairy baby or an elder fairy who was no longer useful to the fairy tribe. This explanation of ex*changed* spirits led to some horrible infanticides or abuse of children in attempts to rid

9 Hopkins and Sugerman, p320.

the body of the unwanted spirit. It also explains the *archaic* meaning of the word – a simpleton, idiot, or imbecile. But *changeling* also refers to one who is apt to change – be it as a traitor of loyalty or as a vagabond to the shifting world of opportunities and demands.

And The Doors song reflects the expediency of being apt to change – of living uptown, downtown and all around; of having money and having none; of flowing with the swarming streets or leaving town on a midnight train. This is a considerable distance from earlier days of stumbling in neon groves as cars crawl by stuffed with eyes. Jim knows how to change which is so necessary to survive. He sings about leaving town on a *midnight train*, another journey to the bright midnight, yet with the same foreboding hue rendered in other Doors songs – a trip into the unknown, a trip on which the fading refrain and accompanying clapping easily carries us.

Typical of how their albums are arranged, The Doors juxtapose this song about a journey with a song about love, as they slide into a song many labelled reminiscent of their earlier, more commercial sound. Robby penned 'Love Her Madly', a funky blues with a bouncy bass line, and it was released as a single in late March 1971, topping out at Number Eleven in mid-May. Characteristic of The Doors, the 45rpm single was backed by the their cover of Willie Dixon's gravelly blues number, '(You Need Meat) Don't Go No Further'.

The urgent flame of Robby's earlier come on to *light my fire* has mellowed to a more resigned funky blues tone with the hint of a businesslike relationship of a sugar daddy who provides for services rendered – treasures for pleasures. But the melodies are upbeat, happy – major key all the way, not the usual minor mode renderings. Yet the contrast between upbeat music and self-deprecating words that seem to be simple bravado gives the song a sense of subtle desperation. The popish, upbeat song bouncing along with cursory lyrics sketches a transparent portrait of love compared to the earthy, blues-rendered portrait of 'Maggie M'Gill' an album earlier and to the gritty urban tone of 'LA Woman' that follows. Jim sings the closing refrain in a light, funky tone and leaves the subtle impression that *madly* can easily become *maddening*, the chill of a cold lover in a darkened room. Or the growing realisation that accepting life as it is and being adaptable doesn't mean you can continue walking out the door from the refuge of love.

Excessive changeability can make life meaningless.

The sing-song tone shifts dramatically with 'Been Down So Long', a stark psychological sketch of life as a prisoner. Richard Farina's book, *Been Down So Long It Looks Like Up To Me*, provided the title and refrain for the song. The book, published in 1966 two days before Farina's death in a motorcycle accident, catalogues events of college student (then campus hippie), Gnossos Pappadopoulis. The book's cataloguing of our culture's banality, as Maybelle Lacey wrote in her review of the book in *Library Journal*, "rolls with its own momentum," but "coarse language and the last possible word in sex and physiological descriptions does exceed all limits of good taste."[10] At that time. Basically a culturally saturated cynic whose actions reflect his lingering adolescent perspective of the world, Gnossos probably provided a kindred spirit with whom Morrison identified.

In this song, the absence of Manzarek's keyboards allows the relentless downbeat of the bass to drag against Krieger's stifling, frustrated pulsating guitar, etching an aggressive backdrop for the anger and apprehension the lyrics evoke. On a one level, this song depicts a gutsy blues portrait of a prisoner lamenting to the warden to open the lock while longing to gain a sense of freedom and control through the implicit sexual come on for his baby to get down on her knee and give her love to him. Morrison can just as easily be lamenting his own self-made warden to free his soul. The erotic politician, the Lizard King, the Dionysus of the Sixties unabashedly reveals a side of being human, of feeling entrapped. Having been forced over the years to be a changeling, Jim naturally has fundamental doubts about the meaning of existence. Setting yourself apart, as Jim (and the group) did, leaves you without anything permanent to hold on to. It becomes a struggle, forcing you to become a changeling, and changes bring about fundamental doubts about the meaning of existence as a human. The struggling shamanic spirit is singing the blues.

The portrait of internal alienation in 'Been Down So Long' shifts to one of external alienation in 'Cars Hiss By My Window'. If the previous songs haven't, the tone of this song interjects us into a steamy, smoke-filled dark nightclub scene. With the absence of keyboards, the brooding guitar and bass melodies with the soft back beats of Densmore's drumming – all having an uncanny similarity to John Lee Hooker's

---

10 Maybelle Lacey (book review of Richard Farina's *Been Down So Long It Looks Like Up To Me*), Library Journal, 1st April 1966, p1924.

'Nightmare' – set the tone for Jim to shift from one prison to another, from the desire for the lover at his command to the emptiness of a cold lover. The lyrics, Hopkins and Sugerman noted, were lifted from one of Jim's Venice Beach notebooks.[11]

The image of a traditional sanctuary, the house, again becomes a strange room, penetrated by the relentless waves of cars hissing by the window, and the alienation between these lovers is a different alienation than the inability to communicate as between the two lovers in 'Strange Days' who were living on surface love. This song, so much simpler in musical tone, laments a far deeper rift between two people. The song begins to touch the fears that can chill a human soul.

Long, drawn out vowels and consonants of stanza one shift to shorter, harder vowels and consonants of the last stanza. The uncertainty is no longer an anxious waiting for the next journey to the new and unknown; there is a chilling reality of expected anticipation from repeated experience, like the waves and cars. The beach puts us on the edge of water and in a world where transition happens, where one form yields to another, where the deep blue dream of 'Love Her Madly' becomes a soft parade of waves and headlights shining on the wall. And this lover isn't walking out the door. The alienation between these lovers is embedded in the relationship, as Morrison croons that he can't hear his baby though he calls and calls.

Though more subtle, the song's images are more powerful than the blatant sarcasm in earlier songs because this relationship has the power to explode and cause more devastation than previous portrayed relationships. As Jim closes the song with a vocalised electric guitar blues solo, the windows within his soul start trembling with the chilling reality that when this music is over, he may well have his lights turned out. Whereas Morrison was mostly aloof from and condescending of the lovers portrayed in previous songs, here he realises others have the power to destroy him – or at least he recognises his personal vulnerability.

Side one of the album closes with a return to town – a funky, blues ode to Los Angeles, 'LA Woman'. A discordant organ crescendo signals the return to town, and then guitar, drums and keyboards take us on what what Terry Rompers called, "a perfect California car song: bright, steady and energetic."[12] But this is more than just another car song. The lover persona Jim sang about in previous albums has been anthropo-

11 Hopkins and Sugerman, p320.
12 Rompers p4.

morphised into the city, allowing The Doors, as Pichaske noted, "to infuse the song with typical sexuality while maintaining an essentially sociological theme."[13] Robert Pielke, in his book *You Say You Want A Revolution*, echoed a similar assessment of the song:

> "The city (which metaphorically represents the state) is personi-fied as a whore whose hair is burning and whose wanderings are confined to freeways, midnight alleys, and topless bars. The imagery is as dominated by the dark as the Beach Boys' is by light; neither give any promise of ending. We are confronted with the unmistakable indications of destruction, disease, disaster, and disillusionment."[14]

And the music in a minor key complements this melancholic lyrical valentine to LA.

As with many aspects of his life, Jim had a love/hate relationship with LA. Sugerman wrote that Morrison lived longer there than anywhere else, loved the city harder than anyone he knew, and said goodbye in a "love letter, a delicious song of longing and lust."[15] Hopkins and Sugerman later wrote in *No One Here Gets Out Alive* that 'LA Woman' was Jim's "despairing salute" a city he now perceived as "diseased and alienated".[16]

Los Angeles, the *city of light* is, for Jim, "a city of night," a phrase he borrowed from a novel by John Rechy. Several of the phrases and images in Rechy's book, *City of Night* (published in 1963) must have stimulated Morrison's own creative imagination, for they surfaced in various lyrics he wrote. What also must have appealed to Morrison was the vivid, descriptive tour, both physical and psychological, of a vagabond world of deviance and homosexuality – a vivid tour from Times Square in New York City to Pershing Park in Los Angeles to the Navy docks of San Diego, to San Francisco to the grandest parade of masks, the Mardi Gras in New Orleans. Like Rechy's unnamed narrator who perpetually seeks solitude from the world of sexual hustling in the cities of night only to return, a behaviour quite natural for people seeking personal worth and security, so Jim continually returns to his city of night, LA Woman.

Instead of expressing the cynicism exemplified in earlier albums or

---

13 Pichaske, p84.
14 Robert G Pielke, *You Say You Want A Revolution: Rock Music In American Culture* (Chicago: Nelson-Hall 1986), p241.
15 Danny Sugerman, *A Shaman's Journey Through The Doors*, Creem, Special Edition: *The Doors*, summer 1981, p39.
16 Hopkins and Sugerman, p320.

the blues in recent songs, Jim accepts his unresolved relationship which is no longer with a lost little girl, but a *woman*, an image of considerably more depth than *girl*. We return to LA for a Sunday afternoon drive, but this isn't a trip down Love Street as Ray's ragtime piano melody cruises us into the blues of twentieth century LA, of twentieth century America, of the Western dream. In the "Soft Parade" The Doors accept that successful hills are part of life's landscape. But in 'LA Woman', the San Gabriel mountains of the Angeles and San Bernardino National Forests which surround Los Angeles, hills of western pine forests which frequently renew themselves via fire – the beautiful hair of the LA Woman, are alive with fire. The hills are changing and yet they aren't. Echoing the opening lines from 'Light My Fire', Morrison sings that if they say he never loved LA, you know they are a liar. Come on, LA, city of light, try to set the night on fire.

The song then creates a lusty urban scene that slithers out from the darkened night club scene into the free flowing imagery of freeway driving. The Doors create a museum-like image of LA penetrated by freeways, a prison of love and blues, of alienation and disease. And when the mood changes from "glad to sadness", the shift is effortless. But Mr Mojo is going to rise, he's going to keep on risin', keep on resurrecting. Hopkins and Sugerman noted in the same tone of jest they believed Jim used when he said "Mr Mojo" was not only part of an anagram for his name, but also the name he would use when contacting LA after he had escaped to Africa.[17]

In his book, *Riders On The Storm*, Densmore recalled how Morrison showed the group how he derived "Mr Mojo Risin" from "Jim Morrison" and John wrote that since *mojo* was a black slang word for sexual prowess, he would "steadily increase the tempo back up to the original speed, a la orgasm."[18] Or was *mojo* inspired by the greasy and diminutive character, Oswald Mojo who married Pamela, a British girl who turned out to be an oil heiress, in Farina's *Been Down So Long It Looks Like Up To Me*?

Like the acceptance in 'Ship of Fools' that this world is our only home, so Jim accepts that LA is his woman. LA Woman is also a changeling, but The Doors, who in previous albums oscillated between breaking through to the other side and seeking refuge in love, have reached an understanding with this city of night that Rechy's narrator

17 Hopkins and Sugerman, p343.
18 Densmore p259.

didn't. LA is Jim's home, but also an extension and reflection of himself, as he has become of her.

> "Every culture that has lost myth has lost, by the same token, its natural, healthy creativity. Only a horizon ringed about with myths can uniform a culture. The forces of imagination and of Apollonian dream are saved only by myth from indiscriminate rambling."
> Friedrich Nietzsche, *The Birth Of Tragedy*

SIDE 2
'L'America'
'Hyacinth House'
'Crawling King Snake'
'The WASP (Texas Radio And The Big Beat)'
'Riders On The Storm'

We leave 'LA Woman', and a marching drum cadence takes us into the museum of 'L'America'. Written and recorded months earlier for Michelango Antonioni's *Zabriskie Point* (a 1970 movie) the song had been rejected by Antonioni. Though the song was spared from being part of what movie critics almost universally panned as a bomb by the Italian film director, The Doors' artistic vision seemed quite similar in focus to Antonioni's. The images and impulses of America that Antonioni clumsily pieced together, The Doors draw into a more fluid impression, their music exposing what the film couldn't. After Densmore had explained how Morrison tried telling Antonioni the apostrophe after the "L" was short for Latin America or anywhere south of the border, John described the recording session with Antonioni, surmising the director didn't understand the "cryptic references to money (beads) and grass (gold – as in Acapulco)" and the song, with its "dark, dissonant chords" of the cold steel resonance of Robby's guitar overshadowing Jim's strong singing, summarised the movie.[19]

The song drew a portrait of the America into which the Sixties had began to dissolve. When Jim sings about trading beads for a pint of gold, there is the implied reference to Acapulco gold – marijuana. But this image transcends more than its slang meaning. The journey of innocence has drifted into the sins of the Western dream. Beads are muse-

19 Densmore, p255.

um pieces of periods of history, but gold – that's an eternal pursuit in the Western dream.

The brash persona of earlier sociological songs has become a rainman, and the conquest of the Lizard King re-entering the town has become a seduction of the townsfolk, or at least the women. The rainman offers the epitome of what many labelled as Morrison therapy: the rainman can change the weather and luck and then teach you how to – as Morrison pauses and rhyme suggests intercourse – find yourself. Fucking equals finding salvation, freeing oneself, breaking through to the other side. Or maybe this is subtle sarcasm, Jim playing the lyric off what people expected from the arrogance of the younger Lizard King. Jim, now older, begins to realise he can't take shelter in his Lizard King persona like he used to because he has matured enough to recognise his vulnerabilities – and the foolishness of being forever the Lizard King and all it implied…although legions of subsequent fans don't. The older Lizard King now comes as a rainman.

Manzarek drapes a curtain of disquieting uneasiness with his organ, sounding like very unfriendly raindrops, made even uneasier by Krieger repeatedly playing a descending four-note guitar line. And the organ interlude between the second and third stanzas echoes the organ melody of 'Strange Days', a reminder that these strange days haven't been washed away. The music is in a mutated minor mode with a lot of funky rhythmical syncopation which creates a weird dissonance. 'L'America' is one of The Doors' most musically innovative pieces.

We then walk into a disquieting sanctuary, 'Hyacinth House'. The song seems another version of the house on 'Love Street'. Neither house offers sanctuary or imprisonment, seemingly just something to pass through with curiosity, the seemingly disjointed images not meant to be interpreted but to evoke gut responses. Jim's images are almost too mundane (or perhaps just neutral with no specific feeling intended) to invoke any sense of despair and tragedy. And the almost moanful tone in which Morrison sings underscores a sense of resignation to the mundane. Jim realises he needs a new friend who doesn't trouble or need him – perhaps a friend like, as he closes the song, *the end*.

However, this isn't the same *end* as in the debut album, for Morrison is acknowledging the blues of being human. Those blues can be expressed in love – or sex, as in The Doors' cover of John Lee Hooker's

'Crawling King Snake'. Jim's gravelly rendition of Hooker's much smoother, even delivery reveals aggression and frustration, feelings that Hooker if he had ever felt in his younger days, had come to terms with. Nonetheless, the musical arrangement of this song isn't as aggressive as in other songs, like Willie Dixon's 'Back Door Man'. The portrait rendered by the music is confident, but not as urgent as in previous portraits. The changeling dons the persona of masculine sexuality, of the Lizard King, if just momentarily before the more mature Morrison acknowledges vulnerabilities he now recognises, like trusting a girl with a wrought-iron soul. It is time to ride the storm, and the electric piano ending to 'Crawling King Snake' preludes the forthcoming 'Riders On The Storm'.

We move from the blues of a man who was born in the Mississippi Delta and couldn't write or read into the 'The WASP (Texas Radio And The Big Beat)' of a Southern-aristocratic, college-educated Morrison. Some of the lyrics were published in a 1968 Doors souvenir book and another version surfaces in the recording of The Doors' Denmark television appearance (17 September 1968). The lyric also formed part of a well-honed reinterpretation on the posthumous album, *An American Prayer*.

As trite as the technique of speaking lyrics over music can be, The Doors deliver a potent impression with the primal drum beat and bass line. The *big beat* is organic yet precise, not the contrite self-conscious pop and rock music of which Morrison had become so critical. The *Western dream* promises precision and predictability, a brilliant dream which some call heavenly, but is shrouded in a shadow as The Doors weave a dense, malevolent texture and take us into a landscape of alluring, yet disquieting images. The allure of azure forests takes Morrison and the listener to a perimeter where there aren't any stars. Out on this edge, we are stoned and immaculate, free from moral blemish, free from fault, undefiled, pure. Primal and free. The wild child. Leaving town to be the changeling. Breaking through to the other side. But there are no stars for guidance, for navigation, for orientation. And the drug imagery of being stoned to get to that forest of azure is no more reassuring than the journey to a strange night of stone in 'Strange Days'.

From living in such an alienated landscape created by the Western dream, Morrison draws forth some of our deepest fears: heartaches, no God, the hopeless night, hungry souls, and a lover with a *wrought-iron soul*. And the shamanic voice of the artistic spirit speaks forth to let it be known that no eternal reward can forgive us for destroying the dawn, for wasting Eden, Earth, our fair sister. The song ends, trailing off with the very cool image of wandering in the *hopeless night* and the image of a maiden who has internalised the iron bars of the prison of her own device.

The last Doors' song on this album was, as Ray said in the radio program, *History Of Rock 'n' Roll*, the last one Jim ever sang, the last one The Doors as a quartet recorded and the last one for the album.[20] 'Riders On The Storm' was released just before Jim's announced death, the song never rising higher than Number 14 on *Billboard*'s Top 100 and lasting only three months on the chart.

Many labelled the song "nightclub cocktail piano music" or any combination of those words, which reflected what a disenchanted Rothchild had told The Doors – their studio playing sounded like "cocktail lounge music" – before he decided not to produce this album.[21]

But the entire album creates, suggests and caters to the darkened atmosphere of a nightclub. The opening waves of thunder draw us in to take a journey, a journey begot by being thrown into this twentieth century world of L'America. Morrison's standard pun of *dog* as backwards *god* slides in as does the notion we are all but acting out a part in this life, souls on loan to this world. But this world can be harsh, evident in the sedate presentation of the deadly reality of killer hitchhikers on freeways of LA, of L'America, on highways to the bright midnight. The imagery is blunt, and the gentle undercurrent of the song's music and lyrics now harbours the threatening edge of death. Everyone is a rider on the storm, a journey that continually risks losing security. This journey is vividly dangerous, and Jim quietly appeals to love. But love has become more than just another brief sanctuary; it gives life meaning.

The image of the killer's brain "squirming like a toad" evokes a far different tone and feeling to the usual parade of snake images; it is an image that doesn't immediately fit into our normal scheme of symbols. Someone can easily rationalise, as many have, that the rhyming of *toad* with *road* is forced and another example of Morrison's mediocre poetry. But even after having rationalised this image, one is still left reacting to it. That is why the image, like so many other images The Doors created in their music, is effective. The image is as blunt and rational as death, and the gentle undercurrent of the song's music and lyrics now

20 *History Of Rock 'n' Roll*, aired 29th April 1978, WOWO Radio, 1190 AM, Fort Wayne, IN.
21 Jackson *BAM*, 3rd July 1981, p20. Densmore, in *Riders On The Storm*, remembered Rothchild calling this song "cocktail jazz" p251.

harbours the threatening edge of death.

The water-like sounding harmonies of Robby's guitar and Ray's electronic piano backed by John's soft, steady, uptempo drum beat render a seductively alluring contrast to the threatening storm, its thunder peeling behind the portrait the lyric's paint. The continuously spiralling bass line echoes the storm's turbulent nature, and Ray's descending electronic piano runs create the cadence of a gentle rain, quite a different feeling of rain than the one created in 'L'America'.

The Doors don't end with a bang, but a rainstorm. Rather than the apocalyptic exit many expected of such raucous erotic politicians seemingly bent on sinister intent, like a gentle rain that falls, The Doors leave as they began: artistic spirits trying to render their artistic vision to share with others. Fading into the storm and its potentially drowning waters seals this closing statement by The Doors with Jim Morrison. Jim fades away into the storm: how could he possibly follow that up?

The Doors artistic vision has settled down from earlier anger and arrogance; thus the music can grow and become deeper, which it does. The emotion is much more subtle, making it more powerful, just as ambiguous images are more powerful than pointedly crafted portraits of raw anger and sarcasm. A piece that portrays strong, pointed feeling evokes immediate reaction, but once that moment of connection is broken, the emotion subsides. With a piece that is more subtle, emotional reaction doesn't occur right away, its impact usually evoking many reactions. Because you can't experience the immediate emotion and purge yourself of it, it lingers and works upon you in ways you may not expect or understand. It is like the difference between the explosive anger that causes you to lash out and the quiet, enduring anger that gradually motivates you to change yourself or the circumstances of your life. To let that kind of emotion work upon you, you have to accept it and try to understand how it is affecting you.

The Doors rendered an artistic vision for the consciousness, painting many scenes which had remained behind the closed doors of the facades of twentieth century foxes, of soft parades, of living in these strange days of L'America. As long as the human world remains a world demanding conformity and grinding away behind plastic images and values imposed upon our existence, the artistic vision rendered by The Doors remains a vivid portrait of the landscape we move across.

chapter 8

LET IT ROLL...

"Without conflict, change is impossible; but without satisfactory resolution,
the changes won't last. It is the overriding task of this current generation
of revolutionaries to resolve the potentially destructive conflicts
bequeathed to them, while encouraging the healthy tensions."
Robert G Pielke, *You Say You Want A Revolution: Rock Music In American
Culture*, p210.

The Doors' artistic orientation was shamanic, not commercial. Change
was inevitable as the six albums evolved. You can't sing revolution all
your life. Hence, The Doors would mature.

Their music isn't validated by isolating the composition and dissecting
it into tangible components. Any music's validity is as rooted in the audience's response as in the performer's artistic endeavours. Analysis of rock
'n' roll doesn't validate its revelations and inspirations. What is *is*. Rock 'n'
roll began as an expression of an emerging revolution of values and consciousness. But *revolution* isn't a solution, nor does it achieve solutions; it
is a process. As a more mature Morrison would realise, evident in his interview with John Tobler at the Isle of Wight Festival in 1970, "you have to be
in a constant state of revolution, or you're dead...[revolution] has to be
every day."[1] For a revolution to avoid becoming the status quo, it must
remain revolutionary. *Victory* promptly kills the revolution. The ultimate
purpose of any worthy revolution is not victory, but the emergence of a
process that enhances a culture's relationship with life. That is shamanic.

When a revolution is under way, there are plenty who want heard what
they have to say. But one easily stuck criticism (and often desired) of rock
is that its lyrics are unintelligible. Transcribe "Tutti Frutti" or try to pin down
any intrinsic meaning to "Louie, Louie." Yet The Doors made it clear that
they wanted people to listen to what their music was saying. An interviewer in the BBC's special, *The Doors Are Open*, asked Ray Manzarek if he
wanted people to like The Doors. Ray replied, "I'd like them to listen; I'd

---

1 Tobler interview with Morrison, Isle of Wight Festival 1970.

like them to give the music a chance and...[pauses]...just to listen."

Who Jim Morrison was as a person, a friend, a buddy, and who Jim Morrison is as a dead rock idol aren't essentially the same, nor can anyone set the correct image of who Jim was, is, or will be. We are witnessing a birth and growth of a legend. Only a germ of truth is needed to nurture the image people choose to believe. The public image of Jim Morrison, lead singer of The Doors and young Dionysus of the Sixties rock scene, fluctuates with the public perceptions and values of the moment. Yet Jim never wavered from the statement he made in the original 1967 Elektra Records biographical sheets: "But the main thing is that we are The Doors."[2]

I close with a translation of words written by Friedrich Nietzsche and published in 1872 in his book, *The Birth Of Tragedy*, a book Morrison said was the one book to read if you wanted to understand his thoughts:[3]

"Though the favourites of the gods die young, they also live eternally in the company of the gods. Of what is noblest on earth we cannot reasonably expect that it have the durable toughness of leather."[4]

After all the reading, listening and writing I have done on The Doors, I will say two things about Jim Morrison: he is quite dead and he is very much alive.

"What the new rebels are doing is jeering at the mass of us for not knowing that beneath the solid middle-class house there is a cellar stacked with dynamite. But with no training as mining engineers or fire-watchers, they go down there with lighted matches and hail the subsequent explosions as art...out of this explosion of 'total honesty, total freedom' may come such a tyrannical reaction, an impulse to censor and police and restrain, that the Rebels – or, let us hope, the sons and daughters of the Rebels – will pull back in time and save their free society by recognising that the first guarantee of liberty is the willingness not to demand too much of it. The fly-wheel of liberty is responsibility."
Alistair Cooke, *Focus On The Arts*, *The 1968 World Book Year Book: A Review Of The Events Of 1967*, p55.

2 Danny Sugerman and Benjamin Edmonds (eds) *The Doors: The Illustrated History* (New York: William Morrow and Company 1983) p9.
3 Mike Jahn *Jim Morrison And The Doors* (an unauthorised book) (New York: Grosset & Dunlap 1969) p73.
4 Friedrich Nietzsche *The Birth Of Tragedy And The Genealogy Of Morals* translated by Francis Golffin (New York: Doubleday Anchor Books 1956) p125.

chapter 9

THE SCENE
notes, stories and tidbits

"The deepest problem before America, then, is moral or psychological.
Since much of the current uneasiness reflects a search less for
solutions than for meaning, remedies depend for their effectiveness
on the philosophy or values which inspire them. The student unrest
is impressive, not because some of it is fomented by agitators,
but because it includes some of the most idealistic elements
of our youth. In fact, much that disquiets us today gives cause
for hope, for it reflects not cynicism but disappointed idealism."
New York Governor Nelson A Rockefeller, *Policy And The People*,
Foreign Affairs, January 1968, p240.

Many stories and interesting anecdotes accompany the recordings done
by The Doors during the late 1960s. These ensuing various notes, stories and other tidbits on the songs recorded by The Doors (with Jim
Morrison) attempt to cite possible sources or inspirations for lyrics,
cross-references lyrics and lines in the songs with other printed poetry
by Jim Morrison, and discusses ambiguities. This information on each of
the six studio albums includes notes, stories and tidbits on the individual songs of that album which include sales chart histories as recorded
by *Billboard* magazine. Framing each album are listings of concurrent
popular albums and singles, top selling books, movies and television
programs to help set the scene for each album.
The following were used as sources for the lyrics.
First and foremost, I relied upon the actual recordings, which I began
trying to transcribe in the 1970s when I was an undergraduate in college
and started researching for printed versions of the lyrics. To clarify fuzzy
passages, I turned to live recordings, especially those on bootlegs. The
printed lyrics on inner sleeves of albums and in the songbooks, *The
Doors/Complete* (1970) and *Morrison Hotel* (1970), provided initial written formats, though these sources proved unreliable for accuracy.[1]

1 In a personal correspondence, Heinz Gerstenmeyer detailed his criticism of The Doors songbooks. He wrote
that Robby Krieger told him that the sheet music was commissioned by Jac Holzman and that The Doors
never read these sheets and that these were what were also delivered to ASCAP for copyright purposes.

Years later, Danny Sugerman edited *The Doors: The Complete Illustrated Lyrics* (Hyperion, hardback edition, 1991; Dell, paperback revised edition, 1992). Though the book provided verification of ambiguous passages and presented an enlightening edition of the lyrics with essays from that time period, it is not a thoroughly accurate transcription of the lyrics as recorded on the six studio albums. But this printed edition controls the copyrights of the lyrics and remains the sole resource (American published) of complete printed lyrics.

In 1993, I met Heinz Gerstenmeyer, a German who began in 1977 trying to transcribe the lyrics as The Doors had recorded them. In 1992, Heinz's book of the English lyrics for the studio albums, *Jim Morrison And The Doors: Die Songtexte Der Studio-LPs*, was published in Germany, although it too has incongruous parts, many of which Heinz indicated were due to the demands by the previous copyrighted edition. Nevertheless, Heinz's transcriptions and personal correspondences provided the most complete and challenging work to which to compare my transcriptions of Doors lyrics.

There probably can be no definite work that reproduces these lyrics with complete accuracy. Jim Morrison mumbled, screamed, slurred, dropped and, as Heinz repeatedly has said, "swallowed" words that cannot be transcribed; moreover, given the spontaneity of Morrison's artistic liberty, a handwritten lyric doesn't necessarily mean he sang it that way.

Listeners should use discretion – and their own imaginations.

ACKNOWLEDGEMENTS

As credited on Elektra recordings, all songs are written by The Doors (lyrics by Jim Morrison or, where noted, Robby Krieger) except:

– the songs on the fourth album, *The Soft Parade* and the fifth album, *Morrison Hotel*, where individual songs were credited;

– *'Alabama Song'*, music by Kurt Weill and lyrics by Bertolt Brecht (Warner/Chappell Music ASCAP);

– *'Back Door Man'*, written by Willie Dixon (Hoochie Coochie Music BMI);

– *'Crawling King Snake'*, written by John Lee Hooker and Bernard Besman (LaCienega Music, BMI).

Sources for poetry of Jim Morrison cited as cross references to the lyrics are as follows:

(1) Jim Morrison, *The Lords And The New Creatures (poems)* (New York: Simon and Schuster, Touchstone Books edition, 1971 paperback edition of 1970 printing);

(2) Jim Morrison, *Wilderness: The Lost Writings Of Jim Morrison, Volume I* (New York: Villard Books, 1988);

(3) Jim Morrison, *The American Night: The Writings of Jim Morrison, Volume II* (New York: Vintage Books, 1990);

(4) Frank Lisciandro, *Jim Morrison: An Hour For Magic* (New York: Delilah Communications Ltd., 1982).

The texts used for printed versions of lyrics are as follows:

(1) Heinz Gerstenmeyer, ed, *Jim Morrison And The Doors: Die Songtexte der Studio-LPs* (English lyrics to studio albums) (Munich, Germany: Schirmer/Mosel, 1992);

(2) Heinz Gerstenmeyer, personal correspondences;

(3) Danny Sugerman, ed, *The Doors: The Complete Illustrated Lyrics* (New York: Hyperion, 1991);

(4) Danny Sugerman, ed, *The Doors: The Complete Lyrics* (New York: Delta Book [Dell Publishing of Bantam Doubleday Dell Publishing Group], November 1992); paperback version with revisions of *The Doors: The Complete Illustrated Lyrics* (Hyperion, 1991);

(5) my own transcription and annotation of lyrics of The Doors' six studio albums.

Unless otherwise noted, any reference to *The Doors: The Complete Lyrics* is valid for the previous edition, *The Doors: The Complete Illustrated Lyrics*.

A comparison of several lyrical transcriptions in Jerry Hopkins and Danny Sugerman's *No One Here Gets Out Alive* (New York: Warner Books, Inc., 1980) to the later transcriptions in Danny Sugerman's edited *The Doors: The Complete Lyric* reveals differences, which exemplify the uncertainty of trying to transcribe these lyrics – which is further indicated with differences in some of the lyrical transcriptions in John Densmore's *Riders On The Storm: My Life With Jim Morrison And The Doors* (New York: Delacorte Press, 1990).

Fred Baggen of The Netherlands is an adamant connoisseur of the bootlegs, and I am indebted to him for the information concerning lyrics that Morrison interjected on live recordings that I have not listened to.

The *Billboard* chart information used in this book is copyright by BPI Communications Inc "Billboard" is a registered trademark of BPI Communications.

POPULAR SONGS
SEPTEMBER 1966-MARCH 1967

'The Beat Goes On'	Sonny And Cher
'Black Is Black'	Los Bravos
'Bus Stop'	The Hollies
'Cherish'	The Association
'Cherry, Cherry'	Neil Diamond
'Devil With A Blue Dress On'/ 'Good Golly Miss Molly'	Mitch Ryder And The Detroit Wheels
'Eleanor Rigby'	The Beatles
'Georgy Girl'	Seekers
'Gimme Some Lovin'	Spencer Davis Group
'Good Vibrations'	Beach Boys
'I Had Too Much To Dream (Last Night)'	Electric Prunes
'I'm A Believer'	The Monkees
'Kind Of A Drag'	Buckinghams
'Last Train To Clarksville'	The Monkees
'Mellow Yellow'	Donovan
'Nashville Cats'	The Lovin' Spoonful
'96 Tears'	? And The Mysterians
'98.6'	Keith
'Poor Side Of Town'	Johnny Rivers
'Reach Out I'll Be There'	Four Tops
'Ruby Tuesday'	The Rolling Stones
'See You In September'	The Happenings
'Snoopy vs The Red Baron'	Royal Guardsmen
'Sugar Town'	Nancy Sinatra
'Summer In The City'	The Lovin' Spoonful
'Sunshine Superman'	Donovan
'(We Ain't Got) Nothin' Yet'	Blue Magoos
'Winchester Cathedral'	New Vaudeville Band
'Wipe Out'	The Surfaris
'Wouldn't It Be Nice'	Beach Boys
'Yellow Submarine'	The Beatles
'You Can't Hurry Love'	The Supremes
'You Keep Me Hangin' On'	The Supremes

POPULAR AND RELEASED ALBUMS
SEPTEMBER 1966-MARCH 1967

Aftermath	The Rolling Stones
And Then...Along Comes The Association	The Association
Best Of The Animals	The Animals
Best Of The Beach Boys – Vol.1	Beach Boys
Best Of Herman Hermits – Vol.2	Herman's Hermits
Blonde On Blonde	Bob Dylan
Dr Zhivago	(soundtrack to movie)
Golden Greats	Garry Lewis And The Playboys
Got Live If You Want It	The Rolling Stones
Jefferson Airplane Takes Off	Jefferson Airplane
Je M'Appele Barbra	Barbra Streisand
The Kinks Greatest Hits	Kinks
Lou Rawls Soulin'	Lou Rawls
The Mamas and The Papas	The Mamas And The Papas
The Monkees	The Monkees
More Of The Monkees	The Monkees
Parsley, Sage, Rosemary And Thyme	Simon And Garfunkel
Pet Sounds	Beach Boys
Revolver	The Beatles
Sergio Mendes And Brasil '66	Sergio Mendes And Brasil '66
Sinatra At The Sands	Frank Sinatra
The Sound Of Music	(soundtrack to movie)
SRO	Herb Albert and The Tijuana Brass
Sunshine Superman	Donovan
Supremes A' Go-Go	The Supremes
The Temptations' Greatest Hits	Temptations
That's Life	Frank Sinatra
What Now My Love?	Herb Albert And The Tijuana Brass
Yesterday...And Today	The Beatles

SOME OF THE BEST-SELLERS AND PUBLISHED BOOKS
1966

FICTION

The Adventurers	Harold Robbins
All In The Family	Edwin O'Connor
Been Down So Long It Looks Like Up To Me	Richard Farina
The Billion Dollar Brain	Len Deighton
The Embezzler	Louis Auchincloss
The Fixer	Bernard Malamud
Giles Goat-Boy	John Barth
The Kremlin Letter	Noel Behn
The President's Plane Is Missing	Robert Serling
S Is For Space	Ray Bradbury
The Secret Of Santa Vittoria	Robert Crichton
The Soft Machine	William Burroughs
Tai-Pan	James Clavell
Tell No Man	Adela Rogers St Johns
The Time Is Noon	*Pearl* Buck
Valley Of The Dolls	Jacqueline Susann

NON-FICTION

Against Interpretation	Susan Sontag
Anyone Can Make A Million	Morton Shulman
Everything But Money	Sam Levenson
Games People Play	Eric Berne MD
Hell's Angels	Hunter S Thompson
Human Sexual Response	William Masters
In Cold Blood	Truman Capote
The Last Battle	Cornelius Ryan
Phyllis Diller's Housekeeping Hints	Phyllis Diller
Rush To Judgment	Mark Lane
A Thousand Days:	
John F Kennedy in the White House	Arthur M Schlesinger Jr

POETRY

Ariel	Sylvia Plath

MOVIES OF 1966

Alfie
An American Dream
Agent 38-24-36
Batman
The Bible
Blow-Up [Italian]
Born Free
Fantastic Voyage
Fahrenheit 451
Fireball 500
A Funny Thing Happened On The Way To The Forum
Gambit
Georgie Girl
The Ghost And Mr Chicken
Grand Prix
Harper
Hawaii
Hotel Paradiso
Lady L
Lt Robin Crusoe US
The Liquidator
Love, The Italian Way
A Man For All Seasons
The Naked Prey
Nevada Smith
Operation Bikini
Our Man Flint
Return Of The Magnificent Seven
The Russians Are Coming!
The Singing Nun
Stop The World – I Want To Get Off
Torn Curtain
The Trouble With Angels
What's Up Tiger Lily?
Who's Afraid Of Virginia Woolf?

● THE DOORS (album)
Elektra Records, EKL-74007 Mono, EKS-74007, Stereo, January 1967.

Side 1: 'Break On Through (To The Other Side)'; 'Soul Kitchen'; 'The Crystal Ship'; 'Twentieth Century Fox'; 'Alabama Song (Whisky Bar)'; 'Light My Fire'

Side 2: 'Back Door Man'; 'I Looked At You'; 'End Of The Night'; 'Take It As It Comes'; 'The End'

Producer: Paul A Rothchild
Production Supervisor: Jac Holzman
Engineer: Bruce Botnick
Additional Musicians: Larry Knechtal, bass

In a 1972 interview by John Tobler with the three surviving Doors, Krieger said that he wrote the lyrics for 'Light My Fire' and the rest of the songs were Morrison's lyrics (*ZigZag*, September 1972, p29).

According to John Densmore in *Riders On The Storm*, The Doors do recording and mixing sessions for *The Doors* in November 1966 at Sunset Sound Recording Studios in Los Angeles. September and October, according to Riordan and Prochnicky's *Break On Through*.

Billboard's Top LPs: debuted at Number 163 on 25 March 1967; peaked at Number Two for two weeks, 16 and 23 September; finally dropped out of the top 100 selling albums on 9 November 1968; was out of the charts after 15 March 1969; and then reappeared on *Billboard*'s Top LPs and Tapes on 20 September 1980 and was out of the charts after 10 January 1981.

◉ BREAK ON THROUGH

'Break On Through' b/w 'End of the Night' was released by Elektra as a 45rpm single (#45611) January 1967. *Billboard*'s Hot 100: single hit

Number 126 on 8 April 1967 and that was it.

In an interview with Jan Morris and published in *The Doors Collectors Magazine* (summer/fall 1995) Jac Holzman explained why Elektra released 'Break On Through' as the first single:

> "In the context of its day and at the time it was the right thing to do because if we were going to learn our way we were not going to learn our way on 'Light My Fire' rather with 'Break On Through' and get the marketplace prepared. It was just too early to start with 'Light My Fire'" (p28).

According to Densmore, Krieger stated that Paul Butterfield's 'Shake Your Money Maker' inspired the guitar melody for 'Break On Through' (*Riders On The Storm* pp86-87). Densmore described the drumbeat he used as a fast bossa nova rhythm from Brazilian music (pp102-3).

In the September 1967 issue of *Hit Parader*, Jim Morrison is quoted as answering the question about how did he write 'Break On Through':

> "I wrote that one morning down in Venice in the canals. I was walking over a bridge. I guess it's one girl, a girl I knew at that time. I think Ray wrote a lot of the music on that one." (p41).

The song, as Manzarek said on the 1991 radio special *In The Studio*, "is about expansion of consciousness; the other side is freedom." Ray, in *Light My Fire: My Life With The Doors*, stated the song was influenced by Stan Getz and Joao Gilberto's bossa nova album, *Getz/Gilberto* (p78).

In *The Lords And The New Creatures (poems)*, Morrison writes about a door to "the other side" where the soul can free itself (p90). In *The American Night*, Morrison writes about going to morning's "other side" (p12). In the piece titled, *The Celebration Of The Lizard* Morrison writes about releasing control and "breaking through" (*The American Night*, p41; and inside sleeve of the album, *Waiting For The Sun*).

Morrison no doubt read John Rechy's 1963 novel, *City Of Night* and borrowed some of Rechy's imagery (see notes to song, 'LA Woman' on the sixth album, *LA Woman*). The Rechy's nameless narrator uses the label "The Other Side" to describe the sexual boundary of the Hollywood world of hustling vagrants and wanderers where the most active members are confident that "unreciprocating vagrants and wanderers" who come to this hustling world will eventually "cross the sexual boundary that separates them now – and they wait almost vengefully for the crossing of that line – to the Other Side – *their* side" (pp200-201).

The recorded chorus, "She gets" omits a final word, *high*, which was censored from the studio version but which was often explicitly resounded in live recordings.

The imagery of the lyric about making the scene from week to week, day to day and hour to hour is practically verbatim from Rechy's novel, *City of Night*. The unnamed narrator of the story describes a scene with Pete, a familiar and streetwise figure in the world of Times Square in New York City, who comments about shacking up with someone permanently to avoid the difficulties of hustling during the bitter cold of winter: "[Pete] added hurriedly, 'I don't dig that scene – I guess I'm too Restless.' He made it, instead, from place to place, week to week, night to night" (p43).

 SOUL KITCHEN

Lyric as written by Jim Morrison is published in *The American Night* (pp101-102).

John Densmore, in his book *Riders On The Storm*, states the song was a tribute to Olivia's, a small soul food restaurant Morrison frequented during his stay on Venice Beach (p40). But Morrison probably intended to suggest the obvious sexual metaphor of warming his head next to her oven: of staying all night in her "soul kitchen" and warming his "mind" next to her "gentle stove".

In the first stanza, do the street lights *share* or *shed* their "hollow glow"? In *The Doors: The Complete Lyrics*, it is *shed* (p26). Densmore, in *Riders On The Storm*, transcribes the lyric with *shed* (p101). Gerstenmeyer, in a personal correspondence, argues that *shed* should be *share*, but had to print *shed* in his book (p13). Part of Gerstenmeyer's argument is based on examining a Morrison handwritten copy of this lyric. In *The American Night*, the verb printed in the line is *share* (p101). Even after listening to live recordings, I still hear *shed* (*shared?*), though either word would fit within the context of the lyrics.

THE CRYSTAL SHIP

'Light My Fire' b/w 'The Crystal Ship' was released by Elektra as a 45rpm single (#45615), April 1967.

In *Riders On The Storm*, Densmore stated that Morrison wrote this song "in the middle of breaking up with an early girlfriend" before the group had their first gig (p96).

In his 1998 book, *Light My Fire: My Life With The Doors*, Manzarek wrote that he created a descending chord structure to harmonise with Morrison's descending melody line and he made it radical for rock 'n' roll using a B flat major seventh chord which he details in the book (p109).

 TWENTIETH CENTURY FOX

Given Morrison's admiration for the French poet Arthur Rimbaud, this lyric is a wonderful contrast to Rimbaud's "Vénus Anadyom`ne" (see Wallace Fowlie's translation in *Rimbaud: Complete Works, Selected Letters*, p41).

Richard Blackburn, a fellow film student with Morrison at UCLA, wrote an elaborate biographic article on those college days which was printed in the May 1976 issue of *Crawdaddy*. He wrote that Ray Manzarek's long-term girl friend (to-be-wife) Dorothy Fugikawa, inspired the lyrics to this song (*Jim Morrison's School Days, Tripping Through The College Jungle* p52).

Manzarek, in *Light My Fire: My Life With The Doors*, quoted the opening seven lines of the song and said that was for Dorothy, his wife (p5).

ALABAMA SONG (WHISKY BAR)
(Music by Kurt Weill [1900-1950], lyrics by Bertolt Brecht [1898-1965], Warner/Chappell Music ASCAP)

Lyrics were written in English and are printed in Bertolt Brecht, *Gesammelte Werke*, a 19-volume work published in German (Frankfurt Am Main, 1967 Band 2, "Aufstieg Und Fall Der Stadt Mahagonny," p504). Brecht did not use "Whisky Bar" as a subtitle for this song. "Mahagonny" is pronounced, *MA-ha-GO-ne-y*.

According to Manzarek in an interview with John Tobler of *ZigZag* magazine, the group was inspired by this song on an album he had of Brecht and Weill songs (*The Doors In A Nutshell; 64 Quick Questions* September 1972, p28). In his 1998 book, *Light My Fire: My Life With The Doors*, Manzarek wrote that his wife Dorothy had a record of the original cast recording from 1932 of Brecht and Weill's *Threepenny Opera* and it inspired the group to use this song (p174). He also wrote that Rothchild brought to the studio a Marxophone, a turn-of-the-century autoharp which could be played flat like a keyboard, and Manzarek used it for an overdub on this song (p208).Densmore, in *Riders On The Storm*, wrote that he thought the song was "a bit odd" when Manzarek first played it to the group from the original cast album for *Mahagonny*, but realised its relevancy as the group began creating their own arrangement of the song (p78).

Jim Morrison sings the first stanza of the song, "Oh, show me the way/To the next whisky bar" which is the way the lyric appears in Brecht's complete works and in WH Auden and Chester Kallman's translation, *The Rise And Fall Of The City Of Mahagonny*. The next stanza, Morrison sings, "Oh, show me the way/To the next little girl"; in Brecht's complete works the lyric is "pretty boy" and in Auden/Kallman's translation it is "Mister Right" (p34). In the songplay "Mahagonny," Brecht used "pretty girl" instead of "pretty boy" in the second stanza; but in the opera, Brecht changed the lyric to "pretty boy" because the song is sung by the whores after they arrive in Mahagonny. A third stanza, which The Doors don't include, begins with the lyrics, "Oh, show us the way to the next little dollar!"

In an interview with Paul Williams which was printed in the August 1967 issue of *Crawdaddy* magazine, producer Paul Rothchild offers a couple of tidbits about the recording of 'Alabama Song' (p25). The missing verse, "Show us the way to the next little dollar," is "out of context for the Doors, that's not quite what they had in mind." And Manzarek plays as an over-dub a Marxaphone, a percussion autoharp used in the 1920s: "it's a series of steel springs that are located at an angle above the strings; you push down on the steel springs and a little metal hammer at the end goes *bouoong*."

The following is based on information from these sources: (1) personal correspondences with Heinz Gerstenmeyer; (2) Bertolt Brecht, *The Rise And Fall Of The City of Mahagonny* (Boston: David R Godine, 1976; translated by WH Auden and Chester Kallman, original trans 1960); and (3) Patty Lee Parmalee, *Brecht's America* (Salt Lake City, Utah: no publisher, 1970; unpublished literary study, two volumes, 493 pages, located in libraries of Indiana University).

Auden and Kallman wrote that *The Rise And Fall Of The City Of Mahagonny* "must offend and repel its audience" to succeed, by portraying how in a Paradise city modern capitalism "destroys human choice" and "panders to the darkest and most cruel aspects of individual and community"; the musical accuses the audience of being "members of that society, with self-cannibalism" (p9). Auden and Kallman interpret Mahagonny's change from a "suckerville" of oppressive dictates of financial rules to a "vast panorama of sensual pleasure which also collapses" as representing for Brecht two faces of our capitalism that required either "a grinding obedience which produces empty 'pleasure' or an equally oppressive freedom based on the ability to pay" or both:

> "Whatever cannot be translated into money...[has] no meaning, no value, no effect in Mahagonny... Neither God nor nature can destroy or reform Mahagonny. Only its own internal contradictions can do that..." (pp17-18).

Brecht wrote five Mahagonny poems in the early 1920s and, according to Auden/Kallman, published these songs in 1926 in *Taschenpostille* ("pocket breviary") and then republished them in a larger edition entitled, *Hauspostille* ("domestic breviary"); *Hauspostille* had some melodies for the lyrics, apparently composed by Brecht himself (p10). In the spring of 1927, Weill approached Brecht to collaborate on a show for the Baden-Baden Festival of Modern Music. The two reworked five songs from *Hauspostille* and added a new finale to create *Das kleine Mahagonny*, an one-act show they called a "Songspiel" a "play upon the term *Singspiel* (that is, *opéra comique* or ballad opera)" (Auden/Kallman, p10). The show premiered, according to Gerstenmeyer, on 27 July 1927, at the Baden-Baden Musicweeks, 'Alabama Song' being introduced by Lotte Lenya. From 1927-29, Weill and Brecht continued reworking the piece into an opera which became *Aufstieg und Fall der Stadt Mahagonny (The Rise And Fall Of The City of Mahagonny*), which premiered, according to Gerstenmeyer, in Leipzig on 9 March 1930, again with Lotte Lenya as Jenny, one of the main characters. In essence, the works were more a continuous work, not an original with later revisions. But the work must have appealed to both Weill and Brecht's desire to incite a reaction from their culture, for both shows caused riots, notably provoking the people in the fledgling Nazi movement. Parmalee noted, after researching the reviews of these premieres, "the bourgeoisie, who expected to see classical opera in its opera house, was certainly convinced that it was seeing communist propaganda" (pp285-86).

Auden/Kallman indicated that the three songs 'Off To Mahagonny', 'Who Lives In Mahagonny' and 'God In Mahagonny' were written before 1922, and that "the two most famous songs, the 'Alabama' and 'Benares' pieces, were written around 1925" (p10). According to Parmalee, Weill and Brecht wrote interchangeably on the text and music for the subsequent shows, and, thus it would be difficult to separate the music as that of Weill and the lyrics as that of Brecht (p288). Kind of like The Doors...

 LIGHT MY FIRE

'Light My Fire' b/w 'The Crystal Ship' was released by Elektra as a 45rpm single (#45615) April 1967. *Billboard*'s Hot 100: debuted at Number 131 on 27 May 1967; peaked at Number One for three weeks, 29 July to 12 August; finally dropped out of the Top 100 selling albums on 9 November 1968; was out of the charts after 23 September; and then reappeared for two weeks a year later, 31 August and 1 September 1968.

In *The Doors: The Complete Lyrics*, the by-line is: "Lyrics by Robby Krieger and Jim Morrison" (p30). Robby Krieger wrote most of this lyric.

In an interview published in *Masters Of Rock: The Life And Times Of Jim Morrison* (Winter 1990), Krieger explained that one day Morrison told the group to go home and write some songs since the group needed more; Robby didn't think he could, but he knew he would have to write a pretty "heavy" song about earth, air, fire, or water to impress Morrison and finally came up with the line about "light my fire" (p21). Densmore, in *Riders On The Storm*, narrates a longer version of the first session the group had with Krieger's idea (pp61-64). Manzarek, in *Light*

My Fire: My Life With The Doors, recreates the dialogue and describes the same scene (p149-51).

The stanza about love becoming a "funeral pyre" – or just the second line about wallowing in the mire – is usually credited to Morrison. Manzarek, in an interview published in *Musician* (August 1981), said that Jim added the verse about love becoming a "funeral pyre" (p48). Densmore described the first rehearsal of the song in his book, *Riders On The Storm* and when Morrison got to the second stanza, Densmore wrote that Jim stopped and asked Krieger, "Where's the rest of it?" Robby responded he got stuck on the second verse; Jim mulled about it while Ray and John kept playing the embryonic rhythm and then sang the line about wallowing in the mire before adding "the rest of the lyrics Robby had written" (p64). In an interview published in the 3 July 1981, issue of *BAM*, Paul Rothchild recalled his least favourite line in the song was the one about wallowing in the mire and he told Jim so without knowing Jim was the one who had contributed that lyric to Krieger's song (p20).

The heart of the song is driven by instrumental solos and were based, according to Densmore and Krieger, on chords similar to John Coltrane's jazz version of 'My Favourite Things'. The rudimentary structure from which Manzarek and Krieger build their interplay between the organ and guitar is quite similar to that between Coltrane's soprano sax and McCoy Tyner's piano on their rendition of Richard Rogers and Oscar Hammerstein II's song. The song became one of America's best known songs from the musical *The Sound Of Music* when Julie Andrews sang it in the 1965 film version. Julie Andrews (the wholesome "Mary Poppins" image stuck to her with no less tenacity than the "young lion/Dionysus" image did to Jim Morrison) sings Rodgers and Hammerstein's innocuous 'Favourite Things'; Jim Morrison sings Robby Krieger's fervent 'Light My Fire'; and the two are fused by John Coltrane's soul-probing sax.

Manzarek, in *Light My Fire: My Life With The Doors*, detailed how the solos were based on John Coltrane's "Ole" from the album *Ole Coltrane* (p78). In *Riders On The Storm*, Densmore explains how in later concerts Krieger began incorporating the melody from The Beatles' 'Eleanor Rigby' into his guitar solo which inspired Densmore to develop both a short exchange of his drumming with Krieger's soloing and cues to signal the end of both Krieger's and Manzarek's solos (pp142, 195).

Michael Hicks writes a more detailed account of this evolution in his unpublished *The Evolution Of 'Light My Fire'*. The essay offers an informative, detailed analysis of how the song evolved, much like the evolution of songs by other American musicians such as Ives and Louis Armstrong who composed by "eclecticism and quotation," using "whatever musics were at hand." Hicks writes the song was "a chain of allusions that kept lengthening until the group, if not the song, collapsed under the weight of its fame." (My copy of this article by Hicks, an associate professor of music at Brigham Young University in Utah, originated from Kerry Humpherys' Doors archives.)

In an interview with Alan Paul that was printed in *Guitar World*, March 1994, when asked about his solo in 'Light My Fire', Krieger responded that this solo was typical, though he played it different every time: "To be honest, the one on the record is not one of my better versions. I only had two tries at it." (p64). For a more detailed musical analysis of Krieger's technique on this solo and other Doors songs, see Keith Wyatt's article, *Inside The Goldmine (Krieger's Guitar Style)*, published in the March 1994 issue of *Guitar World* (p70 onwards).

In his 1998 book, *Light My Fire: My Life With The Doors*, Manzarek describes the recording of this song (pp207-8).

Paul Williams, in his discussion of this album in *Rock Is Rock: A Discussion Of A Doors Song* which was printed in *Crawdaddy* (May 1967), wrote "Is there really any point in saying something like, 'The instrumental in 'Light My Fire' builds at the end into a truly visual orgasm in sound when the reader can at any time put the album onto even the crummiest phonograph and experience that orgasm himself?" (p43). There is a transcription of the lyrics and music in the September 1988 issue of *Guitar* (pp35-44).

In his 1991 film *The Doors*, Oliver Stone includes a confrontational scene over selling Ford the rights to use this song in a television commercial. However, The Doors have never given anyone permission to use any of their songs for commercials. Ray Manzarek offered this reaction:

"Buick asked us whether they could use 'Light My Fire' to advertise the Opel, a lovely little sports car and I thought it was great idea. Jim was away in the desert... We had signed the deal, then Jim had come back from the desert and said, "Holy shit, don't go to bed with the corporations." And since The Doors were four equal partners and everyone had veto power, we dropped it. Oliver Stone in the movie makes the commercial a *fait accom-*

pli and Jim throws the TV at me. The conflict within the band that Oliver Stone was always trying to get across never fucking happened." (p77).

In his 1998 book, *Light My Fire: My Life With The Doors*, Manzarek recalls this episode with more detail (pp305-9).

 BACK DOOR MAN

by Willie Dixon (1915-1992)
(C) 1961, 1989 HOOCHIE COOCHIE MUSIC (BMI)/Administered by BUG. All rights reserved.

Krieger stated that the group wanted to do 'Back Door Man' after he had heard John Hammond Jr do the song (Doe and Tobler, *The Doors In Their Own Words*, p20; quote from 1968). Densmore, in *Riders On The Storm*, wrote Hammond inspired their cover of 'Back Door Man' (p51). John Hammond Jr is the son of John Hammond, who was a prominent figure at Columbia records. Hammond Sr was responsible for the signing of Billie Holiday, Aretha Franklin (before she left to find stardom elsewhere), Pete Seeger and Bruce Springsteen; in 1961, he signed what, at first, was called "Hammond's Folly" – Bob Dylan – and produced Dylan's debut album and, according to the record sleeve, his second album, *The Freewheelin' Bob Dylan*. John Hammond Jr is credited for bringing the Hawks (a group which included Robbie Robertson and which would later become The Band) down from Canada to the States in 1964 before Dylan used them as his band for the first tour of playing his electric music.

In an interview with Alan Paul that was printed in *Guitar World* (March 1994), Krieger was asked how faithful to the original version of 'Back Door Man' the group tried to be, and he replied that they "probably weren't good enough musicians to play exact copies" and they knew Morrison would never sing the song anywhere close to the original (p62). In another interview with Page Milliken which was printed in the March 1973 issue of *Guitar Player* magazine, Krieger is asked about copying ideas or even licks from others, and he replies: "You'll never do their thing better than they can" (reproduced in *Rock Guitarists: From The Pages Of Guitar Player Magazine*; New York: Guitar Player Books, 1975; p99).

Versions of this song as sung by Willie Dixon, by Howlin' Wolf (Chester Burnett, 1910-1976) and by John Hammond Jr (a contemporary of The Doors) all vary. A comparison of The Doors' version of this song to those recorded by Dixon, Wolf and Hammond reveals how Howlin' Wolf's version influenced both Hammond and Morrison in the phrasing of delivery and borrowing the of additional lyrics which Dixon didn't use. Recordings consulted were: Willie Dixon's *I Am The Blues* (album) (Columbi, PC9987), *The Best Of John Hammond* (CD) (Vanguard, VCD011/12, 1987; reissue of 1970 double album), and *Howlin' Wolf: His Greatest Sides, Vol 1* (cassette) (Chess Records [MCA Records], CHC-9107, 1984).

 END OF THE NIGHT

'Break On Through' b/w 'End Of The Night' was released by Elektra as a 45rpm single (#45611) January 1967. The song was one of the six songs recorded by the group (before Robby Krieger joined) on a demo at Aura Records (a subsidiary of World Pacific Studios) in Los Angeles on 2 September 1965.

The lyric about taking "the highway to the end of the night" is an image Hopkins and Sugerman wrote Jim borrowed from the novel, *Journey To The End Of The Night*, written by "the French Nazi apologist and adamantine pessimist, Louis-Ferdinand Celine" (p60). According to producer Paul Rothchild, this line was originally, "take a trip into the end of the night," but Morrison in the studio decided to change it because *trip* had been "violently over used" (Paul Williams' interview in *Crawdaddy*, August 1967, p25).

 TAKE IT AS IT COMES

In *The Doors Quarterly Magazine* (Issue 32, June 1995 p29) appears a reproduction of the sheet music to the song, 'Take It As It Comes'. It is credited to "R (Speed) Krieger." According to the *DQ* article, the sheet music was hand written by Ray Manzarek in 1966 and submitted to ASCAP so The Doors could have copyright control of their songs.

In a personal correspondence, Heinz Gerstenmeyer counters this claim. Gerstenmeyer wrote that what was delivered to ASCAP for copyright purposes was the sheet music commissioned by Jac Holzman to be reprinted in the early Doors songbooks by Music Sales. And Gerstenmeyer wrote that The Doors never saw these transcriptions, according to Krieger. Moreover, all songs are copyrighted, "Words and Music by Jim Morrison, John Densmore, Robby Krieger, Ray Manzarek." Hence, no such scrap of paper could have been registered with ASCAP. Moreover, Gerstenmeyer noted that the melody and chord changes in the scrap are markedly different than the recorded version.

In *No One Here Gets Out Alive*, Hopkins and Sugerman wrote that Morrison didn't want to do meditation like Densmore and Krieger were, but Jim attended one of the lectures to look into the Maharishi's eyes and "see if he was happy"; Morrison decided the Maharishi was and dedicated this song to him (p92).

Manzarek, in *Light My Fire: My Life With The Doors*, stated that his organ solo was inspired by JS Bach (p78).

 THE END

Lyric as written by Jim Morrison is published in *The American Night* (pp111-13).

In a 1969 *Rolling Stone* interview with Jerry Hopkins, to the question what did the song 'The End' mean to him, Morrison replied that he didn't know what he was trying to express and that every time he heard the song, it meant something else. Morrison explained the song began as a "simple goodbye song," but he thought the song's imagery was "sufficiently complex and universal" the song "could be almost anything you want it to be" (26 July 1969 p18).

Densmore, in *Riders On The Storm*, recalls during his narrative of the first session the group had with Krieger's idea for 'Light My Fire' that Morrison introduced one of his new songs – the lyrics that would become the opening of 'The End'; Densmore wrote, "A chill ran up my spine. These weren't lyrics, they were an epitaph" (p62).

In an interview with *Guitar World* (May 1991), Robby Krieger says this about 'The End':

> "It's funny because that started out as just a cute little love song: 'This is the end, my friend, my beautiful friend.' And I got the idea to do an Indian tuning because I was into Ravi Shankar in a big way. From there, it started getting long and more weird. And every time we'd play it, Jim would add more weird stuff" (pp40-41).

Manzarek, in *Light My Fire: My Life With The Doors*, wrote this was originally a good-bye song for an earlier long-time girlfriend of Morrison, Mary Werbelow (p200).

In an interview published in the December 1983 issue of *Audio*, Manzarek stated that album version of 'The End' was a combination of the only two takes the group did of the song. The splice was made in the Oedipal section, at the beginning of the line about the killer awaking before dawn; though there is a sound change between these two cuts, Manzarek said the splice works because at this point of the song the "whole tone of the piece changes" (p44).

In a personal correspondence, Gerstenmeyer expresses similar difficulty with transcribing the passage about the "blue bus" following the Oedipal section and transcribes the passage as (which is different from what was printed in his book on p33):

> "And meet me at the back of the
> Blue bus (d'you know)
> Blue rock, on the
> Blue bus (do ne)
> Blue rock
> Come on, yeah..."

I transcribed the last four lines of this passage as:

> "To the blue rock
> On the blue bus
> To the blue love
> Come on, yeah."

There ensues an instrumental passage under which is barely audible a distant vocal, perhaps Morrison's infamous mantra, "Kill the father, fuck the mother." These passages were not transcribed in *The Doors: The Complete Lyrics*, either the Hyperion hardcover (first edition, 1991) or Delta paperback edition (1992).

In Digby Diehl's article Jim Morrison: Love And The Demonic Psyche in the April 1968 issue of *Eye* magazine, Ray Manzarek offered this interpretation of this lyric about the "blue bus":

> "The ancient Egyptian civilisation, in their tires and religious rituals, had the Solar Boat. When you die, you got in the Solar Boat and went wherever you went. That whole big journey after a kind of death is in the Solar Boat. Well, blue being a Heavenly colour, blue being associated with mysticism and trips...the bus also being associated with trips...it's all of the trips could possibly imagine. The Blue Bus."

There is the story of Morrison returning to the studio after or before the recording of 'The End' and spraying the studio down with a fire extinguisher. Three different accounts of this story are offered in Jerry Hopkins' *The Lizard King: The Essential Jim Morrison* (p71), James Riordan and Jerry Prochnicky's *Break On Through* (p115), and Jerry Hopkins and Danny Sugerman's *No One Here Gets Out Alive* (p100). In *Riders On The Storm*, Densmore mentions this story in his recollection of the recording sessions for 'The End' (pp88-89). And Robby Krieger includes his version in an article he penned for the October 1992 issue of *EQ* magazine (see p52). Manzarek, in *Light My Fire: My Life With The Doors*, offers his version also, except has it happening after the recording of 'Light My Fire' (see pp209-12).

Richard Blackburn, a fellow film student with Morrison at UCLA, in his elaborate biographic article on those college days which was printed in the May 1976 issue of *Crawdaddy*, wrote that Morrison while high on acid "had sat for four hours in front of a soundless television set watching endless violent images and then had written 'The End'" (p55).

What ageing does to one's perspective – two recollections of the recording 'The End' by producer Paul Rothchild in separate interviews 14 years apart.

In an interview with Paul Williams published in *Crawdaddy* (August 1967) Rothchild explained that 'The End' was always changing and Morrison used it as an open canvas for his bits and pieces of poetry and images along with things he just wanted to say. But after the group recorded the song and could hear it on record, the song became the statement they wanted to make and, they then performed it that way, with slight variations (p19).

In an interview with Blair Jackson published in *BAM* (3 July 1981), Rothchild responded to Jackson's comment about Morrison's statement that 'The End' and 'When The Music's Over' were free-form pieces that became static when they were recorded by saying "that's very hip, but not quite accurate." Rothchild said he had seen the group do 'The End' no fewer than 100 times, and the song had a very specific form and wasn't that different when The Doors performed it before and after they had recorded it: "What is on the record is *exactly* the way The Doors wanted you to hear 'The End'" (pp18-19).

In an interview from 1968 between The Doors and Tony Glover, Glover asked, "How much of 'The End' was complete when you went into the studio?" Morrison replied the song had a "basic framework" (a "skeleton"), but the group did it "differently every time." The recorded version, Morrison stated, was "just our version of it at that time." Krieger asserted that the song was "still changing" and that he thought that "it's a lot better now than it was then." Morrison added that when they played the song, they "goof around a lot" and "improvise with the music and the lyrics." (*A Coexistent Conversation With The Doors* [part 3], *Circus*, June 1969, pp56-57.

AMERICAN TELEVISION
1966 FALL PRIME TIME SCHEDULE

	7:30	8:00	8:30	9:00	9:30	10:00	10:30	
SUN		Voyage to Bottom of Sea (7-8)	The FBI	The ABC Sunday Night Movie				**ABC**
	It's About Time	Ed Sullivan	Garry Moore Show			Candid Camera	What's My Line?	**CBS**
	Walt Disney's Wonderful World of Colour		Hey Landlord!	Bonanza		Andy Williams Show		**NBC**
MON	Iron Horse	The Rat Patrol Squad	The Felony	Peyton Place		The Big Valley		**ABC**
		Gilligan's Island	Run, Buddy, Run	The Lucy Show	Andy Griffith Show	Family Affair	Jean Arthur Show/I've Got A Secret	**CBS**
	The Monkees	I Dream of Jeannie	Roger Miller Show	The Road West			Run For Your Life	**NBC**
TUE	Combat!	The Rounders	The Pruitts of Southampton	Love on a Rooftop	The Fugitive			**ABC**
	Daktari	Red Skelton Hour			Petticoat Junction	CBS News Hour		**CBS**
	The Girl From U.N.C.L.E.	Occasional Wife	NBC Tuesday Night At The Movies					**NBC**
WED	Batman	The Monroes	The Man Who Never Was	Peyton Place	ABC Stage '67			**ABC**
		Lost in Space	The Beverly Hillbillies	Green Acres	Gomer Pyle, USMC	Danny Kaye Show		**CBS**
	The Virginian		Bob Hope Show And Specials			I Spy		**NBC**
THU	Batman	F Troop	Tammy Grimes Show	Bewitched	That Girl	Hawk		**ABC**
	Jericho	My Three Sons	The CBS Thursday Night Movie					**CBS**
	Daniel Boone		Star Trek	The Hero		Dean Martin Show		**NBC**
FRI	The Green Hornet		The Time Tunnel		Milton Berle Show		12 O'Clock High	**ABC**
	The Wild, Wild West		Hogan's Heroes		The CBS Friday Night Movies			**CBS**
	Tarzan	The Man From UNCLE.		THE Cat	Laredo			**NBC**
SAT	Shane	Lawrence Welk Show		The Hollywood Palace		ABC Scope		**ABC**
	Jackie Gleason Show		Pistols 'n' Petticoats	Mission: Impossible		Gunsmoke		**CBS**
	Flipper	Please Don't Eat the Daisies	Get Smart	Saturday Night At The Movies				**NBC**

AMERICAN TELEVISION
1966-67 SEASON

SOME OF THE SATURDAY MORNING CARTOONS
Atom Ant
The Beatles
Bugs Bunny Show
Bullwinkle Show (Sunday mornings)
Cool McCool
The Flintstones
The Jetsons
Magilla Gorilla
Mighty Mouse
Road Runner Show
Space Ghost
Tom And Jerry
Underdog

SOME OF THE DAYTIME SOAPS
Another World
As The World Turns
Dark Shadows
Days Of Our Lives
The Doctors
Edge Of Night
General Hospital
Secret Storm

NIGHTLY NEWS
ABC Evening News With Peter Jennings
CBS Evening News With Walter Cronkite
Huntley-Brinkley Report (NBC)

MOVIES OF 1967
Barefoot In The Park
The Battle Of Algiers [Italian]
Bonnie And Clyde

Camelot
Casino Royale
The Comedians
Cool Hand Luke
The Dirty Dozen
Divorce American Style
Doctor Doolittle
El Dorado
Far From The Madding Crowd
Falstaff
A Fistful Of Dollars
For A Few Dollars More
The Graduate
Guess Who's Coming To Dinner
A Guide For The Married Man
The Happening
The Happiest Millionaire
Hotel
How I Won The War
How To Stuff A Wild Bikini
In Cold Blood
In the Heat Of The Night
Jungle Book
King Of Hearts
The Love-Ins
The Man Called Flintstone
St Valentine's Day Massacre
The Taming Of The Shrew
Thoroughly Modern Millie
To Sir, With Love
The Trip
Ulysses
Up The Down Staircase
Valley Of The Dolls
The Way West
The Whisperers
You're A Big Boy Now

SOME OF THE BEST-SELLERS AND PUBLISHED BOOKS
1967

FICTION

All The Little Live Things	Wallace Stegner
The Chosen	Chaim Potok
Death Kit	Susan Sontag
The Eighth Day	Thornton Wilder
The Plot	Irving Wallace
The President's Plane Is Missing	Robert Serling
Rosemary's Baby	Ira Levin
The Ticket That Exploded	William Burroughs
Topaz	Leon Uris
Trout Fishing In America: A Novel	Richard Brautigan
Washington, DC: A Novel	Gore Vidal
When She Was Good	Philip Roth
Where Eagles Dare	Alistar MacLean
Why Are We In Vietnam? A Novel	Norman Mailer

NON-FICTION

The Arrogance Of Power	Senator J William Fulbright
Better Homes And Gardens Favourite Ways With Chicken	
The Bitter Heritage: Vietnam And American Democracy, 1941-1966	Arthur M Schlesinger Jr
Black Skin, White Masks	Fanon Frantz
The Collector's Encyclopedia Of Buttons	Sally C Luscomb
Death Of A President	William Manchester
The Essential Lenny Bruce	(ed) John Cohen
How To Talk Dirty And Influence People	Lenny Bruce
The Medium Is The Massage	Marshall McLuhan and Quentin Fiore
McLuhan: Hot And Cold	(ed) Gerald E Stearns
Misery Is A Blind Date	Johnny Carson
A Modern Priest Looks At His Outdated Church	Father James Kavanaugh
The New Industrial State	John Kenneth Galbraith
Phyllis Diller's Marriage Manual	Phyllis Diller
Soul On Ice	Eldridge Cleaver
Where Do We Go From Here: Chaos Or Community?	Martin Luther King Jr

POETRY

Entering Kansas City High	Allen Ginsberg
Stanyan Street And Other Sorrows	Rod McKuen

POPULAR SONGS
APRIL-SEPTEMBER 1967

'All You Need Is Love'	The Beatles
'Bernadette'	Four Tops
'Brown-Eyed Girl'	Van Morrison
'Can't Take My Eyes Off Of You'	Frankie Valli
'Carrie Ann'	The Hollies
'Cold Sweat'	James Brown And The Famous Flames
'Come On Down To My Boat'	Every Mother's Son
'Creeque Alley'	The Mamas And The Papas
'Dedicated To The One I Love'	The Mamas And The Papas
'Ding Dong The Witch Is Dead'	Fifth Estate
'Don't Sleep In The Subway'	Petula Clark
'Don't You Care'	Buckinghams
'For What It's Worth'	Buffalo Springfield
'Girl, You'll Be A Woman Soon'	Neil Diamond
'Groovin''	The Young Rascals
'The Happening	The Supremes
'Happy Together'	Turtles
'I Dig Rock And Roll Music'	Peter, Paul And Mary
'I Got Rhythm'	Happenings
'I Think We're Alone Now'	Tommy James And The Shondells
'I Was Made To Love Her'	Stevie Wonder
'Let's Live For Today'	Grass Roots
'The Letter'	Box Tops
'Little Bit O' Soul'	Music Explosion
'A Little Bit You, A Little Bit Me'	The Monkees
'Mirage'	Tommy James And The Shondells
'My Cup Runneath Over'	Ed Ames
'Never My Love'	The Association
'Ode To Billie Joe'	Bobbie Gentry
'On A Carousel'	The Hollies

'Penny Lane'	The Beatles
'Pleasant Valley Sunday'	The Monkees
'Reflections'	Diana Ross And The Supremes
'Release Me (And Let Me Love Again)'	Engelbert Humperdinck
'Respect'	Aretha Franklin
'Return Of The Red Baron'	Royal Guardsmen
'San Francisco: "Wear Some Flowers In Your Hair"'	Scott McKenzie
'She'd Rather Be With Me'	Turtles
'Society's Child'	Janis Ian
'Somebody To Love'	Jefferson Airplane
'Somethin' Stupid'	Nancy And Frank Sinatra
'Strawberry Fields Forever'	The Beatles
'Sunday Will Never Be The Same'	Spank And The Gang
'Thank The Lord For The Night Time'	Neil Diamond
'There's A Kind Of Hush'	Herman's Hermits
'Up, Up and Away'	The Fifth Dimension
'Western Union'	Five Americans
'White Rabbit'	Jefferson Airplane
'A Whiter Shade Of Pale'	Procol Harum
'Windy'	The Association

POPULAR AND RELEASED ALBUMS
APRIL-SEPTEMBER 1967

Absolutely Free	Frank Zappa And The Mothers Of Invention
Are You Experienced	Jimi Hendrix Experience
Aretha Arrives	Aretha Franklin
The Best Of The Lovin' Spoonful	The Lovin' Spoonful
The Best Of Sonny And Cher	Sonny And Cher
Between The Buttons	The Rolling Stones
Born Free	Andy Williams
Da Capo	Love
Flowers	The Rolling Stones
Greatest Hits	Bob Dylan
Greatest Hits	The Hollies
Groovin'	The Young Rascals

153

Headquarters	The Monkees
I Never Loved A Man The Way I Love You	Aretha Franklin
Insight Out	The Association
Janis Ian	Janis Ian
The Mamas And The Papas Deliver	The Mamas And The Papas
Mellow Yellow	Donovan
Moby Grape	Moby Grape
Mr Fantasy	Traffic
Paul Revere And The Raiders Greatest Hits	Paul Revere And The Raiders
Reach Out	Four Tops
Release Me	Engelbert Humperdinck
Revenge	Bill Cosby
Rewind	Johnny Rivers
Sounds Like Herb	Albert And The Tijuana Brass
Sgt Pepper's Lonely Hearts Club Band	The Beatles
Surrealistic Pillow	Jefferson Airplane
There's A Kind Of Hush All Over The World	Herman's Hermits
Up, Up and Away	The Fifth Dimension
The Velvet Underground And Nico	The Velvet Underground

 STRANGE DAYS (album)
Elektra Records, EKL-74014 Mono, EKS-74014 Stereo,
October 1967.

Side 1: 'Strange Days'; 'You're Lost Little Girl'; 'Love Me Two Times';
'Unhappy Girl'; 'Horse Latitudes'; 'Moonlight Drive'

Side 2: 'People Are Strange'; 'My Eyes Have Seen You'; 'I Can't See Your
Face in My Mind'; 'When The Music's Over'

Producer: Paul A Rothchild
Production Supervisor: Jac Holzman
Engineer: Bruce Botnick
Additional musicians: Doug Lubahn (of Clear Light), bass; Paul Beaver,
moog synthesiser

In a 1972 interview by John Tobler with the three surviving Doors, Krieger said that he wrote the lyrics for 'You're Lost Little Girl' and 'Love Me Two Times' and the rest of the songs were Morrison's lyrics (*ZigZag*, September 1972 p29).

August-October 1967: The Doors do recording sessions for *Strange Days* at Sunset Sound Recording Studios in Los Angeles.

Billboard's Top LPs: debuted at Number 100 on 4 November 1967; peaked at Number Three for four weeks, 18 November to 9 December; finally dropped out of the top 100 selling albums on 9 November 1968; and was out of the charts after 11 January 1969.

 YOU'RE LOST LITTLE GIRL

In *The Doors: The Complete Lyrics*, the song's by-line is, "Lyrics by Robby Krieger" (p70). In an interview with Robert Matheu that was printed in *Creem Special Edition: The Doors* (Summer 1981), Krieger stated he composed the song, 'You're Lost Little Girl (p59).

In *Riders On The Storm*, Densmore narrated part of the recording session for this song, detailing how Morrison's vocal has "a tranquil mood, like the aftermath of a large explosion" probably due to Rothchild's idea of Jim's girlfriend Pam performing oral sex before Jim sang (p132).

 LOVE ME TWO TIMES

'Love Me Two Times' b/w 'Moonlight Drive' was released by Elektra as a 45rpm single (#45624) November 1967. *Billboard*'s Hot 100: debuted at Number 75 on 9 December 1967; peaked at Number 25 on 13 January; and was out of the charts after 20 January.

In *The Doors: The Complete Lyrics*, the song's by-line is, "Lyrics by Robby Krieger" (p72). In Robert Matheu's interview printed in *Creem Special Edition: The Doors* (Summer 1981), Krieger stated he composed the song, 'Love Me Two Times' (p59). A version of these lyrics is printed in the February 1984 issue of *Star Hits* magazine (p13).

In an interview with *Guitar World* (May 1991), Robby Krieger says this about 'Love Me Two Times':

"The lick is very similar to one that Koerner does on 'Downward Train'. I told him that and he didn't see it, didn't think they sounded alike, but that was what inspired me. In fact, those guys inspired a lot of my licks (p44)."

Throughout the song, Morrison drops the 's' on 'times' to make the lyric sound like he is asking his baby to love him "two time". And this rendering is similar on live recordings. Not until the closing lines of the song does he clearly enunciate 'times' with an 's'. Although it clearly appears to be *times*, the twist with the meaning, *two-time*, is somewhat enticing.

 UNHAPPY GIRL

'People Are Strange' b/w 'Unhappy Girl' was released by Elektra as a 45rpm single (#45621), September 1967.

Sugerman and Hopkins noted that Manzarek played "the entire song backwards" and Densmore created a "soft-suck rhythm sound" by playing "backward high-hat" (*No One Here Gets Out Alive* p128). Densmore, in *Riders On The Storm*, wrote that producer Rothchild had Manzarek overdub his piano chord changes backward as Ray listened to the song backward and then Rothchild played it forward (p128).

In his book, *Light My Fire, My Life With The Doors*, Manzarek describes how he did that (p257). He also describes vividly a the sequences of sensual scenes from Jean Genet's film, *Un Chant d'Amour* (*Song of Love*), depicting male prisoners in their individual cells (pp73-74). The film was being shown in Berkeley, 450 miles north of LA, and both Manzarek and Morrison were at this rare US showing. The scenes, as described by Manzarek, could very well have inspired the imagery Morrison used in this song.

 HORSE LATITUDES

Lyric as written by Jim Morrison is published in *The American Night* (p156).

In the selection 'Self Interview' that opens *Wilderness*, Morrison wrote that he wrote 'Horse Latitudes' when he was in high school (p2).

There is a different poem, entitled Horse Latitudes, published in *Wilderness* (pp94-95).

The Horse Latitudes is the name for the ocean regions located between 30° and 35° latitude in the northern and southern hemispheres. These regions separate the easterly trade winds on the equator sides from the prevailing westerly winds on the polar sides; hence, these parts of the oceans are characterised by calm and very light winds and clear and warm weather. The name supposedly originated from 18th-century sailors whose ships to the New World became becalmed and who threw overboard horses not only to lighten the load but also to conserve water and food supplies that could not be extended.

Sugerman and Hopkins, in *No One Here Gets Out Alive*, detail the recording technique used to create the sound effects for this song. Producer Rothchild and engineer Botnik "created a backdrop of *musique concrète*: varied the speed of tape recording white noise by hand-winding it, electronically altered the recording of already strange sounds of The Doors playing musical instruments in unusual ways and created other strange sounds like a Coke bottle dropped into a metal trash can, coconut shells beating on a tile floor, and friends wailing their lungs raw." (pp127-28). In his book, *Light My Fire, My Life With The Doors*, Manzarek describes the scene of creating this part of the song (p259).

In a book of quotes edited by Andrew Doe and John Tobler, *The Doors In Their Own Words*, Morrison said the song was about Spanish sailing ships becoming stuck in the Doldrums and the men had to lighten the vessels by throwing their major cargo overboard – horses for the New World. Morrison imagined that the horses must have started kicking and bucking when brought to the edge of the boat and that "it must have been hell" to watch as the horses lost strength after swimming for awhile and slowly sunk away (p23 quote attributed to 1968).

In *Jim Morrison And The Doors*, Mike Jahn wrote that song depicts "the Doldrums, where sailing ships from Spain would get stuck" and the sailors, to lighten the vessel, threw some of their cargo overboard, the major cargo being horses for the New World (p60).

The Doldrums is the name of the region of the north part of the south Atlantic Ocean northeast of Brazil of South America and southwest of the Grain Coast of Africa (Guinea, Liberia, Sierra Leone area).

In *No One Here Gets Out Alive*, Jerry Hopkins and Danny Sugerman wrote that, in high school, Jim penned the poem (which became this lyric) after being inspired by a "lurid paperback cover" depicting horses being cast overboard from a Spanish ship becalmed in the Sargasso Sea (p19). In *Light My Fire, My Life With The Doors*, Manzarek stated that he never believed that story because the words were too mature (p258).

The Sargasso Sea is an area of relatively still water in the north Atlantic Ocean northeast of the West Indies and lies chiefly between 25°-35° north latitude and 40°-70° west longitude. The Tropic of Cancer lies just north of 20° latitude. The Sargasso Sea is a region of deep blue waters that are relatively clear and warm due to various currents of the North Atlantic which rotate around the margins of this region, notably the Gulf Stream on the west and south. The area is abundant with brown gulfweed, a seaweed that clusters in huge patches resembling meadows on the water. These peculiarities gave rise to the legends from the tales brought back by New World sailors that the Sargasso Sea was where galleons could become entangled in a snare of thickly matted islands of seaweed which were inhabited by huge monsters of the deep.

 MOONLIGHT DRIVE

'Love Me Two Times' b/w 'Moonlight Drive' was released by Elektra as a 45rpm single (#45624) November 1967.

This was the first song that Morrison sang to Manzarek in the infamous crossing of paths on the sands of Venice Beach in LA in the summer of 1965 after they had graduated from college at UCLA. In his 1998 book, *Light My Fire, My Life With The Doors*, Manzarek describes that scene (pp95-97).

The song was one of the six songs recorded by the group (before Robby Krieger joined) on a demo at Aura Records (a subsidiary of World Pacific Studios) in Los Angeles on 2 September 1965.

Lyric as written by Jim Morrison is published in the book *The American Night* (pp97-98).

In a 1972 interview by John Tobler with the three surviving Doors, Manzarek said this song was the first song they recorded as The Doors, "but it was also the weakest" and they left it off the first album (*ZigZag*,

September 1972 p28). In a subsequent interview with Pete Fornatale of *Musician* magazine, Manzarek further expanded that the song was a "funkier, bluesier kind of song" at first, like a James Brown or Otis Redding song; but while recording the song for the second album, the group "fooled around for awhile" before Ray said, "I got it – we're gonna do a tango...a *rock tango*" (August 1981 p48).

 PEOPLE ARE STRANGE

'People Are Strange' b/w 'Unhappy Girl' was released by Elektra as a 45rpm single (#45621) September 1967. *Billboard*'s Hot 100: debuted at Number 102 on 16 September 1967; peaked at Number 12 on 28 October; and was out of the charts after 18 November.

In advertisements in *The Village Voice*, promoting the upcoming Doors engagement at Steve Paul's Scene East (12 June to 2 July 1967 New York City) appears, "The Incredible Tiny Tim...365 Nights A Year." According to Tiny Tim, Jim Morrison approached him during this time he opened for The Doors and suggested he should do a certain Doors song: 'People Are Strange'. But, as Tiny Tim lamented, a week later the group had a hit single with 'Light My Fire' and nothing ever became of the idea. Actually, Jim probably understood the appropriateness of that idea... (Anthe Rhodes *Sometimes I Feel Like A Lonesome Little Rainbow: Tiny Tim And Some Classic Hollywood Moments* in *Shepherd Express* 29 August-5 September 1991 p10.)

In an interview with Alan Paul that was printed in *Guitar World*, March 1994, Krieger describes how Morrison came up with the lyrics. Jim had shown up at Krieger's house in Laurel Canyon in "one of his suicidal, downer" moods, and Densmore suggested they go to the top of the canyon to watch the sunset which they did. As a dazzling display of sunset colours reflected off the top of the clouds, Krieger said Morrison's mood flip-flopped, and Jim said that he realised he felt so depressed because "if you're strange, people are strange." Jim proceeded to write the lyrics right there, and Krieger explained: "I came up with the music" (p68).

In *Riders On The Storm*, Densmore's version of the story is similar, only he recalled he wasn't there, and it was Robby who suggested they walk up the hill from Robby and John's house on Lookout Mountain

Drive to get a spectacular view of LA from Appian Way (pp124-25).

There is a transcription of the song done by Patrick Mabry in the March 1994 issue of *Guitar World* (pp135-38).

 MY EYES HAVE SEEN YOU

In *Riders On The Storm*, Densmore wrote that the group composed this song in the Manzarek's parents' garage before Krieger joined (p127).

In *Light My Fire, My Life With The Doors*, Manzarek stated that this was the second song Morrison sang to him during their infamous crossing of paths on the sands of Venice Beach in LA in the summer of 1965 after they had graduated from college at UCLA (p98).

The song was one of the six songs recorded by group (before Robby Krieger joined) on a demo at Aura Records (a subsidiary of World Pacific Studios) in Los Angeles on 2 September 1965.

 WHEN THE MUSIC'S OVER

Lyric as written by Jim Morrison is published in The American Night (pp105-107).

In the selection entitled "An American Prayer" is printed the image that music "inflames temperament," which echoes the "dance on fire" image in this song (*The American Night* p5; and p7 of the booklet in the posthumous album *An American Prayer*).

Manzarek, in *Light My Fire: My Life With The Doors*, stated Herbie Hancock's 'Watermelon Man' inspired the opening organ passage (p78).

After the opening dirge of lyrics about turning out the lights and music being your only friend until the end, there follows a very masked line which Gerstenmeyer transcribes as, "Aah – fuck you in the ass, baby!" (p50), which is a bit more discernible on live bootleg recordings.

In Densmore's account of the recording session of 'When The Music's Over', he indicates that the lyric about the "scream of the butterfly" is literally an obscure reference to the title of a skin flick "blazing across the marquee" of a porno theatre near Eighth Avenue and 40th Street in New York (*Riders On The Storm*, pp134-35).

In the Alan Paul interview printed in *Guitar World* (March 1994), Krieger explained the two guitar solos played simultaneously were improvised on the spot and he has never been able to reproduce them again: "That solo was a real challenge because the harmony is static. I had to play 56 bars over the same riff." (p66).

POPULAR SONGS
NOVEMBER 1967-FEBRUARY 1968

'Bend Me, Shape Me'	American Breed
'By The Time I Get To Phoenix'	Glen Campbell
'Chain Of Fools'	Aretha Franklin
'Daydream Believer'	The Monkees
'Different Drum'	Stone Ponys
'Going Out Of My Head'/'Can't Take My Eyes Off Of You'	Lettermen
'Green Tambourine'	Lemon Pipers
'Hello, Goodbye'	The Beatles
'Hey Baby (They're Playing Our Song'	The Buckinghams
'I Can See For Miles'	The Who
'I Heard It Through The Grapevine'	Gladys Knight And The Pips
'I Say A Little Prayer'	Dionne Warwick
'I Second That Emotion'	Smokey Robinson And The Miracles
'I Wonder What She's Doing Tonight'	Tommy Boyce And Bobby Hart
'Incense And Peppermints'	Strawberry Alarm Clock
'It Must Be Him'	Vikki Carr
'Itchycoo Park'	The Small Faces
'Judy In Disguise (With Glasses)'	John Fred And The Playboy Band
'Kentucky Woman'	Neil Diamond
'The Last Waltz'	Engelbert Humperdinck
'Little Ole Man (Uptight – Everything's Alright)'	Bill Cosby
'The Look Of Love'	Dusty Springfield
'Love Is Blue'	Paul Mauriat And His Orchestra
'A Natural Woman'	Aretha Franklin
'An Open Letter To My Teenage Son'	Victor Lundberg
'Please Love Me Forever'	Bobby Vinton
'The Rain, The Park And Other Things'	Cowsills

'Soul Man'   Sam And Dave
'Spooky'   Classics IV
'Summer Rain'   Johnny Rivers
'To Sir, With Love'   Lulu
'Woman, Woman'   Gary Puckett And The Union Gap
'Your Precious Love'   Marvin Gaye And Tammi Terrell

POPULAR AND RELEASED ALBUMS
NOVEMBER 1967-FEBRUARY 1968

After Bathing At Baxters	Jefferson Airplane
Bee Gees First	Bee Gees
Camelot	(soundtrack to movie)
Days Of Future Passed	Moody Blues
Diana Ross And The Supremes Greatest Hits	Diana Ross And The Supremes
Disraeli Gears	Cream
Farewell To The First Golden Era	The Mamas And The Papas
Forever Changes	Love
Four Tops Greatest Hits	Four Tops
Golden Hits	Turtles
Greatest Hits	The Byrds
History Of Otis Redding	Otis Redding
Incense And Peppermints	Strawberry Alarm Clock
It Must Be Him	Vikki Carr
The Last Waltz	Engelbert Humperdinck
Love, Andy	Andy Williams
Lumpy Gravy	Frank Zappa
Magical Mystery Tour	The Beatles
Ninth	Herb Albert And The Tijuana Brass
Ode To Billie Joe	Bobbie Gentry
Paul Mauriat And His Orchestra	Paul Mauriat And His Orchestra
Pisces, Aquarius, Capricorn And Jones Ltd	The Monkees
Simply Streisand	Barbra Streisand
Their Satanic Majesties Request	The Rolling Stones
Vanilla Fudge	Vanilla Fudge
White Light/White Heat	The Velvet Underground

AMERICAN TELEVISION
1967 FALL PRIME TIME SCHEDULE

Day	7:30	8:00	8:30	9:00	9:30	10:00	10:30	
SUN	Voyage To The Bottom... (7-8)	The FBI	The ABC Sunday Night Movie And Specials					ABC
	Gentle Ben		Ed Sullivan Show	Smothers Brothers Comedy Hour		Mission: Impossible		CBS
	Walt Disney's Wonderful World Of Colour		Mothers-in-Law	Bonanza	The High Chaparral			NBC
MON	Cowboy In Africa	The Rat Patrol	The Felony Squad	Peyton Place	The Big Valley			ABC
		Gunsmoke	The Lucy Show	Andy Griffith Show	Family Affair	Carol Burnett Show		CBS
	The Monkees		The Man From UNCLE		Danny Thomas Hour		I Spy	NBC
TUE	Garrison's Gorillas		The Invaders	NYPD	The Hollywood Palace			ABC
	Daktari	Red Skelton Hour		Good Morning World	CBS News Hour			CBS
	I Dream Of Jeannie		Jerry Lewis Show			NBC Tuesday Night At The Movies		NBC
WED	Custer Years		Second Hundred			The ABC Wednesday Night Movie And Specials		ABC
	Lost in Space		The Beverly Hillbillies	Green Acres	He And She	Dundee And The Culhane		CBS
	The Virginian			The Kraft Music Hall		Run For Your Life		NBC
THU	Batman	The Flying Nun	Bewitched	That Girl	Peyton Place	Good Company Local		ABC
	Cimarron Strip			The CBS Thursday Night Movies				CBS
	Daniel Boone		Ironside	Dragnet 1968	Dean Martin Show			NBC
FRI	Off To See The Wizard		Hondo	The Guns Of Will Sonnett	Judd, For the Defence			ABC
	The Wild, Wild West		Gomer Pyle, USMC	The CBS Friday Night Movies				CBS
	Tarzan	Star Trek	Accidental Family	NBC News Specials/ Bell Telephone Hour				NBC
SAT	The Dating Game		The Newlywed Game	Lawrence Welk Show		Iron Horse	ABC Scope	ABC
	Jackie Gleason Show		My Three Sons	Hogan's Heroes	Petticoat Junction	Mannix		CBS
	Maya	Get Smart	Saturday Night At The Movies					NBC

AMERICAN TELEVISION
1967-68 SEASON

SOME OF THE SATURDAY MORNING CARTOONS
Atom Ant
The New Beatles
Bugs Bunny Show (Sunday mornings)
Bullwinkle Show (Sunday mornings)
Cool McCool
The Flintstones
George Of The Jungle
Johnny Quest
Shazzan!
Space Ghost
Spiderman
Tom And Jerry (Sunday mornings)
Underdog (Sunday mornings)

SOME OF THE DAYTIME SOAPS
Another World
As The World Turns
Dark Shadows
Days Of Our Lives
The Doctors
Edge Of Night
General Hospital
One Life To Live
Secret Storm

NIGHTLY NEWS
ABC Evening News with Peter Jennings
CBS Evening News with Walter Cronkite
Huntley-Brinkley Report (NBC)

MOVIES OF 1968

Barbarella
The Boston Strangler
Bullitt
Charly
Chitty Chitty Bang Bang
Cogan's Bluff
Funny Girl
The Good, The Bad And The Ugly
The Green Berets
Hang 'Em High
Head
The Heart Is A Lonely Hunter
The Horse In The Gray Flannel
Hot Millions
How To Save A Marriage – And Ruin Your Life
Ice Station Zebra
The Impossible Years
The Odd Couple
Oliver!
Paper Lion
The Party
Planet Of The Apes
The Producers
Rosemary's Baby
The Secret Life Of An American Wife
The Secret War Of Harry Frigg
The Shakiest Gun In The West
The Thomas Crown Affair
2001: A Space Odyssey
War And Peace [Russian]
Where Were You When The Lights Went Out?
Wild In The Streets
With Six You Get Eggroll
Yellow Submarine
Yours, Mine And Ours

SOME OF THE BEST-SELLERS AND PUBLISHED BOOKS
1968

FICTION

Airport	Arthur Hailey
The Armies Of The Night:	
History As A Novel, The Novel As History	Norman Mailer
Cancer Ward	Alexander Solzhenitsyn
Couples	John Updike
Expensive People	Joyce Carol Oates
The First Circle	Alexander Solzhenitsyn
Force 10 From Navarone	Alistar MacLean
In The Heart Of The Heart Of The Country	William Gass
Lost In The Funhouse	John Barth
Mosby's Memoirs And Other Stories	Saul Bellow
Myra Breckenridge	Gore Vidal
The Senator	Drew Pearson
Tell Me How Long The Train's Been Gone: A Novel	James Baldwin
True Grit: A Novel	Charles Portis
Unspeakable Practises, Unnatural Acts	Donald Barthelme
A World Of Profit	Louis Auchincloss

NON-FICTION

The Algiers Motel Incident	John Hersey
Better Homes And Gardens' Eat And Stay Slim	
Better Homes And Gardens' New Cook Book	
Between Parent And Child:	
New Solutions To Old Problems	Haim Ginott
The Case Against Congress	Drew Pearson and Jack Anderson
The Doctor's Quick Weight Loss Diet	Ervin M. Stillman and Samm Sinclair Baker
The Electric Kool-Aid Acid Test	Tom Wolfe
The Indian Heritage Of America	Alvin Josephy
Instant Replay: The Green Bay Diary Of Jerry Kramer	(ed) Dick Schaap
Kiss Kiss Bang Bang	Pauline Kael
McLuhan: Pro And Con	(ed) Raymond Rosenthal
Miami And The Siege Of Chicago: An Informal History	
Of The Republican And Democratic Conventions of 1968	Norman Mailer

The Money Game	Adam Smith (George G Goodman)
The Naked Ape	Desmond Morris
The Politics Of Ecstasy	Timothy Leary
The Pump House Gang	Tom Wolfe
Revolution For The Hell of It	Abbie Hoffman
Slouching Towards Bethlehem	Joan Didion
The Teachings Of Don Juan: A Yaqui Way of Knowledge	Carlos Castaneda
Through The Vanishing Point:	
* Space In Poetry and Painting*	Marshall McLuhan and Harley Parker
Violence: America In The Sixties	Arthur M Schlesinger Jr
War And Peace In The Global Village: An Inventory Of	
* Some Of The Current Spastic Situations That Could Be*	
Eliminated By More Feedforward	Marshall McLuhan
The Weight Watcher's Cook Book	Jean Nidetch

POETRY

Airplane Dreams, Ankor Wat, And Planet News, 1961-67	Allen Ginsberg
Listen To The Warm And Lonesome Cities	Rod McKuen
The Secret Meaning Of Things	Lawrence Ferlinghetti

 WAITING FOR THE SUN (album)
Elektra Records, EKL-74024 Mono, EKS-74024 Stereo, July 1968.

Side 1: 'Hello, I Love You'; 'Love Street'; 'Not To Touch The Earth'; 'Summer's Almost Gone'; 'Wintertime Love'; 'The Unknown Soldier'

Side 2: 'Spanish Caravan'; 'My Wild Love'; 'We Could Be So Good Together'; 'Yes, The River Knows'; 'Five To One'

Producer: Paul A Rothchild
Production Supervisor: Jac Holzman
Engineer: Bruce Botnick
Additional musicians: Doug Lubahn (of Clear Light), fuzz bass; Kerry Magness (of Popcorn), bass ('The Unknown Soldier'); Leroy Vinegar, acoustic bass ('Spanish Caravan')

January- or February-June 1968: The Doors do recording sessions for *Waiting For The Sun* at Sunset Sound Recording Studios, Los Angeles.

Billboard's Top LPs: debuted at Number 110 on 10 August 1968; peaked at Number One for three weeks, 7-21 September and then again on 5 October; was out of the charts after 22 March 1969; and then reappeared for seven weeks beginning 9 August.

 HELLO, I LOVE YOU

'Hello, I Love You'/'Love Street' was released by Elektra as a 45rpm single (#45635), June 1968.

The song was one of the six songs recorded by group (before Robby Krieger joined) on a demo at Aura Records (a subsidiary of World Pacific Studios) in Los Angeles on 2 September 1965. *Billboard*'s Hot 100: debuted at Number 108 on 29 June 1968; peaked at Number One for two weeks, 3 and 10 August; and was out of the charts after 21 September.

In *Riders On The Storm*, Densmore wrote that the arranging of 'Hello, I Love You' made the song sound "contrived" because of the "tons" of guitar distortion via the fuzz box (which was the latest electronic toy) and because of Krieger's suggestion of turning the beat around like Cream did in 'Sunshine of Your Love'. (p160).

On the radio special, *History Of Rock 'n' Roll*, Manzarek describes the song's origins:

> "'Hello, I Love You' was written for a black girl that Jim and I saw walking down the beach. And she was a black girl, a dusky, dark complexion, dark skin and she was just a little jewel walking by. And then Jim went home that night and wrote a song about just walking up to a girl that you didn't know or anything, and saying, 'Hello, I love you.'"

In *No One Here Gets Out Alive* Sugerman and Hopkins wrote that Morrison wrote the lyric in 1965 after sitting on the beach at Venice and "watching a young, long thin black girl insinuate her way toward him" (p59).

Many accused The Doors of cloning Ray Davies and the Kinks' 'All Day And All Of The Night'. In an interview over ten years after the release of the song, Manzarek commented on the alleged Kink-derivative, saying that the group initially thought the song was "a *lot* like a Kinks song" but added, "It's all rock and roll, we're all family, we're not stealing anything from them, we're sort of... (hums melody) ...Yes it *is* a lot like it, isn't it? Sorry, Ray." (Pete Fornatale, *Musician*, August 1981 p49).

 LOVE STREET

'Hello, I Love You' b/w 'Love Street' was released by Elektra as a 45rpm single (#45635), June 1968.

In the poem 'Don't Start That...' in *The American Night*, the images "Love Street parade" and "Love Street brigade" appear (p147).

In *No One Here Gets Out Alive*, Jerry Hopkins and Danny Sugerman wrote the song was written about where Jim and Pam lived in an apartment on Rothdell Trail in Laurel Canyon; Jim often sat with a beer on the balcony and watched people come and go from the neighbouring small grocery store, called the Country Store (pp110, 112). In their book, *Break On Through*, James Riordan and Jerry Prochnicky added that the address was 1812 Rothdell Trail (pp123, 247).

"Love Street" was the name of a street in the Haight Ashbury district of San Francisco, the neighbourhood where the Grateful Dead originated. *Haight Ashbury Love Street* was also one of the titles used by the underground newspaper *Haight Ashbury Tribune* during 1968. Haight Ashbury, thanks in large part to a feature article in the 30 October 1967 issue of *Newsweek*, became the national emigrating centre of the hippie/flower power movement.

 NOT TO TOUCH THE EARTH

A song labelled '(Go) Insane' was one of the six songs recorded by group (before Robby Krieger joined) on a demo at Aura Records (a subsidiary of World Pacific Studios) in Los Angeles on 2 September 1965. This demo included part of 'Not To Touch The Earth' along with another segment of *The Celebration Of The Lizard*.

The lyric is an internal segment in the selection *The Celebration Of The Lizard* written by Jim Morrison and published on the inner sleeve of this third album and in *The American Night* (pp43-44).

Plans for this third album had begun as grandiose with one side devoted to a 20-minute-plus version of a piece by Morrison 'The Celebration of the Lizard'. But the studio recording of the piece proved to be too crude, and the only passage produced for this album was the 'Not To Touch The Earth' segment.

In the 28 June 1968 issue of *Open City*, a weekly underground newspaper in Los Angeles, Morrison talks to interviewer Jerry Hopkins about the failure to record 'The Celebration Of The Lizard', a piece which had been tried three times in concert. Morrison explains:

> "The people were sort of bored. It hadn't been invented and tested
> properly. I guess it's sort of a closet piece."

According to Hopkins and Sugerman in *No One Here Gets Out Alive*, the first two lines of this song about not touching the earth and not seeing see the sun, came from the table of contents of *The Golden Bough* (p179). Actually, the two lines were taken from Sir James George Frazer's *Aftermath: A Supplement To The Golden Bough* (New York: Macmillan Company 1937; included in 1951 multi-volume edition of *The Golden Bough*). Frazer, at the first part of the twentieth century, wrote what became a definitive study and history of magic and religion of the world. The multi-volume work was published in 1921. In the table of contents (p. xviii) of *Aftermath* are listed the following two chapters:

Chapter LXV – Not To Touch The Earth pp443-446;

Chapter LXVI – Not To See The Sun p447.

Both chapters deal with various culture's taboos of not touching the Earth or not looking into the sun after certain events or rites.

 SUMMER'S ALMOST GONE

In *Light My Fire, My Life With The Doors*, Manzarek stated that this was the third song Morrison sang to him during their infamous crossing of paths on the sands of Venice Beach in LA in the summer of 1965 after they had graduated from college at UCLA (p100).

The song was one of the six songs recorded by group (before Robby Krieger joined) on a demo at Aura Records (a subsidiary of World Pacific Studios) in Los Angeles on 2 September 1965.

 WINTERTIME LOVE

In *The Doors: The Complete Lyrics*, the song's by-line is "Lyrics by Robby Krieger" (p89).

The article *Doors' CD Mystery Baffles Experts* in *Ice* (March 1992 p1, 10) discusses an unexplained vocal difference in the rendition of 'Wintertime Love' on the CD release of *Waiting For The Sun*. Furthermore, Heinz Gerstenmeyer wrote to *Ice* to point out a switching of the channels on which the organ and rhythm guitar parts were recorded (*Doors Difference* July 1994 p4).

 THE UNKNOWN SOLDIER

'The Unknown Soldier' b/w 'We Could Be So Good Together' was released by Elektra as a 45rpm single (#45628) March 1968. The song was subsequently banned by several radio chains. *Billboard*'s Hot 100: debuted at Number 79 on 30 March 1968; peaked at Number 39 for three weeks, 4-28 May; and then immediately fell out of the charts.

In a radio special produced by *The Source*, Manzarek explained the song's origins:

> "Jim said, "Let's do a war song." I said, "Everybody's doing a Vietnam song." And he said, "Nah, nah, this isn't a Vietnam song. This is just a song about war.""

Hopkins and Sugerman recalled the song began in October of 1967 and was developed on the road and over the next couple of months, and "the dirge became a celebration…a rhythm that was both military (metronomic) and carnivalesque." (*No One Here Gets Out Alive* pp149-50).

In his book *The Lizard King: The Essential Jim Morrison*, Jerry Hopkins wrote that 'Unknown Soldier' was from Morrison's writings when he lived in Venice Beach the summer of 1965, right after graduating from UCLA (pp93, 95).

In a 1972 interview by John Tobler with the three surviving Doors, Densmore explained that the group did the gun shot on stage by dropping a reverb unit (*ZigZag*, September 1972 p29).

In *Light My Fire, My Life With The Doors*, Manzarek describes the antics of the firing squad used for the studio recording, comprising a bunch of rock critics, including Paul Williams and Richard Goldstein (pp280-81).

Mitchell Cohen viewed the short film, which promoted the song at a Doors concert at the Fillmore East in March 1968, and he wrote in retrospect for an article in *Fusion* magazine that he felt that the film was a "crude work and filled with Morrison-as-martyr iconography" and simulated "vomiting and political montage...yet it worked." (June 1974, p19).

In an interview with Jacob Atlas, part one published in the October 1968 issue of *Hullabaloo*, Morrison comments about the film: "We conceived and directed the large sequence, the execution on the beach, but the rest of the film was stock footage that was done in New York. We had nothing to do with the final editing." (p50).

 SPANISH CARAVAN

In *The Doors: The Complete Lyrics*, the song's by-line is, "Lyrics by Robby Krieger" (p91).

In an interview printed in *Creem Special Edition: The Doors* (summer 1981), Krieger stated he composed the song, 'Spanish Caravan' (Matheu, p59). In *Riders On The Storm*, Densmore describes the group playing 'Spanish Caravan' at one of their January 1967 gigs at the Fillmore in San Francisco (pp106-7).

Andalusia (or Andalucia), the area referred to in the first stanza, is the southernmost part of Spain. The region compromises about $1/6$ of Spain and is home to about $1/5$ of the country's population. It has a rich history of conquests by Cathagenians, Romans, Vandals, Visigoths and Moors. Though this region was divided in 1833 into eight provinces, its historical name has remained the most common reference. Andalucia Baja (Lower Andalusia) consists of a fertile, productive plain; mountains rising to more than 11,000 feet dominate the Andalucia Alta (Upper Andalusia). Rather than gold and silver, the wealth of these mountains has been exported in the form of copper, coal and lead.

 MY WILD LOVE

The line "My Wild Love" is the foundation of a different untitled poem published in *Wilderness* (p65).

Heinz Gerstenmeyer wrote to *Ice* magazine and noted that Morrison hums at the end of the song over 6 bars on the LP, but over 12 bars on the CD and that the song is nine seconds longer on the CD (*Doors Difference*, July 1994, p4).

 WE COULD BE SO GOOD TOGETHER

'The Unknown Soldier' b/w 'We Could Be So Good Together' was released by Elektra as a 45rpm single (#45628) in March 1968.

Manzarek, in *Light My Fire: My Life With The Doors*, stated he "quoted verbatim" with his organ a Thelonius Monk line from 'Straight, No Chaser.' (p78).

A middle stanza is deleted on a (West) German CD pressing, done by Polygram (Elektra/Asylum Records 74024-2, Europe: 042 041 August 1985). Gerstenmeyer informs me that, on the second pressing, "the digitally remastered one from 1988, this stanza is not deleted."

In the stanza about angels, Gerstenmeyer only capitalises the first *angel* (p74). In the Hyperion edition, both times, the word *angels* is capitalised (p98); in the Delta paperback edition, only the first *angels* is capitalised (p94). I believe the lyric suggests the proper nominative of *Angels* – the human aspirations and values we ascribe to the profound realm rather than to our profane world, those angels we knowingly and unknowingly destroy.

YES, THE RIVER KNOWS

In *The Doors: The Complete Lyrics*, the song's by-line is "Lyrics by Robby Krieger" (p91).

In the Matheu interview that appeared in *Creem Special Edition: The Doors* (Summer 1981), Krieger stated that he composed the song 'Yes, The River Knows', and that it was one of his favourites (p59).

FIVE TO ONE

Densmore wrote in *Riders On The Storm* that Morrison kept bugging him to play a very primitive drumbeat and when John finally relented with the "dumbest 4/4 beat" he knew, Jim started singing the opening lyrics 'Five To One'. Robby added a guitar riff, and Ray joined with the organ (pp160-61).

Morrison offered an explanation of the title to Hank Zevallos in an 1970 interview published in *Poppin*. The song, which Morrison said he didn't think of as political, was an idea he got while waiting in the audience before starting a concert at San Jose, California: "It was one of those big ballroom places and the kids were milling around and I just got an idea for a song." (*Jim Morrison* (interview) March 1970 p50). On 19 November 1967, The Doors performed at the San Jose Continental Ballroom in San Jose, California.

In *The Doors: The Complete Lyrics*, the spoken passage at the end of the song includes the line about getting "fucked up" (p100), which is not on the studio released recording, but is on bootlegs of live recordings.

POPULAR SONGS
MARCH-NOVEMBER 1968

'Ain't Nothing Like The Real Thing'	Marvin Gaye And Tammi Terrell
'Born To Be Wild'	Steppenwolf
'Classical Gas'	Mason Williams
'Cry Like A Baby'	Box Tops

'Dance To The Music'	Sly And The Family Stone
'Do You Know The Way To San Jose?'	Dionne Warwick
'Fire'	The Crazy World Of Arthur Brown
'For Once In My Life'	Stevie Wonder
'The Good, The Bad And The Ugly'	The Hugo Montenegro Orchestra And Chorus
'Journey To The Centre Of Your Mind'	Amboy Dukes
'Harper Valley PTA'	Jeannie C Riley
'Hey Jude'	The Beatles
'Honey'	Bobby Goldsboro
'Hurdy Gurdy Man'	Donovan
'Hush'	Deep Purple
'In-A-Gadda-Da-Vida'	Iron Butterfly
'Indian Lake'	Cowsills
'I've Got To Get A Message To You'	Bee Gees
'Jennifer Juniper'	Donovan
'Jumpin' Jack Flash'	The Rolling Stones
'Just Dropped In (To See What Condition My Condition Was In)'	Kenny Rogers And The First Edition
'Lady Madonna'	The Beatles
'Lady Willpower'	Gary Puckett And The Union Gap
'Light My Fire'	Jose Feliciano
'Love Child'	Diana Ross And The Supremes
'MacArthur Park'	Richard Harris
'Magic Bus'	The Who
'Magic Carpet Ride'	Steppenwolf
'Midnight Confessions'	Grass Roots
'The Mighty Quinn'	Manfred Mann
'Mony Mony'	Tommy James And The Shondells
'Mrs Robinson'	Simon And Garfunkel
'People Got To Be Free'	The Rascals (formerly The Young Rascals)
'Revolution'	The Beatles
'Scarborough Fair'/'Canticle'	Simon And Garfunkel
'Simon Says'	1910 Fruitgum Company
'(Sittin' On) The Dock Of The Bay'	Otis Redding
'Stoned Soul Picnic'	The Fifth Dimension
'Sunshine Of Your Love'	Cream

'Suzie Q'	Creedence Clearwater Revival
'Those Were The Days'	Mary Hopkins
'Time Has Come Today'	Chamber Brothers
'Tuesday Afternoon'	Moody Blues
'This Guy's In Love With You'	Herb Albert
'Valleri'	The Monkees
'Walk Away Renee'	Four Tops
'White Room'	Cream
'Young Girl'	Gary Puckett And The Union Gap
'Yummy, Yummy, Yummy'	Ohio Express

POPULAR AND RELEASED ALBUMS
MARCH-NOVEMBER 1968

Anthem Of The Sun	The Grateful Dead
Aretha Now	Aretha Franklin
At Folsom Prison	Johnny Cash
Axis: Bold As Love	Jimi Hendrix Experience
The Best Of The Brass	Herb Albert And The Tijuana Brass
The Birds, The Bees And The Monkees	The Monkees
Bookends	Simon And Garfunkel
By The Time I Get To Phoenix	Glenn Campbell
Cheap Thrills	Big Brother And The Holding Company (with Janis Joplin)
Child Is Father To The Man	Blood, Sweet And Tears
Crazy World Of Arthur Brown	Crazy World Of Arthur Brown
Creedence Clearwater Revival	Creedence Clearwater Revival
Crown Of Creation	Jefferson Airplane
The Dock Of The Bay	Otis Redding
Donovan In Concert	Donovan
Electric Ladyland	Jimi Hendrix Experience
Feliciano!	Jose Feliciano
Funny Girl	(soundtrack to movie)
Gentle On My Mind	Glen Campbell
God Bless	Tiny Tim
Goin' Out Of My Head	Lettermen
The Good, The Bad And The Ugly	(soundtrack to movie) Ennio Morricone

The Graduate	(soundtrack to movie) Simon And Garfunkel
Honey	Bobby Goldsboro
In Search Of The Lost Chord	Moody Blues
In-A-Gadda-Da-Vida	Iron Butterfly
John Wesley Harding	Bob Dylan
Lady Soul	Aretha Franklin
A Long Time Comin'	Electric Flag (with Mike Bloomfield)
Look Around	Sergio Mendes And Brasil '66
Magic Bus	The Who
Once Upon A Dream	The Rascals (formerly The Young Rascals)
The Papas And The Mamas	The Mamas And The Papas
Quicksilver Messenger Service	Quicksilver Messenger Service
Realisation	Johnny Rivers
Reflections	Diana Ross And The Supremes
Steppenwolf	The Second Steppenwolf
Shades Of Deep Purple	Deep Purple
Steppenwolf	Steppenwolf
Super Sessions	Mike Bloomfield, Al Kooper, Steve Stills
Time Has Come	Chamber Brothers
Time Peace: Greatest Hits	The Rascals (formerly The Young Rascals)
To Russell, My Brother, Whom I Slept With	Bill Cosby
Together Country	Joe And The Fish
Truth	Jeff Beck
Unicorn	Irish Rovers
We're Only In It For The Money	Frank Zappa And The Mothers Of Invention
Wheels Of Fire	Cream
Wildflowers	Judy Collins
Woman, Woman	Gary Puckett And The Union Gap
Wow	Moby Grape
Young Girl	Gary Puckett And The Union Gap

AMERICAN TELEVISION
1968 FALL PRIME TIME SCHEDULE

	7:30	8:00	8:30	9:00	9:30	10:00	10:30	
SUN	Land Of The Giants (7-8)		The FBI	The ABC Sunday Night Movie				**ABC**
	Gentle Ben		Ed Sullivan Show		Smothers Brothers Comedy Hour		Mission: Impossible	**CBS**
	Walt Disney's Wonderful World Of Colour		Mothers-In-Law	Bonanza		Beautiful Phyllis Diller Show		**NBC**
MON	The Avengers			Peyton Place	The Outcasts		The Big Valley	**ABC**
	Gunsmoke		Here's Lucy	Mayberry RFD	Family Affair	Carol Burnett Show		**CBS**
	I Dream Of Jeannie		Rowan And Martin's Laugh-In		NBC Monday Night At The Movies			**NBC**
TUE	Mod Squad		It Takes A Thief		NYPD		That's Life	**ABC**
	Lancer	Red Skelton Hour			Doris Day Show/ 60 Minutes		CBS News Hour	**CBS**
	Jerry Lewis Show			Julia	NBC Tuesday Night At The Movies/ News Special (once a month)			**NBC**
WED	Here Come The Brides			Peyton Place	The ABC Wednesday Night Movie			**ABC**
		Daktari	The Good Guys	The Beverly Hillbillies	Green Acres	Jonathan Winters Show		**CBS**
	The Virginian			The Kraft Music Hall		The Outsider		**NBC**
THU	The Ugliest Girl In Town		The Flying Nun	Bewitched	That Girl	Journey To The Unknown	Local	**ABC**
	Blondie	Hawaii Five-O		The CBS Thursday Night Movies				**CBS**
	Daniel Boone		Ironside		Dragnet 1969	Dean Martin Show		**NBC**
FRI	Operation: Entertainment Squad			The Felony Show	Don Rickles	The Guns of Will Sonnett	Judd, For The Defence	**ABC**
	The Wild, Wild West		Gomer Pyle, USMC	The CBS Friday Night Movies				**CBS**
	The High Chaparral		The Name Of The Game			Star Trek		**NBC**
SAT	The Dating Game		The Newlywed Game	Lawrence Welk Show	The Hollywood Palace	Local		**ABC**
	Jackie Gleason Show		My Three Sons	Hogan's Heroes	Petticoat Junction	Mannix		**CBS**
	Adam-12	Get Smart	The Ghost And Mrs Muir	NBC Saturday Night At The Movies				**NBC**

AMERICAN TELEVISION
1968-69 SEASON

SOME OF THE SATURDAY MORNING CARTOONS
Archie Show
Banana Splits Adventure Hour
The New Beatles (Sunday mornings)
Bugs Bunny/Road Runner Hour
Bullwinkle Show (Sunday mornings)
The Flintstones
George Of The Jungle
Johnny Quest
Shazzan!
Spiderman
Tom And Jerry (Sunday mornings)
Underdog

SOME OF THE DAYTIME SOAPS
Another World
As The World Turns
Dark Shadows
Days Of Our Lives
The Doctors
Edge Of Night
General Hospital
Guiding Light
One Life To Live
Secret Storm

NIGHTLY NEWS
ABC Evening News with Frank Reynolds
CBS Evening News with Walter Cronkite
Huntley-Brinkley Report (NBC)

MOVIES OF 1969
Alice's Restaurant
A Boy Named Charlie Brown

Bob And Carol And Ted And Alice
The Brotherhood
Butch Cassidy And The Sundance Kid
Cactus Flower
Che!
The Comic
The Damned
Death Of A Gunfighter
Easy Rider
Fanny Hill [Swedish]
Goodbye, Columbus
Goodbye, Mr Chips
The Great Bank Robbery
Guns Of The Magnificent Seven
The Happy Ending
Hard Contract
Hell In The Pacific
Hellfighters
Hello, Dolly!
Hell's Angels
Hook, Line And Sinker
I Am Curious (Yellow) [Swedish]
If...
The Illustrated Man
The Love Bug
The Loves Of Isadora
The Maltese Bippy
Marooned
Midnight Cowboy
On Her Majesty's Secret Service
Once Upon a Time In The West
Paint Your Wagon
Popi
The Prime Of Miss Jean Brodie
The Rain People
Staircase
The Sterile Cuckoo

Support Your Local Sheriff
Sweet Charity
Take The Money And Run
Tell Them Willie Boy is Here
They Shoot Horses, Don't They?
Those Daring Young Men In Their Jaunty Jalopes
Three In The Attic
Topaz
True Grit
The Wedding Party
Where Eagles Dare
The Wild Bunch
Z [French]

SOME OF THE BEST-SELLERS AND PUBLISHED BOOKS
1969

FICTION

The Andromeda Strain	Michael Crichton
Bullet Park	John Cheever
The Godfather	Mario Puzo
I Sing The Body Electric	Ray Bradbury
The Inheritors	Harold Robbins
The Love Machine	Jacqueline Susann
Naked Came The Stranger	Penelope Ashe (pseudonym for 25 reporters)
Nightfall And Other Stories	Isaac Asimov
Pictures Of Fidelman: An Exhibition	Bernard Malamud
Portnoy's Complaint	Philip Roth
The Pretenders	Gwen Davis
The Promise	Chaim Potok
Puppet On A Chain	Alistar MacLean
The Seven Minutes	Irving Wallace
Slaughterhouse Five: Or The Children's Crusade	Kurt Vonnegut Jr
Them	Joyce Carol Oates
The Three Daughters Of Madame Liang	Pearl Buck

NON-FICTION

Being Busted	Leslie Fiedler
Between Parent And Teenager	Dr Haim G Ginott
Civilisation: A Personal View	Kenneth Clark
Custer Dies For Your Sins: An Indian Manifesto	Vine Deloria Jr
Counterblast	Marshall McLuhan
Do It! Scenarios Of The Revolution	Jerry Rubin
Everything You Always Wanted To Know About Sex (But Were Afraid To Ask)	David Reuben
The Graham Kerr Cookbook	The Galloping Gourmet
Growing Up Underground	Jane Alpert
Jennie: The Life Of Lady Randolph Churchill	Ralph Martin
The Kingdom And The Power: Are Healing And The Spiritual Gifts Used By Jesus And The Early Church Meant For The Church Today?	Gay Talese
Linda Goodman's Sun Signs	Linda Goodman
The Lives Of Children: The Story Of The First Street School	George Dennison
Living Room War	Michael J. Arlen
The Making Of A Counter Culture: Reflections On The Technocratic Society And Its Youthful Opposition	Theodore Roszak
The Making Of The President, 1968	Theodore H White
Miss Craig's 21-Day Shape-Up Program For Men And Women	Marjorie Craig
My Life And Prophecies	Jeane Dixon with René Noorbergen
The 900 Days: The Siege Of Leningrad	Harrison Salisbury
The Peter Principle	Laurence Peter and Raymond Hull
The Selling Of The President 1968	Joe McGinnis
Styles Of Radical Will	Susan Sontag
Woodstock Nation: A Talk-Rock Album	Abbie Hoffman

POETRY

In Someone's Shadow And Twelve Years Of Christmas	Rod McKuen
Leaflets: Poems 1965-68	Adrienne Rich
Pieces	Robert Creeley

THE SOFT PARADE (album)
Elektra Records, EKS-75005, July 1969

Side 1: 'Tell All The People'/'Touch Me'/'Shaman's Blues'/'Do It'/'Easy Ride'

Side 2: 'Wild Child'/'Runnin' Blue'/'Wishful Sinful'/'The Soft Parade'

Producer: Paul A Rothchild
Production Coordinator: Jac Holzman
Engineer: Bruce Botnick
Additional musicians: Harvey Brooks (of Electric Flag), bass; Curtis Amy, saxophone; George Bohanan, trombone; Champ Webb, cor anglais; Jesse McReynolds, mandolin; Jimmy Buchanan, fiddle; Reinol Andino, congas

In an interview printed in the July 1995 issue of *20th Century Guitar*, session bassist Harvey Brooks talked about the recording of the album *The Soft Parade*, and he immediately mentioned seeing hippie pillows and a lot of other stuff all over the studio. He recalled how he would show up at noon or one o'clock and it would be seven or eight at night before everyone collected themselves and the recording would finally come together. He said he should have been given writer's credit for many of the songs because he did a lot of the arrangements. Brooks also noted that all the horn and strings charts on the album were done by Paul Harris. (Mark Lotito and Don Celenza *Harvey Brooks* p113.)

November 1968-July 1969: The Doors do recording sessions for *The Soft Parade* at Elektra Sound Recorders, Los Angeles.

Billboard's Top LPs: debuted at Number 24 on 9 August 1969; peaked at Number Six for two weeks, 23 and 30 August; and was out of the charts after 14 February 1970.

 TELL ALL THE PEOPLE (Krieger)

'Tell All The People' b/w 'Easy Ride' was released by Elektra as a 45rpm single (#45663) in May 1969. *Billboard*'s Hot 100: debuted at Number 100 on 14 June 1969; peaked at Number 57 for two weeks, 2 and 9

August, and then fell immediately out of the charts.

In an interview printed in *Creem Special Edition: The Doors* (summer 1981), Krieger stated he composed the song 'Tell All The People' (Matheu p59).

In his book *The Lizard King: The Essential Jim Morrison*, Jerry Hopkins wrote that Morrison didn't want people to think he wanted others to follow him because he neither trusted leaders nor wanted to be a leader (p120).

In *Riders On The Storm*, Densmore retold a similar story that Krieger had thought the song was perfect for Morrison, but Jim, after months of silence, finally said he didn't want people to think they should get guns and follow *him* (p187).

In a handwritten response to questions submitted to him by Dave Marsh, Morrison replied to the question, "What was your reaction to...'Tell All The People'?": "Terrible, corny lyrics. Nice song though."

 TOUCH ME (Krieger)

'Touch Me' b/w 'Wild Child' was released by Elektra as a 45rpm single (#45646), December 1968. *Billboard*'s Hot 100: debuted at Number 72 on 28 December 1968; peaked at Number Three on 15 February 1969; and was out of the charts after 22 March.

In the Robert Matheu interview in *Creem Special Edition: The Doors* (summer 1981), Krieger said that he composed the song and that originally the song was 'Hit Me', not 'Touch Me', but Jim said that he wouldn't sing that lyric (p59). Densmore expounded on this, writing that Robby had written, "Come on, come on, come on, now, hit me, babe!", from one of the many rumoured intense domestic squabbles between him and his girlfriend, but he had apparently offered no resistance when Jim suggested the change to "touch me" (*Riders On The Storm* p190).

In some earlier live recordings of the track 'When The Music's Over', Morrison interjected a section which included the lines "Something wrong, something not quite right/Touch me baby/All through the night, yeah."

At the end of the song, the boys in the band chant "Stronger than dirt!" At the time, Ajax detergent was running an often viewed commercial with a white knight galloping across the television screen and zapping things clean; the slogan for the commercial was: "Stronger than dirt!" Session bassist Harvey Brooks recalls in an interview printed in the July 1995 issue of *20th Century Guitar* that The Doors "had to pay tribute to where [this last line] came from. It was such an embarrassing lick [laughs]." (Mark Lotito and Don Celenza, *Harvey Brooks* p113.)

 SHAMAN'S BLUES (Morrison)

On the vinyl album, the line "and your mind" is repeated four times, and six times on the CD.

According to Densmore, the spoken coda which ends the song was created to "schizophrenic multitracking" – sliding in and out ad lib bits from various vocal takes of Morrison's (*Riders On The Storm* p205).

 DO IT (Morrison/Krieger)

'Runnin' Blue' b/w 'Do It' was released by Elektra as a 45rpm single (#45675) in August 1969.

In *The Doors: The Complete Lyrics*, the song's lyrics are credited to Jim Morrison (p109).

 EASY RIDE (Morrison)

'Tell All The People' b/w 'Easy Ride' was released by Elektra as a 45rpm single (#45663) in May 1969. Manzarek, in *Light My Fire: My Life With The Doors*, cites lyrics and who inspired them; he indicated the lyric about the "coda queen" being his bride and reigning in darkness at his side was for Jim's longtime girlfriend, Pam (p4).

 WILD CHILD (Morrison)

'Touch Me' b/w 'Wild Child' was released by Elektra as a 45rpm single (#45646) in December 1968.

Manzarek, in *Light My Fire: My Life With The Doors*, cites lyrics and who inspired them; he indicated this song (or at least parts of it) was for Danny Sugerman (p5).

 RUNNIN' BLUE (Krieger)

'Runnin' Blue' b/w 'Do It' was a released by Elektra as a 45rpm single (#45675), August 1969. *Billboard*'s Hot 100: debuted at Number 89 on 6 September 1969; peaked at Number 64 on 4 October; and was out of the charts after 11 October.

On the singles, albums (except *Weird Scenes Inside The Gold Mine*), and CDs released by Elektra, the song is titled 'Runnin' Blue'. In the book *The Doors: The Complete Lyrics*, the song is titled 'Runnin' Blues' (p120). On *Weird Scenes Inside The Gold Mine*, the song is titled 'Running Blue'.

In a piece of personal correspondence, Fred Baggen writes that Morrison used the opening three lines of this song (about "poor Otis" being dead and gone and the "pretty little girl" wearing a red dress) during two live performances recorded on bootlegs: during the song 'When The Music's Over' at one of the performances during their three-day engagement at Winterland in San Francisco on 26-28 December 1967. (Morrison sang these lyrics just before the final refrain of 'When the music's over') and during 'Soul Kitchen' at a concert in the Chicago Coliseum on 10 May 1968. 'Runnin' Blue' is a tribute to Otis Redding, who had died in a plane crash on 10 December 1967; Redding had been scheduled to play with The Doors at Winterland.

 WISHFUL SINFUL (Krieger)

'Wishful Sinful' b/w 'Who Scared You?' was released by Elektra as a 45rpm single (#45656) in February 1969. *Billboard*'s Hot 100: debuted at Number 79 on 29 March 1969; peaked at Number 44 for two weeks, on 19 and 26 April; and was out of the charts after the following week.

In an interview printed in *Creem Special Edition: The Doors* (Summer 1981), Krieger said that he composed the song 'Wishful Sinful' (Matheu p59).

 THE SOFT PARADE (Morrison)

In a 1981 interview with *Bam*, producer Paul Rothchild stated that a lot of the song was composed with bits of poetry out of Jim's notebooks that he and Jim thought fit rhythmically and conceptually (3 July 1981, p19). In his book *The Lizard King: The Essential Jim Morrison* Jerry Hopkins wrote that the song was Morrison's images of "people walking along Sunset Boulevard" in Los Angeles (p121).

Lyric as written by Jim Morrison is published in *The American Night* (pp49-52). The image "soft parade" also appears as a line in these selections written by Morrison: (1) as "The Soft Parade" in an untitled selection in *Wilderness* (p19); and (2) as "Soft Parade" in the poem 'Don't Start That...' in *The American Night* (p147).

In *The Lords And The New Creatures*, a poem opens with a line about the "soft parade" having begun "on Sunset" and includes a line about "the soft parade" soon beginning (p130). For a more poetically rendered version of what Jim called our "universe of organic gears", see the selection titled 'Dry Water' in *Wilderness* (p157-58) and also in *Jim Morrison: An Hour For Magic* (p111).

In an untitled selection in *Wilderness* are printed lines which are also used in this song, about "calling to the dogs" and a radio "moaning softly" while some animals are still "left in the yard" (p110).

In *Wilderness*, the poem entitled *Horse Latitudes* includes lines, which are also used in this song, about people having difficulty "describing sailors" to what Morrison called the "undernourished" (p94).

In the printed versions in *The Doors: The Complete Lyrics* (p123) and in *The American Night* (p52), the confusing passage at the end about meeting at the crossroads is very close to the lyrics Morrison vocalised for the recording of 'The Soft Parade' taped for the NET television special, *Critique* (13 May 1969).

Morrison repeatedly uses the crossroads imagery in several poems in his two books, *Wilderness* and *The American Night*. Two notable usages offer an extensive description of the "crossroads": on p46 in *Wilderness* and the poem entitled *The Crossroads* on p64 in *The American Night*.

In *Wilderness*, a poem entitled *Horse Latitudes* (p95) includes many of the lines sung and spoken at the end of the song 'The Soft Parade'.

 WHO SCARED YOU? (Morrison/Krieger)

'Wishful Sinful' b/w 'Who Scared You' was released by Elektra as a 45rpm single (#45656) in February 1969. 'Who Scared You?' was not included on the album, *The Soft Parade*.

In a personal correspondence, Fred Baggen writes that Morrison used the opening lyrics to this song within a rendition of 'When The Music's Over' during The Doors' Matrix Club show on 7 March, 1967. Baggen also writes that Morrison used a variation of the lyrics about a rider carrying a sack of gold in a rendition of 'The End' during a concert at Danbury High School Auditorium, 17 October 1967: "I see a rider coming down the road/He had a burden carrying a heavy sack of gold/One bag of silver and one sack of gold." Morrison uses these lines just before the Oedipal section of 'The End'.

POPULAR SONGS
DECEMBER 1968-NOVEMBER 1969

'Abraham, Martin And John'	Dion
'And When I Die'	Blood, Sweat And Tears
'Aquarius'/'Let The Sunshine In'	The Fifth Dimension
'Atlantis'	Donovan
'Bad Moon Rising'	Creedence Clearwater Revival
'The Ballad Of John And Yoko'	The Beatles
'Both Sides Now'	Judy Collins
'The Boxer'	Simon And Garfunkel
'A Boy Named Sue'	Johnny Cash
'Build Me Up Buttercup'	The Foundations
'Cherry Hill Park'	Billy Joe Royal
'Cloud Nine'	Temptations

'Come Together'	The Beatles
'Crimson And Clover'	Tommy James And The Shondells
'Crossroads'	Cream
'Crystal Blue Persuasion'	Tommy James And The Shondells
'Dizzy'	Tommy Roe
'Easy To Be Hard'	Three Dog Night
'Eli's Coming'	Three Dog Night
'Everybody's Talking'	Nilsson
'Everyday People'	Sly And The Family Stone
'Galveston'	Glen Campbell
'Get Back'	The Beatles
'Good Morning Starshine'	Oliver
'Hair'	Cowsills
'Hang 'Em High'	Booker T And The MG's
'Hawaii Five-O'	Ventures
'Hello, It's Me'	Nazz
'Holly Holy'	Neil Diamond
'Honky Tonk Woman'	The Rolling Stones
'Hooked On A Feeling'	BJ Thomas
'Hot Fun In The Summer Time'	Sly and The Family Stone
'I Heard It Through The Grape'	Marvin Gaye
'I'm Gonna Make You Love Me'	Diana Ross And The Supremes
'In The Ghetto'	Elvis Presley
'In The Year 2525'	Zager And Evans
'Indian Giver'	1910 Fruitgum Company
'It's Your Thing'	Isley Brothers
'I've Gotta Be Me'	Sammie Davis Jr
'Jean'	Oliver
'Lay Lady Lay'	Bob Dylan
'Love Child'	Diana Ross And The Supremes
'Love Theme from Romeo And Juliet'	Henry Mancini And Orchestra
'My Cherie Amour'	Stevie Wonder
'Na Na Hey Hey Kiss Him Goodbye'	Steam
'One'	Three Dog Night
'One Tin Soldier'	The Original Caste
'Pinball Wizard'	The Who
'Proud Mary'	Creedence Clearwater Revival

'Ramblin' Gamblin' Man'	Bob Seger
'Ruby, Don't Take Your Love To Town'	Kenny Rogers And The First Edition
'Something'	The Beatles
'Son Of A Preacher Man'	Dusty Springfield
'Spinning Wheel'	Blood, Sweat And Tears
'Stormy'	Classics IV
'Sugar Sugar'	Archies
'Suite: Judy Blue Eyes'	Crosby Still And Nash
'Suspicious Minds'	Elvis Presley
'Sweet Caroline'	Neil Diamond
'Take A Letter, Maria'	RB Greaves
'These Eyes'	The Guess Who
'Time Of The Seasons'	Zombies
'Traces'	Classics IV
'Undun'	The Guess Who
'Wedding Bell Blues'	The Fifth Dimension
'Wichita Lineman'	Glen Campbell
'You've Made Me So Very Happy'	Blood, Sweat And Tears

POPULAR AND RELEASED ALBUMS
DECEMBER 1968-NOVEMBER 1969

Abbey Road	The Beatles
Age Of Aquarius	The Fifth Dimension
Alice's Restaurant	Arlo Guthrie
Aretha's Gold	Aretha Franklin
The Association, Greatest Hits Vol 1	The Association
At San Quentin	Johnny Cash
Aoxomoxoa	The Grateful Dead
The Band	The Band
Bayou Country	Creedence Clearwater Revival
The Beatles (White Album)	The Beatles
Beck-Ola	Jeff Beck
Beggar's Banquet	Rolling Stone
Best Of Cream	Cream
The Best Of Bee Gees	Bee Gees

Bless Its Pointed Little Head	Jefferson Airplane
Blind Faith	Blind Faith
Blood, Sweat And Tears	Blood, Sweat And Tears
Brave New World	Steve Miller Band
Chicago Transit Authority	Chicago
Clouds	Joni Mitchell
Crimson And Clover	Tommy James And The Shondells
Crosby Stills And Nash	Crosby, Stills And Nash
Cruising With Ruben And The Jets	Frank Zappa And The
	Mothers Of Invention
Diana Ross And The Supremes Join	Diana Ross And The Supremes/
The Temptations	The Temptations
Elvis	Elvis Presley
Feliciano/10 To 23	Jose Feliciano
Fool On The Hill	Sergio Mendes And Brasil '66
From Elvis In Memphis	Elvis Presley
Galveston	Glen Campbell
Goodbye	Cream
Greatest Hits	Donovan
Green River	Creedence Clearwater Revival
Hair	(soundtrack to movie)
Happy Heart	Andy Williams
Happy Trails	Quicksilver Messenger Service
Help Yourself	Tom Jones
Hot Buttered Soul	Isaac Hayes
It's A Beautiful Day	It's A Beautiful Day
I've Got Dem Ol' Kozmic Blues Again, Mama!	Janis Joplin
Kickin' Out The Jams	MC5
Last Exit	Traffic
Led Zeppelin	Led Zeppelin
Livin' The Blues	Canned Heat
Love Child	Diana Ross And The Supremes
Nashville Skyline	Bob Dylan
Nazz, Nazz	Nazz
On The Threshold Of A Dream	Moody Blues
On Time	Grand Funk Railroad
Portrait Of Petula	Petula Clark

Puzzle People	Temptations
Romeo And Juliet	(soundtrack to movie)
Santana	Santana
Smash Hits	Jimi Hendrix Experience
Songs From A Room	Leonard Cohen
Ssshh	Ten Years After
Stand!	Sly And The Family Stone
Stand Up	Jethro Tull
Stonedhenge	Ten Years After
Suitable For Framing	Three Dog Night
TCB	Diana Ross And The Supremes/The Temptations
The Velvet Underground	The Velvet Underground
Three Dog Night	Three Dog Night
Through The Past Darkly (Big Hits Vol II)	The Rolling Stones
Tommy	The Who
Traffic	Traffic
Uncle Meat	Frank Zappa And The Mothers Of Invention
Wheatfield Soul	The Guess Who
Wichita Lineman	Glen Campbell
Yellow Submarine	The Beatles

AMERICAN TELEVISION
1969 FALL PRIME TIME SCHEDULE

	7:30	8:00	8:30	9:00	9:30	10:00	10:30	
SUN	Land Of The Giants (7-8)			The FBI	The ABC Sunday Night Movie			ABC
	To Rome With Love		Ed Sullivan Show			Leslie Uggams Show	Mission: Impossible	CBS
	Walt Disney's Wonderful World Of Colour		Bill Cosby Show	Bonanza		The Bold Ones		NBC
MON	The Music Scene			The New People		The Survivors	Love, American Style	ABC
	Gunsmoke		Here's Lucy	Mayberry RFD	Doris Day Show		Carol Burnett Show	CBS
	My World And Welcome To It		Rowan And Martin's Laugh-In		NBC Monday Night At The Movies/ Bob Hope Specials/News Specials			NBC
TUE	Mod Squad			Movie Of The Week			Marcus Welby, MD	ABC
	Lancer	Red Skelton Hour			The Governor		CBS News Hour/ 60 Minutes and JJ	CBS
	I Dream of Jeannie		Debbie Reynolds Show		Julia (once a month)	NBC Tuesday Night At The Movies/First Tuesday		NBC
WED	The Flying Nun		Courtship Of Eddies' Father	Room 222	The ABC Wednesday Night Movies			ABC
	Glen Campbell Goodtime Hour			The Beverly Hillbillies	Medical Centre		Hawaii Five-O	CBS
	The Virginian			The Kraft Music Hall		Then Came Bronson		NBC
THU	The Ghost And Mrs Muir		That Girl	Bewitched	This Is Tom Jones		It Takes A Thief	ABC
	Family Affair		Jim Nabors Hour			The CBS Thursday Night Movies		CBS
	Daniel Boone		Ironside		Dragnet 1970		Dean Martin Show	NBC
FRI	Let's Make A Deal		The Brady Bunch	Mr. Deeds Goes To Town	Here Come The Brides		Jimmy Durante Presents The Lennon Sisters Hour	ABC
	Get Smart		Good Guys	Hogan's Heroes	The CBS Friday Night Movies			CBS
	The High Chaparral		The Name Of The Game			Bracken's World		NBC
SAT	The Dating Game		The Newlywed Game	Lawrence Welk Show		The Hollywood Palace	Local	ABC
	Jackie Gleason Show		My Three Sons	Green Acres	Petticoat Junction		Mannix	CBS
	Andy Williams Show		Adam-12	NBC Saturday Night At The Movies				NBC

AMERICAN TELEVISION
1969-70 SEASON

SOME OF THE SATURDAY MORNING CARTOONS
Archie Comedy Hour
Banana Splits Adventure Hour
Bugs Bunny/Road Runner Hour
Bullwinkle Show (Sunday mornings)
The Flintstones
Hot Wheels
The Jetsons
Pink Panther Show
Scooby-Doo, Where Are You?
Spiderman (Sunday mornings)
Tom And Jerry (Sunday mornings)
Underdog

SOME OF THE DAYTIME SOAPS
Another World
As The World Turns
Dark Shadows
Days Of Our Lives
The Doctors
Edge Of Night
General Hospital
Guiding Light
One Life To Live
Secret Storm

NIGHTLY NEWS
ABC Evening News (with Frank Reynolds and Howard K Smith)
CBS Evening News (with Walter Cronkite)
Huntley-Brinkley Report (NBC)

MOVIES OF 1970

Airport
Anne Of The Thousand Days
The Baby Maker
Beneath The Planet Of The Apes
Bloody Mama
A Boy Named Charlie Brown
The Boys In The Band
Catch-22
The Cheyenne Social Club
Chisum
The Computer Wore Tennis Shoes
Cotton Comes To Harlem
Diary Of A Mad Housewife
Fellini Satyricon [Italian]
Five Easy Pieces
The Forbin Project
Gimme Shelter
How To Succeed With Sex
Kelly's Heroes
King Of The Grizzlies
The Landlord
Let It Be
Little Big Man
Love Story
Lovers And Other Strangers
Loving
The Magic Christian
A Man Called Horse
*M*A*S*H*
My Lover, My Son
My Night At Maud's
My Sweet Charlie
Myra Breckenridge
On A Clear Day You Can See Forever
The Owl And The Pussycat

The Passion Of Anna
Patton
Rider On The Rain
Ryan's Daughter
Scrooge
Shark!
Soldier Blue
Start The Revolution Without Me
The Strawberry Statement
Sympathy For The Devil
There's A Girl In My Soup
Tora! Tora! Tora!
Two Mules For Sister Sara
Which Way To The Front?
Woodstock
Zabriskie Point

SOME OF THE BEST-SELLERS AND PUBLISHED BOOKS
1970

FICTION

Bech: A Book	John Updike
Caravan To Vaccares	Alistar MacLean
City Life	Donald Barthelme
Deliverance	James Dickey
The French Lieutenant's Woman	John Fowles
The Gang That Couldn't Shoot Straight	Jimmy Breslin
God Is An Englishman	RF Delderfield
Islands In The Stream	Ernest Hemingway
Jonathan Livingstone Seagull	Richard Bach
Love Story	Erich Segal
Mr Sammler's Planet: A Novel	Saul Bellow
Play It As It Lays: A Novel	Joan Didion
QB VII	Leon Uris
Rich Man, Poor Man	Irwin Shaw
The Secret Woman	Victoria Holt

NON-FICTION

Ball Four   Jim Bouton
Better Homes And Garden's Fondue And Tabletop Cooking
Body Language   Julius Fast
Crime In American   Ramsey Clark (former attorney general)
Crisis In The Classroom: The Remaking Of
  American Education   Charles Silberman
Culture And Commitment: A Study Of The Generation Gap   Margaret Mead
Future Shock   Alvin Toffler
Human Sexual Inadequacy   William Masters and Virginia E Johnson
Inside The Third Reich   Albert Speer
My Lai 4: A Report On The Massacre And Its Aftermath   Seymour M Hersh
Nuremberg And Vietnam: An American Tragedy   Telford Taylor
Of A Fire On The Moon   Norman Mailer
Our Violent Society   David Abrahamson
Our Violent Past   Irving Sloan
Points Of Rebellion   William O Douglas (Supreme Court Justice)
Push Comes To Shove: The Escalation Of Student Protest   Steven Kelman
Radical Chic And Mau-Mauing The Flak Catchers   Tom Wolfe
The Rediscovery Of Black Nationalism   Theodore Draper
The Sensuous Woman: The First How-To Book For
  The Female Who Yearns To Be All Woman   J (Joan Terry Garrity)
Sexual Politics   Kate Millett
Thirteen Seconds: Confrontation At
  Kent State   Joe Eszterhas and Michael D Roberts

POETRY
Caught In The Quiet   Rod McKuen
For The Soul Of The Planet Is Wakening...   Allen Ginsberg

MORRISON HOTEL (album)
Elektra Records, EKS-75007, February 1970

Side 1: 'Roadhouse Blues'/'Waiting For The Sun'/'You Make Me Real'/
'Peace Frog'/'Blue Sunday'/'Ship Of Fools'

Side 2: 'Land Ho!'/'The Spy'/'Queen Of The Highway'/'Indian Summer'/
'Maggie M'Gill'

Producer: Paul A Rothchild
Engineer: Bruce Botnick
Additional musicians: Ray Neapolitan, bass; Lonnie Mack, bass;
Giovanni Puglese (John Sebastian of Lovin' Spoonful), harmonica
('Roadhouse Blues')

November 1969-January 1970: The Doors do recording sessions for
Morrison Hotel at Sunset Sound Recording Studios in Los Angeles.

Billboard's Top LPs: debuted at Number 51 on 7 March 1970: peaked at
Number Four for three weeks, 21 March-4 April; and was out of the
charts after 5 September.

 ROADHOUSE BLUES (Morrison/The Doors)

'You Make Me Real' b/w 'Roadhouse Blues' was released by Elektra as a
45rpm single (#45685) in March 1970.

A live version of 'Roadhouse Blues' is part of the opening of side two of
the posthumous album, *An American Prayer*.

In *The Doors: The Complete Lyrics*, the opening lyrics are transcribed
keep your "hands" on the wheel (p129). Gerstenmeyer transcribes the line
with *hand*, rather than *hands* (p111). Live recordings suggest that
Morrison is indeed singing *hand* and is not dropping the '*s*' of *hands*.
According to Sugerman and Hopkins in *No One Here Gets Out Alive*, these
opening lines about keeping your eyes on the road and hand(s) on the
steering wheel are what Jim said to his perpetually on-and-off again girlfriend, Pamela, as she drove to a cottage Jim had bought behind a country
bar and club in Topanga Canyon, located just northwest of LA (p271; see
also Hopkins, *The Lizard King: The Essential Jim Morrison*, p129). So log-
ically, you better keep your eyes on the road and hands on the wheel after
you leave the free-wheeling interstates of LA and drive the tightly curved
Topanga Canyon road winding through the mountains north of Malibu.

But either *hand* or *hands* would fit within the context of the lyrics, though *hand* leaves unaccountable what the other hand is doing...

In *Riders On The Storm*, Densmore recalls how Lonnie Mack on bass (p235) and John Sebastian on harmonica (p236) contributed to the song.

 WAITING FOR THE SUN (Morrison)

In an untitled selection in *Wilderness*, Morrison sketches out similar imagery of a naked couple racing down by the quiet side of a beach that is "vast" and "radiant" under a moon that is "cool" and "jewelled" where they revelled with laughter of "soft mad children" (p136). An almost identical version is part of the selection titled 'Ghost Song' on the posthumous album *An American Prayer* (p1 of booklet).

 YOU MAKE ME REAL (Morrison)

'You Make Me Real' b/w 'Roadhouse Blues' was released by Elektra as a 45rpm single (#45685) in March 1970. *Billboard*'s Hot 100: debuted at Number 97 on 11 April 1970; peaked at Number 50 on 2 May; and was out of the charts after 16 May.

 PEACE FROG (Morrison/Krieger)

Parts of this lyric are published in *The American Night* (pp109-110).

According to Densmore, Krieger had "this great rhythm guitar lick", but Morrison didn't have any lyrics to go with it; eventually though, Rothchild had Jim recorded two poems on top of each other – one poem as a metaphor of Jim's life, the other of Pam (*Riders On The Storm* pp244-45).

In *The Lizard King: The Essential Jim Morrison*, Jerry Hopkins wrote that, in one of Morrison's notebooks, Manzarek found "Abortion Stories", which included the litany of blood sung in 'Peace Frog' (p129).

The lyric about ghosts of dead Indians crowding a youngster's "fragile eggshell mind" alludes to an early childhood memory of an accident Morrison's family came upon on a highway. This image shaped the opening images for Oliver Stone's film *The Doors*. In the posthumous album *An American Prayer*, a narrative of this event in the selection, 'Dawn's Highway' is printed on page 2 of the lyric booklet inside the album. These two lines lead into the narrative and a recorded portion of 'Peace Frog' follows the narrative.

In an untitled selection in *Wilderness*, the imagery about ghosts of dead Indians crowding a youngster's "fragile egg-shell mind" is printed (p139). The lines appear in another untitled selection in *Wilderness* (p180).

A more detailed account of the making and recording of 'Peace Frog', appears in Hopkins and Sugerman's *No One Here Gets Out Alive* (pp270-71).

 SHIP OF FOOLS (Morrison/Krieger)

In *The Doors: The Complete Lyrics*, the song's lyrics are credited to Jim Morrison (p128).

In 1962, Katherine Anne Porter (1890-1980), best known for her short stories, published her first novel, *Ship Of Fools* (Boston: Little, Brown and Co). The story is about the voyage of a German passenger ship from Mexico to Germany in 1931 just before the rise to power of Hitler and the Nazis. Porter weaves together a rich tapestry of threads that detail and intertwine the fascinating and the mundane of the novel's spectrum of characters in this drifting micro-world of humanity. The novel took her twenty years to write, from August 1941 to August 1961 (p497). The movie version of Porter's story was a box office hit in 1965. Porter noted in the paragraph that prefaces her novel that the title of her book was a "translation from the German of *Das Narrenschiff*, a moral allegory by Sebastian Brant (1458?-1521) first published in Latin as *Stultifera Navis* in 1494." She added that earth as a ship on its voyage to eternity is a simple, universal image that transcends the ages, and she concluded her preface paragraph: "I am a passenger on that ship."

After photographs from the Apollo moon flights came back, especially the earthrise photos, many readily perceived the image that Earth was just an shimmering island, a vibrant spaceship in the vast sea of the universe. Whether or not inspired by the title of Katherine Anne Porter's novel, the "ship of fools" image has been rendered in many different shades by many different artists, and in this song the image of a ship is cast into drug imagery.

 LAND HO! (Morrison/Krieger)

In *The Doors: The Complete Lyrics*, lyrics are credited to Morrison (p128).

In *Riders On The Storm*, Densmore wrote that he "worked up a complicated skiffle beat to 'Land Ho!'" (p234). Skiffle was the sound that inspired John Lennon to form a band with Paul McCartney.

In the Hyperion edition, the lyric is transcribed that grandpa "walked our country miles" (p137). The *our* may be simply a typo, but Morrison clearly sings, "for"…or is it "four"? Gerstenmeyer in a personal correspondence argues that this line could be transcribed as *four*. In the Delta paperback edition, *our* has been revised to *for* (p137). There is no really clear distinction between *for* or *four*, in context or in enunciation.

 THE SPY (Morrison)

The imagery of this lyric may well have been borrowed from the 1954 novel, *A Spy In The House Of Love*, by Anais Nin (1903-1977). In the Doors song, the spy in Morrison's house of love knows the secrets, the deepest fears and dreams, and implies a sense of control. In Nin's novel, the main character, Sabina, is completely insecure with her behaviour, constantly fears she will expose herself with careless behaviour, and needs to continuously pretend and improvise. Whether or not Morrison actually read this novel, he certainly shared Nin's artistic perspective. From interviews with and articles by Nin printed in *A Woman Speaks: The Lectures, Seminars And Interviews Of Anais Nin* (1975), Nin uses language quite kindred to ideas Morrison expressed, especially in his interview with Lizze James. Both talk about how the individual inherits his or hers cultural concept of morality; how guilt is induced by your religion, family, and whoever has had prestige over you; and how each individual needs to rid him or herself of things that are not genuine to him or her. (For Lizze James interviews, see either her article, *Jim Morrison: Ten Years Gone* in *Creem Special Edition: The Doors*

(Summer 1981 pp16-23) or the entries included by Danny Sugerman and Benjamin Edmonds in *The Doors: The Illustrated History* (1983) – *Part I: Lizze James Interview With Jim Morrison* (pp64-67) and *Part II: Lizze James Interview With Jim Morrison* (pp122-24).

 QUEEN OF THE HIGHWAY (Morrison/Krieger)

In *The Doors: The Complete Lyrics*, the song's lyrics are credited to Jim Morrison (p128).

 INDIAN SUMMER (Morrison/Krieger)

In *The Doors: The Complete Lyrics*, lyrics are credited to Morrison (p128).
In an interview with Alan Paul that was printed in *Guitar World*, March 1994, Krieger states that 'Indian Summer' not 'Moonlight Drive' was The Doors' first song (p68). In *Riders On The Storm*, Densmore also wrote that 'Indian Summer' was the group's first song, having stayed "in the can" because of a couple of bad notes from Krieger and Morrison (p244).

 MAGGIE M'GILL (Morrison/The Doors)

In *The Doors: The Complete Lyrics*, the song's lyrics are credited to Morrison (p128).
In *Riders On The Storm*, Densmore recounts how the group initially began working out this song after a disastrous concert at the University of Michigan at Ann Arbor (p201, 237-39). The Doors performed at the University of Michigan's Homecoming Concert on 28 October 1967.

 ABSOLUTELY LIVE (live double album)
Elektra Records, EKS-9002, July 1970

Side 1: 'Who Do Love'/'Medley – Alabama Song'/'Back Door Man'/'Love Hides'/'Five To One'

Side 2: 'Build Me A Woman'/'When The Music's Over'
Side 3: 'Close To You'/'Universal Mind'/'Break On Thru #2'

Side 4: 'The Celebration Of The Lizard'/'Soul Kitchen'

Producer: Paul A Rothchild
Production supervisor: Jac Holzman
Engineer: Bruce Botnick

Billboard's Top LPs: debuted at Number 69 on 8 August 1970; peaked at Number Eight on 5 September; and was out of the charts after 19 December.
Part of the lyrics to 'Universal Mind' are printed in a tour book issued in 1968.

 13 (compilation album)
Elektra Records, EKS-74079, November 1970

Side 1: 'Light My Fire'/'People Are Strange'/'Back Door Man'/'Moonlight Drive'/'The Crystal Ship'/'Roadhouse Blues'
Side 2: 'Touch Me'/'Love Me Two Times'/'You're Lost Little Girl'/'Hello, I Love You'/'Land Ho'/'Wild Child'/'The Unknown Soldier'

Producer,: Paul A Rothchild
Production supervisor: Jac Holzman
Engineer: Bruce Botnick

Billboard's Top LPs: debuted at Number 75 on 19 December 1970; peaked at Number 27 for two weeks, 2-9 January 1971; and was out of the charts after 8 May.

POPULAR SONGS

DECEMBER 1969-NOVEMBER 1970

'ABC'	The Jackson 5
'After Midnight'	Eric Clapton
'American Woman'/'No Sugar Tonight'	The Guess Who
'Ain't No Mountain High Enough'	Diana Ross
'Band Of Gold'	Freda Payne
'Big Yellow Taxi'	Joni Mitchell
'Bridge Over Troubled Water'	Simon And Garfunkel
'Candida'	Dawn
'Cecilia'	Simon And Garfunkel
'Celebrate'	Three Dog Night
'Close To You'	The Carpenters
'Come And Get It'	Badfinger
'Cracklin' Rose'	Neil Diamond
'Does Anybody Really Know What Time It Is?'	Chicago
'Down On The Corner'	Creedence Clearwater Revival
'El Condor Pasa'	Simon And Garfunkel
'Everything Is Beautiful'	Ray Stevens
'Evil Ways'	Santana
'Fire And Rain'	James Taylor
'Green-Eyed Lady'	Sugarloaf
'Gypsy Woman'	Brian Hyland
'Hand Me Down World'	The Guess Who
'Hi-De-Ho'	Blood, Sweat And Tears
'Hitchin' A Ride'	Vanity Fare
'(I Know) I'm Losing You'	Rare Earth
'I Think I Love You'	The Partridge Family
'I'll Be There'	The Jackson 5
'I'll Never Fall In Love Again'	Dionne Warwick
'In The Summertime'	Mungo Jerry
'Indiana Wants Me'	R Dean Taylor
'Instant Karma (We All Shine On)'	John Lennon
'It Don't Matter To Me'	Bread
'Julie, Do Ya Love Me?'	Bobby Sherman

'Kentucky Rain'	Elvis Presley
'Leaving On A Jet Plane'	Peter, Paul And Mary
'Let It Be'	The Beatles
'The Letter'	Joe Cocker
'The Long And Winding Road'	The Beatles
'Look What They've Done To My Song, Ma'	New Seekers
'Love Grows (Where My Rosemary Goes)'	Edison Lighthouse
'Make It With You'	Bread
'Make Me Smile'	Chicago
'Mama Told Me (Not To Come)'	Three Dog Night
'Mississippi Queen'	Mountain
'Montego Bay'	Bobby Bloom
'No Matter What'	Badfinger
'No Time'	The Guess Who
'Ohio'	Crosby, Stills, Nash And Young
'Our House'	Crosby, Stills, Nash And Young
'Patches'	Clarence Carter
'Psychedelic Shack'	The Temptations
'Question'	Moody Blues
'Rain Drops Keep Fallin' On My Head'	BJ Thomas
'The Rapper'	Jaggers
'Ride Captain Ride'	Blues Image
'Rubber Duckie'	Ernie (Jim Henson/*Sesame Street*)
'Shilo'	Neil Diamond
'Signed, Sealed, Delivered (I'm Yours)'	Stevie Wonder
'Solitary Man'	Neil Diamond
'Someday We'll Be Together'	Diana Ross And The Supremes
'Spill The Wine'	Eric Burdon And War
'Spirit In The Sky'	Norman Greenbaum
'Teach Your Children'	Crosby, Stills, Nash And Young
'Tears Of A Clown'	Smokey Robinson And The Miracles
Thank You (Falettin Me Be Mice Elf Agin)'	Sly And The Family Stone
'Time Waits For No One'	Friends Of Distinction
'Travellin' Band'/'Who'll Stop The Rain'	Creedence Clearwater Revival
'25 Or 6 To 4'	Chicago
'Up Around The Bend'	Creedence Clearwater Revival
'Vehicle'	Ides Of March

'Venus'	Shocking Blue
'War'	Edwin Starr
'We've Only Just Begun'	The Carpenters
'Whole Lotta Love'	Led Zeppelin
'Woodstock'	Crosby, Stills, Nash And Young
'Yesterme, Yesteryou, Yesterday'	Stevie Wonder

POPULAR AND RELEASED ALBUMS
DECEMBER 1969-NOVEMBER 1970

ABC	The Jackson 5
Abraxas	Santana
After The Goldrush	Neil Young
Alone Together	Dave Mason
American Woman	The Guess Who
Beaucoups Of Blues	Ringo Starr
Benefit	Jethro Tull
Black Sabbath	Black Sabbath
Blood, Sweat And Tears 3	Blood, Sweat and Tears
Bridge Over Troubled Water	Simon And Garfunkel
Butch Cassidy And The Sundance Kid	Burt Bacharach (soundtrack to movie)
Captured Live At The Forum	Three Dog Night
Chicago	Chicago
Close To You	The Carpenters
Closer To Home	Grand Funk Railroad
Cosmo's Factory	Creedence Clearwater Revival
Curtis	Curtis Mayfield
Deja Vu	Crosby, Stills, Nash And Young
The Devil Made Me Buy This Dress	Flip Wilson
Diana Ross	Diana Ross
Easy Rider	(soundtrack to movie)
Ecology	Rare Earth
Elton John	Elton John
Empty Rooms	John Mayall
Engelbert Humperdinck	Engelbert Humperdinck

Eric Burdon Declares War	Eric Burdon and War
Eric Clapton	Eric Clapton
Everybody Knows This Is Nowhere	Neil Young And Crazy Horse
Frijid Pink	Frijid Pink
Gasoline Alley	Rod Stewart
Get Ready	Rare Earth
Get Yer Ya-Ya's Out	The Rolling Stones
Gold	Neil Diamond
Grand Funk	Grand Funk Railroad
Greatest Hits	The Fifth Dimension
Greatest Hits	Gary Puckett And The Union Gap
Greatest Hits	Sly And The Family Stone
Band Of Gypsys	Jimi Hendrix with Buddy Miles and Billy Cox
Here Comes Bobby	Bobby Sherman
Hey Jude	The Beatles
Hot Buttered Soul	Isaac Hayes
I Am The President	David Frye
Idlewild South	Allman Brothers Band
In The Court Of The Crimson King: An Observation By King Crimson	King Crimson
Iron Butterfly Live	Iron Butterfly
The Isaac Hayes Movement	Isaac Hayes
It Ain't Easy	Three Dog Night
James Gang Rides Again	James Gang
Joe Cocker!	Joe Cocker
John Barleycorn Must Die	Traffic
Led Zeppelin II	Led Zeppelin
Led Zeppelin III	Led Zeppelin
Let It Be	The Beatles
Let It Bleed	The Rolling Stones
Live Steppenwolf	Steppenwolf
Live At Leeds	The Who
Live/Dead	The Grateful Dead
Live Cream	Cream
Live In Las Vegas	Tom Jones
Plastic Ono Band – Live Peace In Toronto	Plastic Ono Band
Mad Dogs And Englishmen	Joe Cocker

Marrying Maiden	It's A Beautiful Day
McCartney	Paul McCartney
Metamorphosis	Iron Butterfly
Monster	Steppenwolf
Moondance	Van Morrison
Mountain Climbing	Mountain
New Morning	Bob Dylan
Number 5	Steve Miller Band
On Stage: February 1970	Elvis Presley
On The Waters	Bread
Monterey	Otis Redding and Jimi Hendrix Experience (soundtrack)
The Partridge Family Album	The Partridge Family
Psychedelic Shack	Temptations
A Question Of Balance	Moody Blues
Raindrops Keep Fallin' On My Head	BJ Thomas
Self Portrait	Bob Dylan
Sentimental Journey	Ringo Starr
Sex Machine	James Brown
Signed, Sealed, Delivered	Stevie Wonder
Stage Fright	The Band
Sweet Baby James	James Taylor
10 Years Together	Peter, Paul And Mary
Third Album	The Jackson 5
To Bonnie From Delaney	Delaney And Bonnie
To Our Children's Children's Children	Moody Blues
Tom	Tom Jones
Tom Rush	Tom Rush
Ummagumma	Pink Floyd
USA Union	John Mayall
Volunteers	Jefferson Airplane
Willie And The Poor Boys	Creedence Clearwater Revival
Woodstock	(soundtrack to movie)
Workingman's Dead	The Grateful Dead

AMERICAN TELEVISION
1970 FALL PRIME TIME SCHEDULE

	7:30	8:00	8:30	9:00	9:30	10:00	10:30	
SUN	The Young Rebels (6-7)		The FBI	The ABC Sunday Night Movie				**ABC**
	Hogan's Heroes		Ed Sullivan Show		Glen Campbell Goodtime Hour		Tim Conway Comedy Hour	**CBS**
	Walt Disney's Wonderful World Of Colour		Bill Cosby Show	Bonanza		The Bold Ones		**NBC**
MON	The Young Lawyers		The Silent Force	NFL Monday Night Football (replaced with movies after 14 December)				**ABC**
	Gunsmoke		Here's Lucy	Mayberry RFD	Doris Day Show		Carol Burnett Show	**CBS**
	Red Skelton Show		Rowan And Martin's Laugh-In		NBC Monday Night At The Movies/ Bob Hope Specials/News Specials			**NBC**
TUE	Mod Squad		Movie Of The Week			Marcus Welby, MD		**ABC**
	The Beverly Hillbillies		Green Acres	Hee Haw	To Rome With Love	CBS News Hour/60 Minutes		**CBS**
	Don Knotts Show		Julia	NBC Tuesday Night At The Movies/First Tuesday (once a month)				**NBC**
WED	Courtship Of Eddies' Father		Make Room For Granddaddy	Room 222	Johnny Cash Show		Dan August	**ABC**
	The Storefront Lawyers		The Governor And JJ	Medical Centre		Hawaii Five-O		**CBS**
	The Men from Shiloh		The Kraft Music Hall		Four-In-One			**NBC**
THU	Matt Lincoln		Bewitched	Barefoot In The Park	The Odd Couple		The Immortal	**ABC**
	Family Affair		Jim Nabors Hour		The CBS Thursday Night Movies			**CBS**
	Flip Wilson Show		Ironside		Nancy	Dean Martin Show		**NBC**
FRI	The Brady Bunch		Nanny And The Professor	The Partridge Family	That Girl	Love, American Style	This Is Tom Jones	**ABC**
	The Interns		The Headmaster		The CBS Friday Night Movies			**CBS**
	The High Chaparral		The Name of the Game		Bracken's World			**NBC**
SAT	Let's Make A Deal		The Newlywed Game	Lawrence Welk Show		The Most Deadly Game	Local	**ABC**
	Mission: Impossible		My Three Sons	Arnie	Mary Tyler	Mannix		**CBS**
	Andy Williams Show		Adam-12	NBC Saturday Night At The Movies				**NBC**

AMERICAN TELEVISION
1970-71 SEASON

SOME OF THE SATURDAY MORNING CARTOONS
Archie's Funhouse
Bugs Bunny/Road Runner Hour
Bullwinkle Show (Sunday mornings)
Heckle And Jeckle Show
Hot Wheels
The Jetsons (Saturday afternoons)
Johnny Quest (Sunday mornings)
Josie And The Pussycats
Pink Panther Show
Scooby-Doo, Where Are You?
Tom And Jerry (Sunday mornings)
Woody Woodpecker Show

SOME OF THE DAYTIME SOAPS
Another World
As The World Turns
Dark Shadows
Days Of Our Lives
The Doctors
Edge Of Night
General Hospital
Guiding Light
One Life To Live
Secret Storm

NIGHTLY NEWS
ABC Evening News (with Harry Reasoner and Howard K Smith)
CBS Evening News (with Walter Cronkite)
NBC Nightly News (with David Brinkley,
John Chancellor and Frank McGee)

MOVIES OF 1971

The Abominable Dr Phibes
The Andromeda Strain
Bananas
Bedknobs And Broomsticks
Big Jake
Billy Jack
Black Jesus
Bless The Beasts And Children
Carnal Knowledge
A Clockwork Orange
The Conformist [Italian]
Daughters Of Darkness
Death In Venice
Diamonds Are Forever
Dirty Harry
Escape From The Planet Of The Apes
Fiddler On The Roof
The French Connection
The Go-Between
The Great Chicago Conspiracy Case
The Great White Hope
A Gunfight
Hoa Binh
The Hospital
Investigation Of A Citizen Above Suspicion
Is There Sex After Death?
Klute
Kotch
The Last Movie
The Last Picture Show
Little Murders
McCabe And Mrs Miller
Minnie And Muskowitz
Murphy's War
Play Misty For Me

Rio Lobo
Shaft
Skin Game
Summer Of '42
Sunday Bloody Sunday
Sweet Sweetback's Baadasssss Song
They Might Be Giants
200 Motels
Vanishing Point
The Villain
When Dinosaurs Ruled The Earth
Who Is Harry Kellerman And Why Is He Saying Those
Terrible Things about Me?
The Wild Country
Wild Rovers
Willard
Willie Wonka And The Chocolate Factory

SOME OF THE BEST-SELLERS AND PUBLISHED BOOKS
1971

FICTION

The Autobiography Of Miss Jane Pittman	Ernest J Gaines
The Betsy	Harold Robbins
Bear Island	Alistar MacLean
The Bell Jar	Sylvia Plath
The Book Of Daniel: A Novel	EL Doctorow
The Day Of The Jackal	Frederick Forsyth
Death Of The Fox	George Garrett
The Drifters	James Michener
The Exorcist	William Peter Blatty
Message From Malaga	Helen MacInnes
Love In The Ruins: The Adventures Of A Bad Catholic At A Time Near The End Of The World	Walker Percy
The Other	Thomas Tryon
Our Gang (Starring Tricky And His Friends)	Philip Roth

The Passions Of The Mind: A Novel Of Sigmund Freud	Irving Stone
Rabbit Redux	John Updike
Summer Of '42	Herman Raucher
The Tenants	Bernard Malamud
Wheels	Arthur Hailey
The Winds Of War	Herman Wouk
Wonderland	Joyce Carol Oates

NON-FICTION

Better Homes And Gardens' Blender Cook Book	
Bury My Heart At Wounded Knee:	
An Indian History Of The American West	Dee Brown
The Closing Circle: Nature, Man And Technology	Barry Commoner
Don't Shoot – We Are Your Children!	J Anthony Lukas
Eleanor And Franklin	Joseph P Lash
The Female Eunuch	Germaine Greer
The Greening Of America: How The Youth Revolution	
Is Trying To Make America Livable	Charles Reich
Honour Thy Father	Gay Talese
I'm OK, You're OK	Thomas Harris
Kent State: What Happened And Why	James Michener
The Prisoner Of Sex	Norman Mailer
The Ra Expeditions	Thor Heyerdahl
The Sensuous Man	M
A Separate Reality: Further Conversations With	
Don Juan	Carlos Castaneda
A Special Rage	Gilbert Moore
Steal This Book	Abbie Hoffman
Tet!	Don Oberdorfer
365 Days	Dr Ronald J Glasser
The Vantage Point: Perspectives Of The Presidency,	
1963-1969	Lyndon Baines Johnson
Wunnerful, Wunnerful!	Lawrence Welk

POETRY

Fields Of Wonder	Rod McKuen

LA WOMAN (album)
Elektra Records, EKS-75011, April 1971

Side 1: 'The Changeling'/'Love Her Madly'/'Been Down So Long'/'Cars Hiss By My Window'/'LA Woman'

Side 2: 'L'America'/'Hyacinth House'/'Crawling King Snake'/'The WASP'(Texas Radio And The Big Beat)/'Riders On The Storm'

Producer: Bruce Botnick and The Doors
Additional musicians: Marc Benno, rhythm guitar; Jerry Scheff, bass

In *No One Here Gets Out Alive*, Hopkins and Sugerman wrote that, after hearing the first working tape of *LA Woman*, Jac Holzman, Elektra's president, thought, "I'm listening to Jim's final album as a vocalist" (p341).

November-December: The Doors undertake recording sessions for *LA Woman* at The Doors Workshop (the office for The Doors) in Los Angeles.

Billboard's Top LPs: debuted at Number 56 on 8 May 1971; peaked at Number Nine on 5 June; and was out of the charts after 25 December.

 THE CHANGELING

'Riders On The Storm' b/w 'The Changeling' was released by Elektra as a 45rpm single (#45738) in June 1971.

According to Hopkins and Sugerman, the lyrics for 'The Changeling' were written in 1968 (*No One Here Gets Out Alive* p320).

Among the student films that were shown in 1968 at the University of Southern California was one titled *Changeling*.

In looking up meanings of the word *changeling*, I found several: one apt to change; a disloyal person; a child (usually an infant) secretly substituted for another; (*Archaic* meaning) a simpleton, idiot or imbecile. From various dictionaries and encyclopedias about the world of fairy mythology came the following accounts about *changelings*. A changeling is a fairy substituted for a stolen human baby; the substituted fairy could have been a fairy baby or an elder fairy who was no longer useful to the fairy tribe. Though these tales of changelings were evident in Northern European legends about fairies or dwarfs, the predominant references came from Ireland – the artistic heritage for the drunken Irish poet, Jim Morrison. Usually, according to the accounts, the birth of a handicapped or other exceptionally abnormal child was explained away with the story of a changeling. Kind of appropriate for Morrison's ostracised relationship with his parents…

In her novel *Ship Of Fools* Katherine Ann Porter includes a passage about *changelings*, as one of the main female characters compares her current boyfriend to her childhood memory of what her old Scottish nurse told about changelings (p400).

The "swarming street(s)" image of this song appears in several writings by Morrison: (1) in an untitled selection, Morrison writes of being free of the "swarming streets" while in a womb or tomb (*Wilderness* p9); (2) in an untitled selection, Morrison writes about his ears assembling music out of the "swarming streets" (*Wilderness* p79); and (3) in the selection entitled, *An American Prayer* Morrison writes about fleeing the streets' "swarming wisdom" (*The American Night* p5; and p7 of booklet in the posthumous album, *An American Prayer*).

In an interview with Bob Chorush, Morrison stated he didn't think there had ever been a real riot at any of The Doors' concerts but the commotion had emanated from a "swarming theory" about animal and insect species that swarm together when they start out stripping the food supply: "It's a way of communicating. Working out a solution or signalling an awareness to each other. Signalling that there is a danger…" Jim then extends the idea to discuss people in many big cities feeling crowded: "People are getting very erotic and paranoid and I guess things like rock concerts are a form of human swarming to communicate this uneasiness about overpopulation. I haven't really got it all worked out yet…" (*An Interview With Jim Morrison: The Lizard King Reforms: Taking The Snake And Wearing It, Los Angeles Free Press* 15 January 1971, p24).

LOVE HER MADLY

'Love Her Madly' b/w 'Don't Go No Further' (cover of a Willie Dixon song) was released by Elektra as a 45rpm single (#45726) in March 1971. *Billboard*'s Hot 100: debuted at Number 103 on 3 April 1971; peaked at Number Eleven for two weeks, in 15-22 May; and was out of the charts after 19 June.

In *The Doors: The Complete Lyrics*, the song's by-line is "Lyrics by Robby Krieger" (p146). In an interview with Robert Matheu, Krieger said he composed the song 'Love Her Madly' (*Creem Special Edition: The Doors* Summer 1981 p59).

Manzarek, in *Light My Fire: My Life With The Doors*, wrote that this song was a "chugging, tuneful tribute to a fight" Krieger had with a girl-friend (p12).

 BEEN DOWN SO LONG

The inspiration for the title and refrain of this song was Richard Farina's book *Been Down So Long It Looks Like Up To Me* published in 1966 two days before Farina's death in a motorcycle accident. The book catalogues the events of college student (at the time, "campus hippie"), Gnossos Pappadopoulis. The book's cataloguing of the American culture's banality, as Maybelle Lacey wrote in the review of the book in *Library Journal*, "rolls with its own momentum," but "coarse language and the last possible word in sex and physiological descriptions does exceed all limits of good taste" (1 April 1966, p1924). At that time. Basically a culturally saturated cynic whose actions reflect his lingering adolescent perspective of the world, Gnossos probably provided a kindred spirit with whom Morrison identified.

 CARS HISS BY MY WINDOW

This song has an uncanny similarity to John Lee Hooker's 'Nightmare' as released on John Lee Hooker, *The Hook: 20 Years Of Hits And Hot*

Boogie [CD] (Chameleon Records, D2-74794, 1989; VeeJay Hall of Fame Series).
According to Hopkins and Sugerman, the lyrics were taken from one of Jim's Venice Beach notebooks (*No One Here Gets Out Alive* p320).
In the final lyrical stanza, I transcribe Morrison singing, "A cold girl'll kill you," as it is in *The Doors: The Complete Lyrics*. Gerstenmeyer transcribes it as "Ah, cold girl I'll kill you" (p140). In a personal correspondence, Gerstenmeyer discusses the possibility of either line and states the Krieger said the "cold girl I'll kill you" is correct. In a later correspondence, Gerstenmeyer writes:

> "'Cold girl I'll kill' fits better into the context. He lies in the room with a girl who is absolutely passive and he's active. I'm pretty sure it has to be [this] and that [Morrison] is intentionally mumbling a little bit, so that it does not sound so cruel. And of course he does not mean 'kill' literally... He lies there with a 'cold' girl and at the end he decides to 'kill' her."

But if this song is viewed in the larger landscape of a maturing artistic vision of The Doors (and hence, Jim Morrison) Morrison may be expressing his own passivity to forces he can't control. Images of being the "Lizard King" who can do *anything* have faded since that third album. This song laments a far deeper rift between two people that transcends any superficial sarcasm about a plastic twentieth century fox living on Love Street or being a prisoner of her own device. This relationship isn't superficial; it has the power to explode more forcefully and cause more devastation than previous portrayed relationships because there is a chilling reality of expected anticipation from repeated experience, like the waves and cars in this song. Though more subtle, these images are more powerful than the blatant sarcasm in earlier songs because you don't know when or how the scene will explode. The suddenness of a "sonic boom" punctuates the growing possibility that a *cold girl* will kill him "in a darkened room." Not only emotionally, but very possibly physically. Though Morrison doesn't admit his control has been upset by unexpected forces, there is the undercurrent reality that it has been. No longer condescending toward lovers as in previous songs, Morrison may be realising others have the power to destroy him – or at least may be recognising his personal vulnerability. The song wouldn't fit in the context of the previous albums, but fits the landscape rendered in this last album.

Either line certainly adds a sinister twist to the meaning of the lyric. But such altering between what may have been written and what was sung would not have beyond Morrison's artistic liberty – or intent.

Listener discretion is advised.

 LA WOMAN

Lyric as written by Jim Morrison is published in *The American Night* (pp114-15). Compare imagery of this song with imagery in a poem about the city in *The Lords And The New Creatures* (p12). Also compare Morrison's lyrical portrait of Los Angeles with Arthur Rimbaud's poetic portrait of Paris in Wallace Fowlie's translation of *Parisian Orgy Or Paris Is Repopulated* (*L'Orgie Parisienne, Ou Paris Se Repeuple*) (*Rimbaud: Complete Works, Selected Letters* pp82-87).

Morrison uses the phrase "city of night," from John Rechy's book, *City Of Night*. Published in 1963, the novel portrays a world of "sexual perversion and homosexuality," a – as Lloyd W. Griffin wrote in his book review in the *Library Journal* – "cool, level, extremely graphic account of a piece of sub-cultural America as true, unfortunately, as the facets of America revealed by Tom Wolfe or Robert Frost" and follows an unnamed narrator who "has seen it all and has struggled unsuccessfully to break away from a life of loneliness and loss, terror and the search for reality in a hostile (indifferent) and unreal world" (July 1963 pp2228-29). Certainly what must have appealed to Morrison was the vividly descriptive physical and psychological tour from Times Square in New York City to Pershing Park in Los Angeles, to the Navy docks of San Diego to San Francisco to the grandest parade of masks, the Mardi Gras in New Orleans that Rechy provides of this frenzied, wanton sub-culture which Morrison no doubt had journeyed, if but casually, through in the mid-1960s. Like Rechy's unnamed narrator who perpetually seeks solitude from the city of night only to return, evoking the same feeling most people experience when trying to find self-meaning and security, so Morrison continually returns to his city of night, LA Woman.

In *The Doors: The Complete Lyrics*, the lyric, "Mr Mojo risin'" is printed as "Mister Mojo risin'" (pp150-151). In *No One Here Gets Out Alive*, Hopkins and Sugerman transcribe the lyric as "Mr Mojo Risin'" (p320). In *Riders On The Storm*, Densmore details how Morrison showed the group how he could derive "Mr Mojo Risin" from "Jim Morrison" (p259). Sugerman and Hopkins noted in a tone of jest they believed Jim used when he said "Mr Mojo" was not only part of an anagram for his name, but also the name he would use "when contacting the office after he'd split to Africa" (*No One Here Gets Out Alive* p343). If we accept that, then I agree with Gerstenmeyer who wrote that "if you write 'Mister Mojo' instead of 'Mr Mojo'…the anagram is lost." Hence, it is "Mr Mojo," not "Mister Mojo."

Since "mojo" was a black slang word for sexual prowess (Jimmy Smith's blues song 'Got My Mojo Working'), Densmore wrote that he would "steadily increase the tempo back up to the original speed, a la orgasm" (*Riders On The Storm* p259). Or was "mojo" inspired by the greasy and diminutive character, Oswald Mojo who married Pamela, a British girl who turned out to be an oil heiress, in Farina's *Been Down So Long It Looks Like Up To Me*?

The only recorded live performance of 'LA Woman' is on the bootleg recording, *If It Ain't One Thing, It's Another (Live At The Felt Forum NY And Dallas, Texas 1970)* [triple album; Felt Forum 17 and 18 January 1970 – sides 1, 2, 3 and 4; Dallas 11 December 1970 – sides 5 and 6]. In this version, Morrison varies the studio recorded lyric, "Never saw a lady." He sings, "Never saw a lady/look so down and so alone" and "Never saw a lady/look so down and all alone." Soon after, Morrison croons variations around the lyric, "never saw someone look so down and all alone." And he alters the second singing of the line about LA being "just another lost angel, City of Night" to "just another dark witness in the city of night."

There is a transcription of the song appearing in an article written by Robert L Doerschuk *Ray Manzarek Of The Doors: Waiting For The Nubians* printed in the February 1991 issue of *Keyboard Magazine* (p87).

⊙ L'AMERICA

The word 'L'america' appears as *Lamerica*, *LAmerica*, *L'america* and *lamerica* in some of Morrison's poetic tidbits. In an untitled poem, *Lamerica* appears in the first three lines, and then *lamerica* appears in the rest of the poem (*Wilderness*, pp7-8); two other poems shared the title 'LAMERICA'; another had the title 'LAmerica' (*Wilderness*, p87); in another, entitled 'L'AMERICA', *L'america* appears in the first line and then *Lamerica* appears in the rest of the poem (*The American Night*, p140); and in a handwritten copy of the lyrics, the title is spelled 'Lamerica', with the lighter corrections of *'A* written over the original spelling (*The Doors Quarterly Magazine*, issue 25, 1992, p28).

Morrison's enunciation is *la-mer-ee-ca*. Therefore, should it be *La'merica?* Morrison's intent is to shift our perception of *America* – and hence all of the typical implied images and meanings with that word – to a different viewpoint with the exotic and strange-sounding *L'America*.

Written and recorded months before the rest of the songs for this album, the song was intended for Michelangelo Antonioni's *Zabriskie Point*, but it was rejected by Antonioni. Though spared from being part of what critics almost universally panned as a bomb by the Italian film director, The Doors' artistic vision seemed quite similar in focus to Antonioni's; however, The Doors drew the images and impulses of America that Antonioni clumsily pieced together into a more fluid impression. After Densmore had explained how Morrison tried telling Antonioni that the apostrophe after the *L* was short for Latin America, or anywhere south of the border, John described the recording session with Antonioni, surmising that the song was too much for the director, since he wouldn't understand the "cryptic references to money [beads] and grass [gold – as in Acapulco]", and the song, with it's "dark, disso-nant chords" of Robby's guitar resonating like cold steel and overshad-owing Jim's strong singing, summarised the movie (*Riders On The Storm*, pp254-5).

Although the rhyme scheme in the second stanza suggests the word *fuck*, neither *The Doors: The Complete Lyrics* nor Gerstenmeyer note the very faded shriek of *'uck* to close this line. In a personal correspondence, Gerstenmeyer writes: "Ray Manzarek screams 'Uh!' in the background." Manzarek, in an interview printed in the February 1991 issue of *Keyboard* magazine, said about the song: "The song was intended to be the opening theme for *Zabriskie Point*, so that dissonance [in the opening] was for the danger of going across the highway. And the blues section, of course, was 'the Rain Man's coming to town. Change your luck. Teach your women how to *f-f-f-f...find* themselves.' Ooh, Jim! We thought you were gonna say *fuck* [laughs]. Good lyric!" (p88).

In *The Lords And The New Creatures*, Morrison writes that, in ancient communities, the "stranger" was perceived as the "greatest menace" (p12), a contrast to the friendly strangers in this song.

In the piece titled 'The Celebration Of The Lizard', a line appears about rain falling "gently on the town", echoing the image of the strangers in the song coming to town like a "gentle rain" (*The American Night*, p41, and on the inside sleeve of the album *Waiting For The Sun*).

 HYACINTH HOUSE

In *Riders On The Storm*, Densmore suggests a connection with the Greek Hyacinth myth (pp257-8), but somehow the disjointed images of Jim's lyric are too mundane or neutral to invoke any sense of despair and tragedy, as in the myth. The Hyacinth House in question seems to be another version of the house on Love Street; it doesn't offer sanctuary or imprisonment, just something to pass through, like a museum.

In an interview with *Guitar World* in May 1991, Robby Krieger says: "It was a very odd vocal – a very, *very* odd vocal. I didn't know what to make of it then, and I still don't. We wrote that one night when Jim was over at my house, and we were watching these raccons in my back yard. That's where he got the lions." (p46)

In *No One Here Gets Out Alive*, Jerry Hopkins and Danny Sugerman wrote that, after Morrison sang the line about seeing that the "bathroom is clear", Manzarek played a melody from Chopin's "Til The End Of

Time' (p342).

The lyric about throwing away the jack of hearts may be an allusion to the "jack o' diamonds is a hard card to play" line in a Richard Fariña poem (the opening page of *Long Time Coming*).

 CRAWLING KING SNAKE (John Lee Hooker/Bernard Besman)

Bernard Besman provided the following information: the song was recorded at United Sound Studios in Detroit, Michigan, on 18 February 1949, and was released on Modern Records (#20-714); that Besman copyrihgted the song on 21 May 1968; and that the 1949 recording was later transferred to the CD *John Lee Hooker: The Legendary Modern Recordings 1948-1954* (Virgin Records, America [Flair], 7243 8 39658 2 3, 1993).

Morrison's version of the song is closer to a later recording of the song recorded by Hooker on VeeJay Records, for whom Hooker recorded during the 1950s. The song was reproduced on *The Hook: 20 Years Of Hits And Hot Boogie* (CD, Chameleon Records, D2-7494, 1989, VeeJay 'Hall Of Fame' series).

 RIDERS ON THE STORM

'Riders On The Storm' b/w 'The Changeling' was released by Elektra as a 45rpm single (#45738) in June 1971. *Billboard*'s Hot 100: debuted at Number 74 on 3 July 1971, peaked at Number 14 on 4 September, and was out of the charts after 18 September.

According to Densmore, in *Riders On The Storm*, Elektra president Jac Holzman convinced the group to release 'Love Her Madly' as the first single, and if it hit the Top Five on the AM radio stations then 'Riders On The Storm' would garner lots of playing time as a single on FM stations (p266). John added that he and engineer/producer Bruce Botnik edited some of Manzarek's piano solo in order to cut down the length of the song for radio play (p266).

The last Doors song on this album was, as Manzarek said in the radio program *History Of Rock 'n' Roll*, the last one Morrison ever sang, the last one The Doors recorded, and the last one for the album. Segments of the song were used as background music for a narrative piece entitled 'The Hitchhiker' on the posthumous album *An American Prayer*.

In interview Alan Paul which was printed in *Guitar World* in March 1994, Krieger said that the group was "fooling around with 'Ghost Riders In The Sky' one day and somehow it turned into 'Riders On The Storm' (p189).

In *Light My Fire, My Life With The Doors*, Manzarek writes that, after the group had listened to the recorded version of the song, Robby said that the song made him feel like he was out on a desert with big thunderclouds in the distance, and he suggested adding the sound of thunder and rain (p8).

A variation of the lyric about the killer's brain squirming "like a toad" appears in Morrison's roughed-out screenplay entitled *The Hitchhiker (An American Pastoral)*. Jim describes Billy, the murderous hitchhiker, in a car, and he is singing along with "wild abandon" to the Rolling Stones' '(I Can't Get No) Satisfaction' while he "squirms in his seat like a toad" (*The American Night*, p78).

A transcription of the music and lyrics appears in the December issue of *Words And Music* (Vol 1, No 1, pp14-18). There is also a transcription of the song included in an article by Robert L Doerschuk, 'Ray Manzarek Of The Doors: Waiting For The Nubians', printed in the February 1991 issue of *Keyboard* (pp84-5).

POPULAR SONGS
DECEMBER 1970-SEPTEMBER 1971

'Ain't No Sunshine'	Bill Withers
'Amos Moses'	Jerry Reed
'Another Day'	Paul McCartney
'Bangla Desh'	George Harrison
'Beginnings'/'Colour My World'	Chicago
'Black Magic Woman'	Santana
'Bridge Over Troubled Water'	Aretha Franklin
'Brown Sugar'	The Rolling Stones

223

'Chick-A-Boom'	Daddy Dewdrop
'Don't Pull Your Love'	Hamilton, Joe Frank And Reynolds
'Draggin' The Line'	Tommy James
'For All We Know'	The Carpenters
'Get It On'	Chase
'Go Away Little Girl'	Donny Osmond
'Have You Ever Seen The Rain?'	Creedence Clearwater Revival
'Hot Pants Part 1 (She Got To Use What She Got	
To Get What She Wants)'	James Brown
'How Can You Mend A Broken Heart?'	Bee Gees
'I Am...I Said'	Neil Diamond
'I Just Want To Celebrate'	Rare Earth
'If'	Bread
'If I Were Your Woman'	Gladys Knight And The Pips
'If Not For You'	Olivia Newton-John
'If You Could Read My Mind'	Gordon Lightfoot
'I'll Meet You Halfway'	The Partridge Family
'I'm 18'	Alice Cooper
'Immigrant Song'	Led Zeppelin
'Indian Reservation'	Paul Revere And The Raiders
'It Don't Come Easy'	Ringo Starr
'It's Too Late'/'I Feel The Earth Move'	Carol King
'Joy To The World'	Three Dog Night
'Just My Imagination (Running Away With Me)'	Temptations
'Knock Three Times'	Dawn
'Layla'	Derek And The Dominos
'Liar'	Three Dog Night
'Lonely Days'	Bee Gees
'Love Story (Where Do I Begin?)'	Andy Williams
'Love The One You're With'	Stephen Stills
'Lucky Man'	Emerson, Lake And Palmer
'Maggie May'	Rod Stewart
'Me And Bobby McGee'	Janis Joplin
'Me And My Arrow'	Nilsson
'Me And You And A Dog Named Boo'	Lobo
'Mercy Mercy Me (The Ecology)'	Marvin Gaye
'Moon Shadow'	Cat Stevens

'Mr Big Stuff'	Jean Knight
'Mr Bojangles'	Nitty Gritty Dirt Band
'My Sweet Lord'/'Isn't It A Pity?'	George Harrison
'Never Can Say Goodbye'	The Jackson Five
'Never-Ending Song Of Love'	Delaney And Bonnie And Friends
'The Night They Drove Old Dixie Down'	Joan Baez
'One Bad Apple'	Osmonds
'One Less Bell To Answer'	The Fifth Dimension
'One Toke Over The Line'	Brewer And Shipley
'Power To The People'	John Lennon And The Plastic Ono Band
'Put Your Hand In The Hand'	Ocean
'Rainy Days And Mondays'	The Carpenters
'Reason To Believe'	Rod Stewart
'Resurrection Shuffle'	Ashton, Gardner And Dyke
'She's A Lady'	Tom Jones
'Signs'	Five-Man Electric Band
'Smiling Faces Sometimes'	Undisputed Truth
'Sooner Or Later'	Grass Roots
'Spanish Harlem'	Aretha Franklin
'Stoney End'	Barbra Streisand
'The Story In Your Eyes'	Moody Blues
'Superstar'	The Carpenters
'Superstar (*Jesus Christ Superstar*)'	Murray Head With The Trinidad Singers
'Sweet And Innocent'	Donny Osmond
'Take Me Home, Country Roads'	John Denver
'Temptation Eyes'	Grass Roots
'That's The Way I've Always Heard It Should Be'	Carly Simon
'Theme From Love Story'	Henry Mancini And His Orchestra
'Timothy'	Buoys
'Treat Her Like A Lady'	Cornelius Brothers And Sister Rose
'Uncle Albert'/'Admiral Halsey'	Paul And Linda McCartney
'Want Ads'	Honey Cone
'We Gotta Get You A Woman'	Todd Rundgren
'Wedding Song (There Is Love)'	Paul Stookey
'What Is Life'	George Harrison
'What's Going On'	Marvin Gaye

'What The World Needs Now Is Love'/
  'Abraham, Martin And John'   Tom Clay
'When You're Hot, You're Hot'   The Who
'Your Song'   Elton John
'You've Got A Friend'   James Taylor

POPULAR AND RELEASED ALBUMS
DECEMBER 1970-SEPTEMBER 1971

All Things Must Pass	George Harrison
Aqualung	Jethro Tull
Aretha Live At Fillmore West	Aretha Franklin
At Fillmore East	Allman Brother Band
BS&T4	Blood, Sweat And Tears
Best Of The Guess Who	The Guess Who
Blows Against The Empire	Paul Kantner And The Jefferson Starship
Blue	Joni Mitchell
Carly Simon	Carly Simon
Carpenters	The Carpenters
Chase	Chase
Chicago III	Chicago
Cry Of Love	Jimi Hendrix
Elvis Country	Elvis Presley
Emerson, Lake And Palmer	Emerson, Lake And Palmer
Every Good Boy Deserves Favour	Moody Blues
Every Picture Tells A Story	Rod Stewart
Four-Way Street	Crosby, Still, Nash And Young
Golden Biscuits	Three Dog Night
Homemade	Osmonds
If I Could Only Remember My Name	David Crosby
If You Could Read My Mind	Gordon Lightfoot
James Taylor And The Original Flying Machine	James Taylor
Jesus Christ Superstar	Various Artists
John Lennon/Plastic Ono Band	John Lennon And The Plastic Ono Band
Ladies Of The Canyon	Joni Mitchell

Layla And Other Assorted Love Songs	Derek And The Dominos
Live Album	Grand Funk Railroad
Lova Vs Powerman And The Moneygoround	Kinks
Love It To Death	Alice Cooper
Love Story	(soundtrack to movie)
Love Story	Andy Williams
Manna	Bread
Maybe Tomorrow	The Jackson Five
Mud Slide Slim And The Blue Horizon	James Taylor
Nantucket Sleighride	Mountain
Naturally	Three Dog Night
Osmonds	Osmonds
Paranoid	Black Sabbath
Pearl	Janis Joplin
Pendulum	Creedence Clearwater Revival
Poems, Prayers And Promises	John Denver
The Point!	Nilsson
Ram	Paul And Linda McCartney
Rose Garden	Lynn Anderson
Runt	Todd Rundgren
17-11-70	Elton John
Shaft	Isaac Hayes (soundtrack to movie)
Songs For Beginners	Graham Nash
Stephen Stills	Stephen Stills
Sticky Fingers	The Rolling Stones
Stoney End	Barbra Streisand
Super Bad	James Brown
Survival	Grand Funk Railroad
Tapestry	Carole King
Tarkus	Emerson, Lake And Palmer
Tea For The Tillerman	Cat Stevens
Thirds	James Gang
This Is A Recording	Lily Tomlin
To Be Continued	Isaac Hayes
Tumbleweed Connection	Elton John
Up To Date	The Partridge Family
Whales And Nightingales	Judy Collins

What's Going On	Marvin Gaye
Who's Next	The Who
Worst Of Jefferson Airplane	Jefferson Airplane

DISCOGRAPHY AND FILMOGRAPHY

The following sampling of sources reflect the works that contributed to this book:

A) Audio recordings of The Doors (chronological listing up through 1991 releases)
B) A sampling of radio and television specials on The Doors (alphabetical listing)
C) Videos (alphabetical listing)
D) Books, magazines, and newspapers (alphabetical listing)

I owe many thanks to Kerry Humpherys who shared with me his extensive personal collection of Doors recordings.

The following recordings were referred to in regards to The Doors' recordings of 'Back Door Man', 'Cars Hiss By My Window', 'Crawling King Snake', 'Light My Fire', 'Little Red Rooster' and 'Who Do You Love'.

Coltrane, John. *The Best Of John Coltrane* [CD]. Altantic, 1541-2, 1970. (For comparison to the dual solos in 'My Favourite Things' which inspired the structure of dual solos in 'Light My Fire'.)

Dixon, Willie. *I Am The Blues* [album]. Columbia, PC 9987. Reissued on CD by Mobile Fidelity Sound Lab, MFCD 872 (Columbia, copyright 1970). *Original Master Recording* series. (Includes 'Back Door Man' and 'The Little Red Rooster'.)

Hammond, John Jr *The Best Of John Hammond* [CD]. Vanguard, VCD-11/2, 1986/87; reissue of 1970 double album. (Includes 'Who Do You Love' and 'Backdoor Man' and Chuck Berry is credited as writer of 'Backdoor Man'.)

Hooker, John Lee. *John Lee Hooker: The Legendary Modern Recordings 1948-1954* [CD]. Virgin Records America (Flair), 7243 8 39658 2 3, 1993. (Includes 'Crawling King Snake'.)

Hooker, John Lee. *The Hook: 20 Years Of Hits And Hot Boogie* [CD]. Chameleon Records, D2-74794, 1989. VeeJay Hall of Fame Series. (Includes 'Crawling King Snake' and 'Nightmare'.)

Howlin' Wolf (Chester Burnett). *Howlin' Wolf: His Greatest Sides, Vol 1* [cassette]. Chess Records (MCA Records), CHC-9107, 1983. (Includes 'The Red Rooster' and 'Back Door Man'.)

SINGLES

'Break On Through'/'End of the Night'
45rpm single, Elektra, 45611, January 1967.

'Light My Fire'/'The Crystal Ship'
45rpm single, Elektra, 45615, April 1967.

'People Are Strange'/'Unhappy Girl'
45rpm single, Elektra, 45621, September 1967.

'Love Me Two Times'/'Moonlight Drive'
45rpm single, Elektra, 45624, November 1967.

'The Unknown Soldier'/'We Could Be So Good Together'
45rpm single, Elektra, 45628, March 1968.

'Hello, I Love You'/'Love Street'
45rpm single, Elektra, 45635, June 1968.

'Touch Me'/'Wild Child'
45rpm single, Elektra, 45646, December 1968.

'Wishful Sinful'/'Who Scared You'
45rpm single, Elektra, 45656, February 1969.

'Tell All The People'/'Easy Ride'
45rpm single, Elektra, 45663, May 1969.

'Runnin' Blue'/'Do It'
45rpm single, Elektra, 45675, August 1969.

'You Make Me Real'/'Roadhouse Blues'
45rpm single, Elektra, 45685, March 1970.

'Love Her Madly'/'Don't Go No Further'
45rpm single, Elektra, 45726, March 1971.

'Light My Fire'/'Love Me Two Times'
45rpm single, "Spun Gold" Series, E-45051, April 1971.

'Touch Me'/'Hello, I Love You'
45rpm single, "Spun Gold" Series, E-45052, April 1971.

'Riders On The Storm'/'The Changeling'
45rpm single, Elektra, 45738, June 1971.

'Tightrope Ride'/'Variety Is The Spice Of Life'
45rpm single, Elektra, 45757, November 1971.

'Ship With Sails'/'In The Eye Of The Sun'
45rpm single, Elektra, 45768, May 1972.

'Get Up And Dance'/'Treetrunk'
45rpm single, Elektra, 454793, July 1972.

'The Mosquito'/'It Slipped My Mind'

45rpm single, Elektra, 45807, August 1972.

'Riders On The Storm'/'Love Her Madly'
45rpm single, "Spun Gold" Series, E-45059, September 1972.

'The Piano Bird'/'Good Rockin''
45rpm single, Elektra, 45825, November 1972.

'LA Woman'/'Roadhouse Blues'
45rpm single, "Spun Gold" Series, Elektra, 45122.

'People Are Strange'/'Break On Through'
45rpm single, "Spun Gold" Series, Elektra, 45123.

'Love Her Madly'/'Riders On The Storm'//'Touch Me'/'Light My Fire'
45rpm EP, Elektra, EPE 230 MX 165842, 1980 (Australian release).

'Roadhouse Blues' (stereo)/'Roadhouse Blues' (mono)
45rpm promotional single, Elektra/Asylum Records, E-46005-A, 1978.

'Roadhouse Blues'/'Albinoni Adagio'
45rpm single, Elektra, E-46005, January 1979.

'Hello, I Love You'/'Love Me Two Times'//'Ghost Song'/'Roadhouse Blues'
(both from *An American Prayer*)
45rpm double pack, Elektra, K 12215, 1979 (UK pressing).

'The End'/'The Delta' (Carmine Coppola and Francis Coppola) (in con-
junction with Francis Coppola's movie *Apocalypse Now*)
45rpm single, Elektra K 12400 (EF-90166), 1979.

'Gloria'/'Love Me Two Times'
33⅓rpm single from *Alive, She Cried*, Elektra, E 9774T, 1983 (UK
pressing).

'Gloria' (clean edit)/'Gloria' (dirty album version)
33⅓rpm promotional single, Elektra/Asylum Records, EAOR 4942, 1983.

'Love Me Two Times'/'Moonlight Drive' (includes 'Horse Latitudes') 33¹/₃rpm promotional single, Elektra/Asylum Records, EAOR 4955, 1983.

'Light My Fire' (album version, 1985)'/'Light My Fire (edit of live version, *Live At The Hollywood Bowl*, 1987) 33¹/₃rpm promotional single, Elektra/Asylum/Nonesuch Records, 5245.

'Break on Through'/'Love Street'//'Hello, I Love You'/'Touch Me' 33¹/₃rpm promotional copy, Elektra Entertainment, 7559-66556-0, 1991 (UK pressing).

'Light My Fire'/'People Are Strange' and 'Soul Kitchen' 33¹/₃rpm single, Elektra Entertainment, 7559-66537-0, 1991 (UK pressing).

'Riders On The Storm'/'Roadhouse Blues' (live) and 'Love Her Two Times' (live) 33¹/₃rpm single, Elektra, 7559-66509-0, 1991 (UK pressing).

'The Unknown Soldier' (The Doors)/'A Soldier's View Of Vietnam' (Doc Kennedy) 33¹/₃rpm single, Elektra/Asylum/Nonesuch Records, PR 8001, no date (circa 1980s). Special limited edition twelve-inch single from 98 KZEW in support of the Vietnam Veterans Memorial Fund of Texas.)

'Break On Through' (from Oliver Stone's film *The Doors*) CD single, Elektra, PRCD 8314-2, 1991.

'Light My Fire' (3:04)/'Love Me Two Times' (3:15) CD single, Elektra, 45051-2, no date.

'The Ghost Song' CD single, Elektra, EKR 205CD 7559-66119-2, 1995 (UK pressing). Includes 'The Ghost Song', 'Roadhouse Blues' (live), 'Love Me Two Times' (live), Jim Morrison Interview (1:25).

ALBUMS/COMPACT DISCS

The Doors (album). Elektra Records, EKL-74007 mono, EKS-74007 stereo, January 1967.
The Doors (cassette), TC5-4007.
The Doors (eight-track cassette). ET8-4007.
The Doors (album). Mobile Fidelity Sounds Lab, MFSL 1-051, 1980. Half-speed production and mastering; "Original Master Recording" series.
The Doors (CD). Elektra/Asylum Records, 74007-2, November 1983. (The version pressed by PolyGram in West Germany lists Robby Krieger as "Bobby Krieger".)
The Doors (24ct gold-plated CD). DDC Compact Classics, Inc. (Northridge, CA), GZS-1023, July 1992. (Pressed in Japan.)

Strange Days (album). Elektra Records, EKL-74014 mono, EKS-74014 stereo, October 1967.
Strange Days (cassette), TC5-4014.
Strange Days (eight-track cassette), ET8-4014.
Strange Days (CD). Elektra/Asylum Records, 74014-2, September 1985.
Strange Days (24ct gold-plated CD). DDC Compact Classics, Inc. (Northridge, CA), GZS-1026, October 1992. (Pressed in Japan.)

Waiting For The Sun (album). Elektra Records, EKL-74024 mono, EKS-74024 stereo, July 1968.
Waiting For The Sun (cassette), TC5-4024.
Waiting For The Sun (eight-track cassette), ET8-4024.
Waiting For The Sun (cassette), 60156-4, August 1982.
Waiting For The Sun (CD). Elektra/Asylum Records, 74024-2, August 1985.
Waiting For The Sun (24ct gold-plated CD). DDC Compact Classics, Inc. (Northridge, CA), GZS-1045, October 1993. (Pressed in Japan.)

The Soft Parade (album). Elektra Records, EKS-75005, July 1969.
The Soft Parade (cassette), TC5-5005.
The Soft Parade (eight-track cassette), ET8-5005.
The Soft Parade (CD). Elektra/Asylum Records, 75005-2, May 1988.
Morrison Hotel (album). Elektra Records, EKS-75007, February 1970.
Morrison Hotel (cassette), TC5-5007.
Morrison Hotel (eight-track tape), ET8-5007.
Morrison Hotel (CD). Elektra/Asylum Records, 75007-2, May 1985.

Absolutely Live (double album). Elektra Records, EKS-9002, July 1970.
Side 1: 'Who Do Love'/'Medley – Alabama Song'/'Back Door Man'/ 'Love Hides'/'Five To One'
Side 2: 'Build Me A Woman'/'When The Music's Over'
Side 3: 'Close To You'/'Universal Mind'/'Break On Thru #2'
Side 4: 'The Celebration Of The Lizard'/'Soul Kitchen'
Absolutely Live (cassette), C2-9002.
Absolutely Live (eight-track cassette), T8-9002.

13 (album). Elektra Records, EKS-74079, November 1970.
Side 1: 'Light My Fire'/'People Are Strange'/'Back Door Man'/ 'Moonlight Drive'/'The Crystal Ship'/'Roadhouse Blues'
Side 2: 'Touch Me'/'Love Me Two Times'/'You're Lost Little Girl'/'Hello, I Love You'/'Land Ho!'/'Wild Child'/'The Unknown Soldier'
13 (cassette), TC5-4079.
13 (eight-track cassette), ET8-4079.

LA Woman (album). Elektra Records, EKS-75011, April 1971.
LA Woman (cassette), TC5-5011.
LA Woman (eight-track cassette), EET8-5011.
LA Woman (CD). Elektra/Asylum Records, 75011-2, March 1985.
LA Woman (CD). HMV Classic Collection (London), C88 1-6. Includes twelve-page booklet with text by Max Bell and reprints of three reviews

of album. 2,500 pressed.
LA Woman (24ct gold-plated CD). DDC Compact Classics, Inc. (Northridge, CA), GZS-1034, March 1993. (Pressed in Japan.)

Other Voices (album [without Jim Morrison]). Elektra Records, EKS-75017, November 1971.
Side 1: 'In The Eye Of The Sun'/'Variety Is The Spice Of Life'/'Ships w/ Sails'/'Tightrope Ride'
Side 2: 'Down On The Farm'/'I'm Horny, I'm Stoned'/'Wandering Musician'/'Hang On To Your Life'

Weird Scenes Inside The Gold Mine (double album). Elektra Records, 8E-6001, January 1972.
Side 1: 'Break On Through'/'Strange Days'/'Shaman's Blues'/'Love Street'/'Peace Frog'/'Blue Sunday'/'The WASP (Texas Radio And The Big Beat)'/'End Of The Night'
Side 2: 'Love Her Madly'/'Spanish Caravan'/'Ship Of Fools'/'The Spy'/ 'The End'
Side 3: 'Take It As It Comes'/'Running Blue'/'LA Woman'/'Five To One'/ 'Who Scared You'/'(You Need Meat) Don't Go No Further'
Side 4: 'Riders On The Storm'/'Maggie M'Gill'/'Horse Latitudes'/ 'When The Music's Over'
Weird Scenes Inside The Gold Mine (cassette), C2-6001.
Weird Scenes Inside The Gold Mine (eight-track cassette), T8-6001.

Full Circle (album [without Jim Morrison]). Elektra Records, EKS-75038, July 1972.
Side 1: 'Get Up And Dance'/'4 Billion Souls'/'Verdilac'/'Hardwood Floor'/'Good Rockin''
Side 2: 'The Mosquito'/'The Piano Bird'/'It Slipped My Mind'/'The Peking King And The New York Queen'

The Best Of The Doors (Quadrophonic album). Elektra Records, EQ-

5035, September 1973.
Side 1: 'Who Do You Love'/'Soul Kitchen'/'Hello, I Love You'/'People Are Strange'/'Riders On The Storm'
Side 2: 'Touch Me'/'Love Her Madly'/'Love Me Two Times'/'Take It As It Comes'/'Moonlight Drive'/'Light My Fire'
The Best Of The Doors (cassette), TC5-5035.
The Best Of The Doors (eight-track cassette), ET8-5035.

Morrison, Jim (Music by The Doors). *An American Prayer* [album].
Elektra/Asylum Records, 5E-502, November 1978; re-issued 1995 with CD version and with bonus tracks (see CD listing).
Side 1: 'Awake' ('Ghost Dance', 'Dawn's Highway', 'Newborn Awakening')/'To Come of Age' ('Black Polished Chrome'/'Latino Chrome', 'Angels And Sailors', 'Stoned Immaculate')/'The Poet's Dream' ('The Movie', 'Curses Invocations')
Side 2: 'World On Fire' ('American Night', 'Roadhouse Blues', 'Lament', 'The Hitchhiker')/'An American Prayer'
An American Prayer (cassette), 5C5-502.
An American Prayer (eight-track cassette), 5T8-502.
An American Prayer (CD), 61812-2.
Bonus tracks: 'Babylon Fading',' Bird Of Prey', 'The Ghost Song'

Greatest Hits (album). Elektra/Asylum Records, 5E-515, October 1980.
Side 1: 'Hello, I Love You'/'Light My Fire'/'People Are Strange'/'Love Me Two Times'
Side 2: 'Break On Through'/'Roadhouse Blues'/'Not To Touch the Earth'/'Touch Me'/'LA Woman'
Greatest Hits (cassette), 5C5-55.
Greatest Hits (eight-track cassette), 5T8-515.

Alive, She Cried (album). Elektra/Asylum Records, 60269-1, October 1983.
Side 1: 'Gloria'/'Light My Fire'/'You Make Me Real'

Side 2: 'Texas Radio And The Big Beat'/'Love Me Two Times'/'Little Red Rooster'/'Moonlight Drive'
Alive, She Cried (cassette), 60269-4.
Alive, She Cried (CD). Elektra/Asylum Records, 60269-2, June 1984.

Classics (album). Elektra/Asylum Records, 60417-1, May 1985.
Side 1: 'Strange Days'/'Love Her Madly'/'Waiting For The Sun'/'My Eyes Have Seen You'/'Wild Child'/'Crystal Ship'/'Five To One'
Side 2: 'Roadhouse Blues' (live)/'Land Ho!'/'I Can't See Your Face In My Mind'/'Peace Frog'/'The WASP'/'The Unknown Soldier'
Classics (cassette), 60417-4.

The Best Of The Doors (double album). Elektra/Asylum Records, 60345-1, June 1987.
Side 1: 'Break On Through'/'Light My Fire'/'The Crystal Ship'/'People Are Strange'/'Strange Days'/'Love Me Two Times'
Side 2: 'Five To One'/'Waiting For The Sun'/'Spanish Caravan'/'When The Music's Over'
Side 3: 'Hello, I Love You'/'Roadhouse Blues'/'LA Woman'/'Riders On The Storm'
Side 4: 'Touch Me'/'Love Her Madly'/'The Unknown Soldier'/'The End'
The Best Of The Doors (cassette), 60345-4.
The Best Of The Doors (double CD). Elektra/Asylum Records, 9 60345-2, July 1987.
Disc 1: sides 1 and 2 of double album
Disc 2: sides 3 and 4 of double album

Live At The Hollywood Bowl (album). Elektra/Asylum Records, 60741-1, June 1987.
Side 1: 'Wake Up'/'Light My Fire'
Side 2: 'The Unknown Soldier'/'A Little Game'/'The Hill Dwellers'/'Spanish Caravan'
Live At The Hollywood Bowl (cassette), 60741-4.

Live At The Hollywood Bowl (CD). Elektra/Asylum Records, 60741-2, July 1987. Includes a bonus track: an edit of the live version of 'Light My Fire'

The Doors: An Oliver Stone Film (album soundtrack). Elektra Entertainment, 61047-1 (European release only), March 1991.

Side 1: 'The Movie'/'Riders On The Storm'/'Love Street'/'Break On Through'/'The End'

Side 2: 'Light My Fire'/'Ghost Song'/'Roadhouse Blues'/'Heroin' (performed by Velvet Underground and Nico)/'Carmina Burana': Introduction (performed by the Atlanta Symphony Orchestra and Chorus, conducted by Robert Shaw)/'Stoned Immaculate'/'When The Music's Over'/'The Severed Garden (Adagio)'/'LA Woman'

The Doors: An Oliver Stone Film (CD soundtrack). Elektra Entertainment, 61047-2, March 1991.

The Doors: An Oliver Stone Film (cassette soundtrack), 61047-4.

In Concert (three albums). Elektra/Asylum Records, 7559-61082-1 (European release only), May 1991. (Compilation of the live recordings from *Absolutely Live*; *Alive, She Cried*; and *Live At The Hollywood Bowl*.)

Side 1: 'House Announcer'/'Who Do You Love'/'Medley – Alabama Song'/'Back Door Man'/'Love Hides'/'Five To One'/'Build Me A Woman'

Side 2: 'When The Music's Over'/'Universal Mind'/'Petition The Lord With Prayer'/'Medley – Dead Cats Dead Rats'/'Break on Through #2'

Side 3: 'The Celebration of the Lizard'/'Soul Kitchen'

Side 4: 'Roadhouse Blues'/'Gloria'/'Light My Fire' (including *Graveyard Poem*)

Side 5: 'You Make Me Real'/'Texas Radio And The Big Beat'/'Love Me Two Times'/'Little Red Rooster'/'Moonlight Drive'

Side 6: 'Close To You'/'The Unknown Soldier'/'The End'

In Concert (double CD). Elektra/Asylum Records, 61082-2, May 1991. (Compilation of the live recordings from *Absolutely Live*; *Alive, She Cried*; and *Live At The Hollywood Bowl*.)

Disc 1: sides 1, 2 and 3 of triple album.
Disc 2: sides 4, 5 and 6 of triple album.
In Concert (cassette), 61082-4.

RADIO AND TELEVISION SPECIALS

The Continuous History Of Rock And Roll: The Doors Profile (two hours). Show #32. New York: Rolling Stone Magazine Productions, aired 15-16 May 1982.

The Doors: From The Inside With Jac Holzman (six hours). Valley Isle Productions Ltd and Media America, Inc, 1988. Produced by Sandy Gibson.

THE DOORS – Setting The Record Straight (7 hours). Culver City, CA: Westwood One.
Show #91-42 (one hour), aired week of 14 October 1991;
Show #91-43 (one hour), aired week of 21 October 1991;
Show #91-44 (one hour), aired week of 28 October 1991;
Show #91-45 (one hour), aired week of 4 November 1991;
Show #91-46 (one hour), aired week of 11 November 1991;
Show #91-47 (one hour), aired week of 18 November 1991;
Show #91-48 (four hours), aired week of 25 November 1991.

The Doors 25th Anniversary Radio Special (three hours). New York: Unistar, aired 20-22 April 1990. Host: Ed Sciaky.

Goodnight America (ABC-TV midnight specials). Aired 1 May 1974.

History Of Rock 'n' Roll (personal tape recording). Aired 29 April 1978, WOWO Radio, 1190 AM, Fort Wayne, IN.

In The Studio: The Doors – The Doors (one hour). Show #135. Burbank, CA: Album Network and Bullet Productions, aired week of 21 January 1991. Host: Ray Manzarek.

In The Studio: The Doors – LA Woman (one hour). Show #146. Burbank, CA: Album Network and Bullet Productions, aired week of 8 April 1991. Host: Ray Manzarek.

In The Studio: The Doors – Strange Days (one hour). Show #145. Burbank, CA: Album Network and Bullet Productions, aired week of 1 April 1991. Host: Ray Manzarek.

Inner View: The Doors – Parts One, Two, Three And Four (one hour each). Series #14, Shows #1, #2, #3 and #4. Beverly Hills, CA: Inner View, 1976. Host: Jim Ladd.

Off The Record Special – Featuring: The Doors (one hour). Show #91-12. Culver City, CA: Westwood One, aired March 1991 (repeated week of 16 December 1991). Host: Mary Turner.

Rock And Roll Never Forgets – Jim Morrison (five hours). Culver City, CA: Westwood One, aired week of 25 July 1983.

The Source: The Doors Special (two hours). Show #NBC 81-9. New York: NBC Radio's Young Adult Network, aired 4-6 December 1981.

The Source: The Doors Special Encore (three hours). Show #NBC 82-23. New York: NBC Radio's Young Adult Network, aired 2-4 July 1982.

Supergroups Presents Light My Fire: Commemorating The 20th Anniversary Of The Doors (three hours). Los Angeles: ABC Rock Radio Network, aired 20-25 May 1987. Hosts: Ray Manzarek, John Densmore, Robbie Krieger. Produced by Denny Somach Productions.

Three Hours For Magic: The Jim Morrison Special (three hours).

New York: London Wavelength, 1981. Frank Lisciandro. Produced by Jon Sargent.

A 20th Anniversary Salute To The Doors (two hours). New York: Radio International, aired 10-26 April 1987. Host: Robby Krieger. Produced by Jon Sargent.

Up Close: The Doors (two hours). Media America Radio, Near Perfect Productions, 1994.

VIDEOS AND FILMS

The Best Of The 60s (video of various footage and of the complete NET show *Critique*, on The Doors). (No acknowledged label.)

Break On Thru (three-minute promotional film). Los Angeles: Elektra Records, 1966.

The Doors. A Feast Of Friends (40-minute documentary film). Los Angeles, 1969.

The Doors: A Tribute To Jim Morrison. Burbank, CA: Warner Home Video, Inc, 1982.

The Doors: An Oliver Stone Film. Van Nuys, CA: LIVE Home Video, 1991.

The Doors Are Open: The Roundhouse, London, September 1968. Douglas Music Video (manufactured and distributed by Warner Reprise Video, a division of Warner Bros. Records) reproduction of BBC show first broadcast on 17 December 1968 by Granada Television International Limited.

The Doors: Dance On Fire. Universal City, CA: MCA Home Video, 1985.

The Doors: Light My Fire (video single). New York: A Vision Entertainment, 1988.

The Doors: Live At The Hollywood Bowl. Universal City, CA: MCA Home Video, 1987.

The Doors: Live In Europe 1968. New York: HBO Video, 1988.

The Doors: The Soft Parade, A Retrospective. Universal City, CA: MCA Home Video, 1991.

McClure, Michael and Ray Manzarek. Love Lion. New York: Mystic Fire Video, 1991.

Morrison, Jim, Frank Lisciandro and Paul Ferrara. *HWY* (50-minute film). Los Angeles, 1969.

The Unknown Soldier (three-minute promotional film). Los Angeles: Elektra Records, 1968.

SELECTED BIBLIOGRAPHY
OF WORKS

Albums (review of Morrison Hotel). *Fusion* (Boston), 1 May 1970, p20.

Archies' 'Jingle, Jingle' Wins 'Em A Gold Disc; Doors Cop 5th Straight. *Variety*, 4 March 1970, p43.

Bangs, Lester: *Jim Morrison: Bozo Dionysus A Decade Later, Musician*, August 1981 pp40-45.

Bangs, Lester: *Jim Morrison, Oafus Laureate Creem* special edition: *The Doors*, summer 1981, pp24, 29.

Bangs, Lester: *Morrison Hotel* (record review) *Rolling Stone*, 30 April 1970, p53.

Blackburn, Richard: *Jim Morrison's School Days, Tripping Through The College Jungle, Crawdaddy*, May 1976, pp50-55.

Benjamin, Franklin V and Duane Schneider: *Anais Nin: An Introduction*. Athens, OH: Ohio University Press, 1979.

Book Review Digest: Sixty-Second Annual Cumulation (March 1965-February 1966). Josephine Samudio (ed), New York: The HW Wilson Company, 1966. Farina, Richard: *Been Down So Long It Looks Like Up To Me*, pp360-61.

Book Review Digest: Fifty-Ninth Annual Cumulation (March 1963-February 1964). Dorothy P Davison (ed) New York: The HW Wilson Company, 1964. Rechy, John: *City Of Night*, p837.

Brecht, Bertolt: *Gesammelte Werke* (19-volume work published in German). Frankfurt Am Main, 1967. Band Two contains *Aufstieg Und Fall Der Stadt Mahagonny*.

Brecht, Bertolt: *The Rise And Fall Of The City Of Mahagonny*. Translated by WH Auden and Chester Kallman, original trans 1960. Boston: David R Godine, 1976.

Burt, Rob and Patsy North (ed): *West Coast Story*. London: Phoebus Publishing Company, 1977. (Published in USA by Chartwell Books Inc, Secausuc, NJ.) (Entry on The Doors, pp38-42.)

Chorush, Bob: *The Lizard King Reforms: Taking The Snake And Wearing It; An Interview With Jim Morrison, Los Angeles Free Press*, 15 January 1971, pp23-24.

Cline, Rob: *The Soft Parade* (record reviews). *Northwest Passage* (Bellingham, WA), 19 August 1969, p20.

Cohen, Mitchell: *Remembering Morrison, Fusion*, June 1974, pp18-19.

Cohn, Nik: *Rock From The Beginning*. New York: Stein and Day, 1969. (The Doors are discussed on pp235-36.)

Contemporary Literary Criticism. Sharon R Gunton (ed). *Morrison, Jim: 1943-1971* on pp285-96, Vol 17. Detroit: Gale Research Company, 1981.

Contemporary Authors. Francis Carol Locher (ed). *Morrison, James Douglas: 1943-1971* on pp450-52, Vols 73-76. Detroit: Gale Research Company, 1978.

Cott, Jonathan: *Doors, Airplane In Middle Earth, Rolling Stone*, 26

October 1968, pp1, 12.

Curb Inks Morrison In New Now Artist-To-Film Movie, Billboard, 2 May 1970, p3.

Cuscuna, Michael: *Behind The Doors, Down Beat*, 28 May 1970, pp13, 32.

Dalton, David and Lenny Kaye: *Rock 100*. New York: Grosset and Dunlap, Publishers, 1977. (Entry on The Doors, pp163-66.)

Densmore, John: *Riders On The Storm: My Life With Jim Morrison And The Doors*. New York: Delacorte Press, 1990.

Didion, Joan: *Waiting For Morrison, The Saturday Evening Post*, 9 March 1968, p16.

DiMartino, Dave: *Morrison In Miami: Flesh And Memories, Creem* special edition: *The Doors*, summer 1981, pp30-32.

The Doors: *The Doors/Complete* (songbook). Leo Alfassy, piano arrangements. New York: Music Sales Corporation, 1970. Includes reprint of *Stage Doors* by Harvey Perr as introduction.

The Doors: *Morrison Hotel* (songbook). Edited by Herbert Wise; piano arrangements by Leo Alfassy. New York: Music Sales Corporation, 1970.

The Doors (record review of *Waiting For The Sun*). *Harbinger* (Toronto), August 1968, p21.

Farina, Richard: *Been Down So Long It Looks Like Up To Me*. New York: Dell Publishing Co, Inc (paperback version of Random House hardback, 1966), 1967.

Farina, Richard: *Long Time Coming And A Long Time Gone*. New York: Random House, 1969.

Fornatale, Pete: *Strange Days: Doors' Organist Ray Manzarek*, *Musician*, August 1981, pp46-51, 60.

Fowlie, Wallace: *Rimbaud*. Chicago: The University of Chicago Press, 1965 (first Phoenix edition [paperback], 1967). This is a rewrite of two earlier works: *Rimbaud: The Myth Of Childhood* and *Rimbaud's Illuminations*.

Fowlie, Wallace: *Rimbaud And Jim Morrison: The Rebel As Poet*, Durham, NC: Duke University Press, 1993 and 1994.

Francis, Miller Jr: 'Callin' On The Gods' (review of *The Soft Parade*). *The Great Speckled Bird* (Atlanta), 20 October 1969 p18.

Garbarini, Vic: *Blues For A Shaman: Doors' Producer Paul Rothschild* (sic), *Musician*, August 1981, pp52-57.

Gerstenmeyer, Heinz: *Jim Morrison And The Doors: Die Songtexte Der Studio-LPs* (English lyrics to studio albums). Munich, Germany: Schirmer/Mosel, 1992.

Gilmore, Mikal: *The Legacy Of Jim Morrison And The Doors, Rolling Stone*, 4 April 1991, pp30-31, 33-34, 62.

Goldstein, Richard (ed): *The Poetry Of Rock*. New York: Bantam Books, 1969 (first published 1968). ('Twentieth Century Fox' p85; 'Horse Latitudes' p142; 'The End' pp143-44.)

Griffin, Lloyd W: (book review of John Rechy's *City Of Night*). *Library Journal*, July 1963, pp2228-29.

Halpert, Stephen: *Get Back: The Doors Are Closed, Fusion* (Boston), 20 March 1970, p38.

Hendrickson, Mark: *The Doors: The Legend Lives On...And On* (interview with Ray Manzarek). *Only Music*, December 1987, pp32-35, 53.

Hibbard, Don J with Carol Kaleialoha: *The Role Of Rock*, Englewood

Cliffs, NJ: Prentice-Hall, Inc, 1983.

Hopkins, Jerry: *The Lizard King: The Essential Jim Morrison*. New York: Charles Scribner's Sons, 1992.

Hopkins, Jerry: *The Rolling Stone Interview: Jim Morrison*, *Rolling Stone*, 26 July 1969, pp15-24.

Hopkins, Jerry and Danny Sugerman: *No One Here Gets Out Alive*. New York: Warner Books, Inc, 1980.

Houghton, Rob: *LA Woman* (record review). *Creem* special edition: *The Doors*, summer 1981, p54.

Hunter, Ross: *Sounds: Strange Doors* (record review of *Strange Days*). *IT (International Times*, London), 5-19 January 1968, p12.

Jackson, Blair: *Paul Rothchild: The Doors' Producer Recalls The Agony And The Ecstasy Of Working With The Doors*, *BAM*, 3 July 1981, pp18-20, 25.

Jahn, Mike: *Jim Morrison And The Doors* (an unauthorised book). New York: Grosset and Dunlap, 1969.

James, Lizze: *Jim Morrison: Ten Years Gone Creem* special edition: *The Doors*, summer 1981, pp16-23.

Jilek, Ed: *Records, The Paper* (Michigan State University, East Lansing, MI), 9 May 1967, p12.

Johnson, Pete: *Doors Rattle Hinges At Whisky A Go Go, Los Angeles Times*, 18 May 1967, Part IV, p13.

Johnson, Pete: *Popular Records: Latest Stones Album Best Yet, Los Angeles Times*, calender section, 26 February 1967, p30. (Includes record review of *The Doors* under the subtitle *Doors Open Up.*)

Kapor, Mitch: *The Soft Parade* (record review). *View From The Bottom*

(New Haven, CN), 7 August 1969, p13.

Kennely, Patricia: *Pop Record Reviews: The Doors, Morrison Hotel, Jazz And Pop*, May 1970, pp54-55.

Kennely, Patricia: *Pop Record Reviews: The Doors, The Soft Parade, Jazz And Pop*, October 1969, pp40-41.

Kerouac, Jack: *On The Road*. New York: Penguin Books, 1976 (first published New York: Viking Compass edition, 1959; copyrighted Jack Kerouac, 1955, 1957).

Kordosh, J: *Soft Parade* (record review). *Creem* special edition: *The Doors*, summer 1981, p51.

Kordosh, J: *Strange Days* (record review). *Creem* special edition: *The Doors*, summer 1981, pp48, 51.

Krieger, Robby: *Take It As It Comes* (reprint of Manzarek handwritten sheet music of song). *The Doors Quarterly Magazine*, Issue 32, June 1995, pp29.

KT: *Records* (review of *The Soft Parade*). *Octopus* (Ottawa, Canada), Vol 2-11 (1969), p26.

Lacey, Maybelle: Book review of Richard Farina's *Been Down So Long It Looks Like Up To Me*. *Library Journal*, 1 April 1966, p1,924.

Laurence, Paul: *Ray Manzarek* (interview). *Audio*, December 1983, pp40-45.

Lisciandro, Frank: *Jim Morrison: An Hour For Magic*. New York: Delilah Communications Ltd, 1982.

Lisciandro, Frank: *Morrison: A Feast Of Friends*. New York: Warner Books, Inc, 1991.

Lowe, Steven: *The Lighter Side/The Doors: Strange Days* (record review). *High Fidelity Magazine*, January 1968, p98.

Ludlow, Liz and Jesse Nash: *Robbie Krieger* (interview). *Masters Of Rock: The Life And Times Of Jim Morrison*, winter 1990, Vol 1 #3, pp21-23.

Mangelsdorff, Rich: *Doors Stuck?* (record review of *Waiting For The Sun*). *Kaleidoscope* (Milwaukee), 23 August-12 September 1968, p6.

Mangelsdorff, Rich: *Music Wheel* (record review of *The Soft Parade*). *Kaleidoscope* (Milwaukee), 12-25 September 1969, p15.

Manzarek, Ray: *Light My Fire: My Life With The Doors*. New York: GP Putnam's Sons, 1998.

Marsh, Dave: *Morrison Hotel – The Doors* (record review). *Creem* (Detroit) Vol 2 #10 (February 1970), p25.

Matheu, Robert: *Through The Doors Again: Manzarek, Krieger And Densmore Today, Creem* special edition: *The Doors*, summer 1981, pp56-66.

Miller, Jim (ed): *The Rolling Stone Illustrated History Of Rock And Roll*. New York: Rolling Stone Press, 1976. (Entry on The Doors by Lester Bangs, pp262-63.)

Morrison Hotel (record review). *Amazing Grace* (Tallahassee), Vol 1 #5 (1970), p12.

Morrison, Jim: *The American Night: The Writings Of Jim Morrison, Volume II*. New York: Vintage Books, 1990.

Morrison, Jim: *Anatomy Of Rock: Jazz And Pop*, September 1970, pp18-19.

Morrison, Jim: *From Dry Water, The Los Angeles IMAGE*, 3-16 October 1970, p20.

Morrison, Jim: *Jim Morrison's An American Prayer*. Baton Rouge: B Of A Company, Louisiana, 1984.

Morrison, Jim: *Jim Morrison Raps...Eye*, October 1968, pp53-55.

Morrison, Jim: *Jim Morrison's Tribute To Brian Jones, Datebook*, November 1969, pp15-17.

Morrison, Jim: *The Lords And The New Creatures*. New York: Simon and Schuster, Touchstone Book edition, 1971 paperback edition of 1970 printing.

Morrison, Jim: *The Lords And The New Creatures*. New York: Simon and Schuster, first Fireside edition, 1987.

Morrison, Jim: *The Lost Writings Of Jim Morrison* (excerpts from *Wilderness: The Lost Writings Of Jim Morrison*). *Rolling Stone*, 6 October 1988, pp69-70.

Morrison, Jim (opening lines to 'Soft Parade'). *The Los Angeles IMAGE*, 3-16 October 1969, p8.

Morrison, Jim: *Poems From Dry Water Rock*, 2 February 1970, p4.

Morrison, Jim: Reproduction of personal letter to Dave Marsh, editor of *Creem*. *The Doors Collectors Magazine*, spring 1994 (Issue #4), pp28-33.

Morrison, Jim: *Sounds For Your Soul* (poem reprinted from *The Doors Program Book*). *16 Spec*, summer 1968, p54.

Morrison, Jim: *Wilderness: The Lost Writings Of Jim Morrison, Vol I*. New York: Villard Books, 1988.

Nietzsche, Friedrich: *The Birth of Tragedy And The Genealogy of Morals*. Translated by Francis Golffin. New York: Doubleday (Anchor Books), 1956.

Nin, Anais: *A Spy In The House of Love*. New York: Pocket Books (a division of Simon and Schuster), 1994. (First published Chicago: The Swallow Press Inc, 1959; copyrighted Anais Nin, 1954).

Nin, Anais: *A Woman Speaks: The Lectures, Seminars And Interviews Of Anais Nin*. Edited by Evelyn J Hinz. Chicago: The Swallow Press Inc, 1975.

Nirkind, Bob (Turk): *The Doors – Follow Them Down* (record review of *The Soft Parade*). *The South End* (Wayne State, Detroit), 21 August 1969, p8.

Noname, Hugh: *Doors: LA Woman* (record review). *IT (International Times*, London), 26 August-9 September 1971, p18.

Opening The Doors (review of WOR-Stereo's Birthday Anniversary Rock Show at the Village Theatre). *The East Village Other* (New York), 1-15 July 1967, p11.

Parmalee, Patty Lee: *Brecht's America*. Salt Lake City, Utah: no publisher, 1970. (An unpublished literary study, two volumes, 493 pages, located in libraries of University of Indiana).

Paul, Alan: *Strange Days* (interview with Krieger). *Guitar World*, March 1994, pp58-62, 64, 66, 68, 112, 186, 189.

Perr, Harvey: *Stage Doors* (concert review). *Los Angeles Free Press*, 8 August 1969, p26.

Pichaske, David R: *The Poetry Of Rock: The Golden Years*. Peoria, IL: The Ellis Press, 1981. (Chapter 5 on The Doors, pp75-84.)

Pielke, Robert G: *You Say You Want A Revolution: Rock Music In American Culture*. Chicago: Nelson-Hall, 1986.

Porter, Katherine Anne: *Ship Of Fools*. Boston: an Atlantic Monthly Press book (Little, Brown and Company), 1962.

Powledge, Fred: *Wicked Go The Doors, Life*, 12 April 1968, pp86A, 86B, 89-94.

Reabur, Chris: *Morrison Hotel Revisited, Jazz And Pop*, September

1970, pp20-24. 'Chris Reabur' was a pseudonym for Bruce Harris.

Rechy, John: *City Of Night*. New York: Grover Press, Inc, 1963.

'Records 70', *Fusion* (Boston), 22 January 1971, p24.

Riegel, Richard: *Tongues Of Knowledge In The Feathered Night (The Blue Bus Is Double Parked): The Doors On Record*, *Creem* special edition: *The Doors*, summer 1981, pp8-15.

Rimbaud, Arthur: *Rimbaud: Complete Works, Selected Letters*. Translation, introduction and notes by Wallace Fowlie. Chicago: The University of Chicago Press, 1966.

Rimbaud, Arthur: *A Season In Hell* and *The Illuminations*. Translated by Enid Rhodes Peschel. New York: Oxford University Press, 1973.

Rompers, Terry: *Looking Through The Doors,* Trouser Press, September/October 1980, front cover, pp1-4. (Fold-up tabloid so that front cover is half of last page.)

Rolling Stone/Rock Almanac: The Chronicles Of Rock And Roll. New York: Collier Books, 1983.

Root, Robert L Jr: *A Listener's Guide To The Rhetoric Of Popular Music*, *Journal Of Popular Culture*, summer 1986 pp15-26.

Roxon, Lillian: *Rock Encyclopedia*. New York: Grosset and Dunlap, 1969. (Entry on The Doors, pp150-53.)

Ruby, Jay: *Pop Record Reviews: The Doors, Waiting For The Sun*, *Jazz And Pop*, December 1968, pp56-57.

Schlesinger, Arthur Jr: *Movies* (review of Antonioni's *Zabriskie Point*), *Vogue*, 1 April 1970, pp116, 118.

Somma, Robert: *Banging Away At The Doors Of Convention*,

Crawdaddy, October 1968, pp17-20.

Spotlight Singles: Top 60 Pop Spotlight (Doors – 'You Make Me Real').
Billboard, 4 April 1970, p60.

Stambler, Irwin: *Encyclopedia Of Pop, Rock And Soul*, New York: St
Martin's Press, 1974. (Entry on The Doors, pp166-69.)

Stevenson, Salli: *An Interview With Jim Morrison (Part I)*, *Circus*,
January 1971, pp42-45.

Sugerman, Danny: *A Shaman's Journey Through The Doors*, *Creem*
special edition: *The Doors*, summer 1981, pp37-38.

Sugerman, Danny (ed): *The Doors: The Complete Illustrated Lyrics*.
New York: Hyperion, 1991.

Sugerman, Danny (ed): *The Doors: The Complete Lyrics*. New York:
Delta Book (Dell Publishing of Bantam Doubleday Dell Publishing
Group), 1992. Paperback version with revisions of *The Doors: The
Complete Illustrated Lyrics* (Hyperion, 1991).

Sugerman, Danny and Benjamin Edmonds (eds): *The Doors: The
Illustrated History*. New York: William Morrow and Company, 1983.

Tobler, John: *The Doors In A Nutshell; 64 Quick Questions (Interview
With Three Doors)*, *ZigZag*, September 1972 (#25), pp28-29.

Tobler, John: *Opening The Doors Of Perception* (interviews with the
four Doors – "over one hour of rare and intriguing dialogue") (CD).
Raven (RVCD-33), no date. Transcription of interview with Jim Morrison
is printed in Jerry Hopkin's *The Lizard King: The Essential Jim
Morrison*, pp231-36.

Top Singles Of The Week (Doors: 'Riders On The Storm') 16 June 1971 p46.

Tosches, Nick: *The Doors*, *Fusion* (Boston), 25 June 1971, pp47-49.

van Lustbader, Eric: *Jim Morrison: Riding Out The Final Storm*, *Circus*, September 1971, pp37-41. (Also *Circus*, 31 January 1981, pp24-30.)

Walley, David: *The Elektra Company, Or How One Learns To Love The Bombs*, *The East Village Other* (New York), 10 September 1969, p12.

Walls, Richard C: *The Doors* (record review). *Creem* special edition: *The Doors*, summer 1981, p48.

Walls, Richard C: *Waiting For The Sun* (record review). *Creem* special edition: *The Doors*, summer 1981, p51.

Whitcomb, Ian: *Rock Odyssey: A Musician's Chronicle Of The Sixties*. Garden City, New York: Dolphin Books, 1983. (Scattered references to The Doors, plus an interesting account of Morrison on pp336-42.)

Williams, Paul: *Music Without The Myth*, *Rolling Stone*, 11 September 1981, p34.

Williams, Paul: *Rock Is Rock: A Discussion Of A Doors Song* ('Soul Kitchen'). *Crawdaddy*, May 1967, pp42-46.

Williams, Paul: *Rothchild Speaks* (interview). *Crawdaddy*, July/August 1967, pp18-25.

Youngblood, Gene: *Doors Reaching For Outer Limits Of Inner Space* (record review of *Strange Days*). *Los Angeles Free Press*, 1 December 1967, pp6, 15.

Zevallos, Hank: *Jim Morrison* (interview). *Poppin*, March 1970, pp46-53.